BUILDING PEACE IN
WEST AFRICA

INTERNATIONAL PEACE ACADEMY
OCCASIONAL PAPER SERIES

BUILDING PEACE IN WEST AFRICA

Liberia, Sierra Leone, and Guinea-Bissau

Adekeye Adebajo

LYNNE
RIENNER
PUBLISHERS

BOULDER
LONDON

Published in the United States of America in 2002 by
Lynne Rienner Publishers, Inc.
1800 30th Street, Boulder, Colorado 80301
www.rienner.com

and in the United Kingdom by
Lynne Rienner Publishers, Inc.
3 Henrietta Street, Covent Garden, London WC2E 8LU

Library of Congress Cataloging-in-Publication Data
Adebajo, Adekeye, 1966–
   Building peace in West Africa : Liberia, Sierra Leone, and Guinea-Bissau / Adekeye
Adebajo.
      p. cm.—(International Peace Academy occasional paper series)
   Includes bibliographical references (p.) and index.
   ISBN 1-58826-077-1 (alk. paper)
   1. Africa, West—Politics and government—1960–   2. Conflict management—Africa,
West.   3. National security—Africa, West.   4. Political stability—Africa, West.   I.
Title.   II. Series.
DT476.5.A34   2002
327.1'72'0966—dc21

                                                                                    2001048938

British Cataloguing in Publication Data
A Cataloguing in Publication record for this book
is available from the British Library.

Printed and bound in the United States of America

         The paper used in this publication meets the requirements
  ∞   of the American National Standard for Permanence of
         Paper for Printed Library Materials Z39.48-1984.

   5   4   3   2   1

For the victims of war in West Africa,
in the hope that the inhabitants of this troubled subregion
will have the vision, will, and courage
to build a viable political, economic, and security community

Contents

Foreword

As a board member and longtime friend of the International Peace Academy, I feel honored to have been asked to contribute this foreword. It is also a matter of personal pride for me to do so in view of my decade-long acquaintance with the author, whom I first met when he invited me to address Oxford University's Africa Society in 1992. Adekeye Adebajo is definitely among the new generation of African scholar-diplomats, having completed a doctorate at Oxford University on the Liberian civil war and served, with my active encouragement, on UN missions in South Africa, Western Sahara, and Iraq.

While serving as Nigeria's Permanent Representative to the UN between 1990 and 1999, I chaired the UN's Special Committee on Peacekeeping and represented my country on the UN Security Council between 1993 and 1994. Many of the issues described in this monograph, particularly in relation to Liberia and Sierra Leone, were areas of great concern to my country, the West African subregion, the continent as a whole, and the entire international community. The publication of this occasional paper is particularly timely following on the heels of the report of the UN's Inter-Agency Task Force on West Africa in May 2001, which recommended that the UN Security Council adopt a regional approach to managing West Africa's interconnected conflicts in Liberia, Sierra Leone, Guinea, and Guinea-Bissau. This occasional paper also makes an important contribution to the literature, as no study has yet examined the dynamics of West Africa's security complex and offered policy recommendations for building a new post–Cold War security architecture in West Africa based on the three cases of Liberia, Sierra Leone, and Guinea-Bissau.

This study tackles contemporary issues that are of utmost significance to building peace in West Africa. The Economic Community of West African States (ECOWAS) is among the world's avant-garde organizations in its efforts to develop a security architecture in its own subregion. In this regard, the signing of the Protocol Relating to the Mechanism for Conflict Prevention, Management, Resolution, Peacekeeping, and Security at the ECOWAS summit in Lomé in December 1999 was a key development. The ECOWAS Cease-fire Monitoring Group (ECOMOG) interventions in Liberia, Sierra Leone, and Guinea-Bissau were both historic and unprecedented, and their lessons will be crucial for developing a security mechanism in West Africa and beyond. The UN has recently established peacebuilding offices in Liberia and Guinea-Bissau and is likely to establish another in Sierra Leone. The creation of these offices is an important addition to the UN's conflict management armory. The UN must now collaborate with members of ECOWAS and civil society actors in these countries to rebuild these war-torn societies and to prevent the flames of these conflicts from engulfing the entire West African subregion. This is the surest path to the promotion of durable peace and sustainable development.

—*Ibrahim Gambari*
UN Undersecretary-General and
Special Adviser to the UN Secretary-General of Africa

Acknowledgments

I would like first to thank David M. Malone—president of the International Peace Academy (IPA) and the most efficient and energetic taskmaster I have yet encountered—for his support and encouragement, which ensured that this occasional paper was completed. I would also like to thank the IPA staff for enduring my periodic retreats into monastic solitude to complete this study. Ibrahim Gambari, UN Undersecretary-General and Special Adviser to the UN Secretary-General of Africa, was kind enough to contribute a foreword to this occasional paper. I am profoundly grateful that he has been such a devoted mentor and a constant source of advice, encouragement, and inspiration during the course of my career. My students at Columbia University's School of International and Public Affairs helped me to refine my ideas through stimulating and thought-provoking exchanges. I thank Andrea Bartoli, director of Columbia's International Conflict Resolution Program, for giving me this exciting opportunity.

I must also thank other mentors, friends, teachers, and colleagues who took the time to read through early drafts of the chapters in this study and offered many insightful comments and suggestions that helped me to avoid errors of fact and judgment. These individuals include: Ladipo Adamolekun, Daniel Bach, John Hirsch, James Jonah, Kathryn Jones, Jimmy Kandeh, David Keen, Martin Kilson, A. H. M. Kirk-Greene, Chris Landsberg, David M. Malone, Guy Martin, James Mayall, Angela Muvumba, Anthony Ohemeng-Boamah, Donald Rothchild, Amos Sawyer, Stephen Stedman, John Stremlau, W. Scott Thompson, Augustine Toure, Margaret Vogt, Kaye Whiteman, Gavin Williams, and Douglas Yates. All errors that remain in the text are, of course, solely mine. I would also like to acknowledge the excellent copyediting and literary skills of Sara Lodge of Oxford University, which greatly improved the final text. Aida Mengistu, program officer at the IPA, lent crucial assistance in compiling

11

the bibliography and abbreviations in record time. Karin Wermester, senior program officer at the IPA, provided important assistance in coordinating logistical arrangements between the IPA and Lynne Rienner Publishers. I thank my family—"Auntie," Tilewa, Kemi, and Femi—for their enduring support and for tolerating my long absences from the ancestral home.

I would also like to thank all the dedicated officials at the secretariats of the Economic Community of West African States (ECOWAS) in Abuja and the Accord de Non-Aggression et d'Assistance en Matière de Défense in Abidjan for imparting to me some of their knowledge and experience. Officials at the UN Secretariat and key permanent representatives in New York, as well as senior diplomats at the State Department in Washington, D.C., also provided important insights for which I am immensely grateful. I thank all the diplomats, soldiers, priests, journalists, and courageous civil society actors who gave me the benefit of their rich experiences in Liberia, Sierra Leone, Burkina Faso, Côte d'Ivoire, Ghana, Guinea, Nigeria, Senegal, and Togo. Last but certainly not least, the government of the Netherlands generously funded a major research trip to West Africa in 1999 as well as the publication and dissemination of this study through a grant to the IPA. I would like to take this opportunity to express my deep appreciation to the Dutch government for its generous support of the IPA's Africa Program over the years.

—A. A.

For too long in our history, Africa has spoken through the voices of others. Now, what I have called an African Personality in international affairs will have a chance of making its proper impact and will let the world know it through the voices of Africa's own sons.

—Kwame Nkrumah

Economic Community of West African States (ECOWAS)

1

Introduction

Civil wars and civil strifes are but violent reactions to the pervasive lack of democracy, the denial of human rights, the complete disregard of the sovereignty of the people, the lack of empowerment and accountability and, generally bad governance.

—Adebayo Adedeji, Executive Secretary,
UN Economic Commission for Africa, 1975–1991

Among all of Africa's conflict-ridden subregions, West Africa is currently one of the most volatile. Local brush fires have raged in the last decade from Liberia to Sierra Leone to Guinea to Guinea-Bissau to Senegal in an interconnected web of instability. But West Africa has gone further than any other African subregion in efforts to establish a security mechanism to manage its own conflicts.[1] The Economic Community of West African States Cease-fire Monitoring Group (ECOMOG) intervention in Liberia between 1990 and 1997 was the first such action by a subregional organization in Africa relying principally on its own men, money, and military matériel. It was also the first time the UN had sent military observers to support an already established subregional force. The ECOMOG intervention in Sierra Leone to restore the democratic government of Ahmed Tejan Kabbah to power in 1998 was equally unprecedented. The UN currently has its largest peacekeeping force in the world in Sierra Leone and has established peacebuilding offices in Liberia and Guinea-Bissau. ECOMOG undertook a brief but unsuccessful intervention into Guinea-Bissau in 1999. Building on these three experiences, West Africa's leaders are currently attempting to institutionalize a security mechanism to manage future subregional conflicts.

The fact that regional actors took the lead in efforts to manage these three conflicts represents a significant trend in conflict management. The post–Cold War era has seen an increasing division of labor between region-

15

al actors and an overburdened UN. In his 1992 report, *An Agenda for Peace,* former UN Secretary-General Boutros Boutros-Ghali argued that regional security arrangements be used to lighten the UN's heavy peace-keeping burden as foreseen in Chapter 8 of the UN Charter.[2] Peacekeeping debacles in Somalia (1993) and Rwanda (1994) have led to great reluctance on the part of the most powerful members of the UN Security Council to sanction new UN missions, particularly in Africa.[3] This situation has result-ed in efforts by African subregional organizations and the Organization of African Unity (OAU) to develop their own security mechanisms. It has also led to efforts by casualty-shy Western countries to strengthen the capacity of regional security organizations in Africa.

The ECOMOG interventions in Liberia, Sierra Leone, and Guinea-Bissau demonstrated both the advantages and the disadvantages of subre-gional security organizations. Local actors often have the advantage of understanding the complex dynamics of their subregions better and often have the largest stake in ending conflicts due to the destabilizing flow of refugees, factions, and arms across porous borders. Subregional actors can also focus more attention on extinguishing local brush fires than can the OAU or the UN, which have many agendas. But the involvement of local actors in these conflicts can also lead to the pursuit of parochial and self-interested goals. This can result in partisanship and a lack of neutrality, exacerbating rather than alleviating regional conflicts. The involvement of civil society groups and external actors in regional conflict management can, however, contribute to improving the neutrality of these missions, as will be seen in the cases of Liberia, Sierra Leone, and Guinea-Bissau.

The four principal questions that this study seeks to address are the fol-lowing: First, what were the political, economic, and security constraints to establishing a subregional security mechanism and to promoting economic integration in West Africa between 1960 and 1990? Second, what domestic, subregional, and external factors hampered or helped peacemaking efforts in Liberia, Sierra Leone, and Guinea-Bissau, and what factors account for the unresolved security and political processes in all three countries? Third, how successful have efforts at conflict management been in these three cases, and what factors were responsible for similar or different outcomes in these countries? Fourth, what are the lessons that can be derived from the three cases for building sustainable peace in West Africa and, more specifically, for institutionalizing ECOMOG as a permanent security mech-anism in West Africa?

Each chapter attempts to address these questions. In response to the first question, Chapter 2 assesses the constraints to creating a subregional security mechanism and promoting economic integration in West Africa. We highlight particularly the antagonism between Nigeria and a French-led francophone bloc that rendered both economic integration and military cooperation difficult. In response to the fourth question, Chapter 6 draws some lessons from Liberia, Sierra Leone, and Guinea-Bissau for developing a security mechanism in West Africa. The chapter focuses on such issues as the importance of developing proper mandates and securing logistical and financial support for future ECOMOG missions, how to forge subregional unity and alleviate the fears of ECOWAS states about Nigeria's hegemonic ambitions, the role of external actors in supporting peacemaking efforts in West Africa, and devising effective strategies to deal with "spoilers." The chapter also makes more specific recommendations on institutionalizing military cooperation in West Africa.

The three case studies address the second and third questions posed above. In the case of Liberia, the study advances three main arguments to explain the protracted conflict. First, the failure to implement thirteen peace agreements for six years was due to the proliferation of armed factions and the manipulation of ethnic rivalries and plundering of resources by rival warlords. Second, amid fears of Nigeria's hegemonic ambitions by subregional states, ECOWAS members could not agree on a common approach to managing the conflict while several subregional states backed rival factions. In a subregion with strong leaders and weak institutions, personal relationships between leaders often drove state policies, leading to shifting, unstable alliances. ECOMOG also lacked the military and financial tools to engage the warlords in a protracted guerrilla war. Third, international actors failed to support significantly subregional efforts to manage the conflict and were wary of ECOMOG's lack of impartiality as well as Nigeria's repressive military regimes.

Chapter 3 advances three further arguments to explain the (temporary) end of Liberia's war in 1997. First, the warlords, after being handed the spoils of office in 1995, largely cooperated with ECOMOG in disarming their fighters, with the most powerful, Charles Taylor, confident of winning power through elections, having made peace with Nigeria. Second, subregional unity was facilitated by the fact that Nigeria no longer supported factions opposed to the National Patriotic Front of Liberia (NPFL), and francophone Burkina Faso, Côte d'Ivoire, and Niger could contribute troops to ECOMOG. Third, with increased cooperation from the warlords and a more diverse subregional force, the United States and the European Union (EU) provided crucial logistical and financial support to ECOMOG that facilitated the disarmament of the factions and the holding of elections in 1997 with UN support.

A similar pattern emerged in the case of Sierra Leone, for which we put forward three principal arguments to explain the decade-long conflict. First, a combination of diamond-plundering warlords and undisciplined militias as well as often inept politicians and soldiers in Freetown totally dependent on external military support, produced political and military deadlock. Second, a divided ECOWAS saw different members supporting either successive governments in Freetown or rebels in the countryside, while several ECOWAS states complained about Nigeria's military dominance of the ECOMOG High Command as well as its unilateral military and diplomatic actions. Third, as in Liberia, the international community starved ECOMOG and Sierra Leone of the resources and attention that may have made peacemaking efforts more effective. The UN was eventually forced to take over ECOMOG's peacekeeping duties in 2000 after a democratically elected civilian regime emerged in Nigeria.

Finally, in the case of Guinea-Bissau, Chapter 5 makes three main arguments to explain the failed ECOMOG intervention and the fragility of peacebuilding efforts. First, Guinea-Bissau's two belligerents negotiated agreements in bad faith that they had no intention of honoring. The support provided them by various external actors allowed them to continue waging war. Second, a military intervention by Senegal and Guinea in support of one side, amid security concerns in Dakar of arms trafficking to secessionists in Casamance, only hardened the resolve of the other party to keep fighting. The replacement of Seneguinean forces by a more neutral but inadequately sized ECOMOG peacekeeping force entirely dependent on French financial and logistical support meant that the peacekeepers were in no position to defend the capital when the rebel force attacked the incumbent regime. This resulted in the withdrawal of the ECOMOG force from Guinea-Bissau after only four months. Finally, despite the holding of democratic elections and the establishment of a UN peacebuilding office in Guinea-Bissau, continued political instability has dissuaded wary external donors from contributing substantially to peacebuilding in the country.

The three conflicts examined in this study highlight the interdependence of security in West Africa and the importance of a regional approach to conflict management. A UN Inter-Agency Mission to West Africa in May 2001, led by Assistant Secretary-General Ibrahima Fall, recommended that the UN Security Council adopt such an approach to managing the subregion's interconnected conflicts.[4] The civil war in Liberia led to deep political splits within ECOWAS, with francophone states opposing the Nigerian-led intervention, which also initially involved Ghana, Guinea, Sierra Leone, and Gambia. The civil war was triggered from Côte d'Ivoire and the rebels received military support from Burkina Faso (and Libya). The fighting spilled more than 750,000 refugees into Côte d'Ivoire, Guinea, Sierra Leone, Ghana, and Nigeria, and military incursions were launched into Côte d'Ivoire and Guinea by Liberian factions. The continuing instability on the Guinea-Liberia border and the rebel invasion of Liberia's northern

Lofa county in 1999 by a faction calling itself Liberians United for Reconciliation and Democracy (LURD) has seen governments in Conakry and Monrovia supporting opposing rebel movements.

The interdependence of security in West Africa was further undermined when the Revolutionary United Front (RUF), consisting of Sierra Leonean members of the main Liberian faction, Charles Taylor's NPFL, triggered a decade-long civil war in Sierra Leone through an invasion from Liberian territory in March 1991. Nigeria, Ghana, and Guinea sent troops to support the regime in Freetown. Over 500,0000 Sierra Leonean refugees spilled into neighboring Guinea and Liberia as a result of this civil war. Finally, in Guinea-Bissau, Senegal and Guinea intervened militarily in a civil conflict that spilled refugees into Senegal, Guinea, and Gambia. Over 3,000 refugees also entered Guinea-Bissau to flee fighting in Senegal's Casamance region. The conflict in Guinea-Bissau saw alleged arms trafficking by a secessionist group in Senegal, Mouvement des Forces Démocratiques de Casamance (MFDC), which launched attacks into Senegal from Guinea-Bissau. The MFDC also reportedly supported Bissau Guinean general Ansumane Mane's rebellion.

It is important to note from the outset that although this study examines some of the tasks usually associated with postconflict peacebuilding, the term *building peace* employed in the title of this occasional paper does not refer specifically to these tasks. We use the term more broadly to encompass peacemaking and peacekeeping efforts in these three West African cases. Postconflict peacebuilding is often associated with "second-generation" UN missions in the post–Cold War era in places like Namibia, Mozambique, Angola, Somalia, Cambodia, and El Salvador, where efforts have been made to adopt a holistic approach to peace. Not only are diplomatic and military tools employed in building peace, today's peacebuilders also focus on political, social, and economic aspects of societies emerging from civil war in an effort to address the root causes of conflicts. Such tasks often involve disarming and demobilizing warring factions; conducting and observing elections; repatriating and resettling refugees; rehabilitating and reintegrating soldiers into local communities; restructuring and reforming security forces, civil services, and judiciaries; monitoring and investigating human rights abuses; and overseeing transitional civilian authorities.[5] This study addresses some of these issues, but focuses principally on the efforts of a variety of external and domestic actors to make, keep, and enforce peace.

Much has been written on international peacemaking efforts in Liberia, but similar efforts in Sierra Leone and Guinea-Bissau are far less well known. This study aims to make a contribution to the literature and policy debates by filling this critical gap. No study has yet examined all three

ECOMOG interventions comparatively and sought to draw lessons from the cases for the development of an ECOWAS security mechanism. In the course of completing this study, I undertook field research trips to Liberia, Sierra Leone, Burkina Faso, Côte d'Ivoire, Ghana, Guinea, Nigeria, Senegal, and Togo, mainly between 1999 and 2001. Politicians, diplomats, soldiers, priests, scholars, journalists, and other civil society actors and UN officials were interviewed in all nine countries.

These research trips afforded me an opportunity to make a firsthand assessment of the security situation in West Africa. I undertook several research trips to the ECOWAS secretariat in Abuja and also visited the Accord de Non-Aggression et d'Assistance en Matière de Défense (ANAD) secretariat in Abidjan. I also attended two ECOWAS heads of state summits in Lomé (1999) and Dakar (2001). The study is also based on interviews with officials at the UN Secretariat in New York as well as with key Permanent Representatives to the UN. In addition to these interviews, the study employs primary sources based on unpublished ECOWAS and UN documents, as well as the extensive secondary literature on regional security in West Africa.

*   *   *

This occasional paper is divided into five chapters following this brief introduction, after which a political, economic, and security background of West Africa since independence places the discussion in its broader historical and regional context. Three case studies of international interventions in Liberia, Sierra Leone, and Guinea-Bissau are then examined, explaining the reasons for the successes and failures of peacemaking in the three cases. These chapters assess the domestic, subregional, and external dynamics of the three conflicts, and examine the roles and motivations of internal belligerents, civil society actors, ECOWAS, ECOMOG, the OAU, the UN, the EU, the United States, Britain, France, Portugal, and the Community of Portuguese-Speaking Countries (CPLP). The chapters also very briefly examine the role of nonstate actors like Executive Outcomes and International Alert. In the final chapter, the study draws relevant lessons from the three ECOMOG interventions for building peace in West Africa through ECOWAS's 1999 security mechanism.

NOTES

1. See ECOWAS Protocol Relating to the Mechanism for Conflict Prevention, Management, Resolution, Peacekeeping, and Security; Lomé, 10 December 1999.

2. See Boutros Boutros-Ghali, *An Agenda for Peace* (New York: United Nations, 1992); and Boutros Boutros-Ghali, *Supplement to an Agenda for Peace,* S/1995/1, 3 January 1995.

3. See Adekeye Adebajo and Chris Landsberg, "Back to the Future: UN Peacekeeping in Africa," *International Peacekeeping* 7, no. 4 (Winter 2000): 161–188; Christopher Clapham, "The United Nations and Peacekeeping in Africa," in Mark Malan (ed.), *Whither Peacekeeping in Africa?* (Pretoria: Institute for Security Studies, 1999), pp. 25–44; Oliver Furley and Roy May (eds.), *Peacekeeping in Africa* (Aldershot and Brookfield, Vt.: Ashgate, 1998); Marrack Goulding, "The United Nations and Conflict in Africa Since the Cold War," *African Affairs* 98, no. 391 (April 1999): 155–166; and Agostinho Zacarias, *The United Nations and International Peacekeeping* (London: I. B. Tauris, 1996).

4. See Report of the Inter-Agency Mission to West Africa, "Towards a Comprehensive Approach to Durable and Sustainable Solutions to Priority Needs and Challenges in West Africa," UN Security Council document, S/2001/434, 2 May 2001.

5. See Boutros-Ghali, *An Agenda for Peace;* Elizabeth Cousens and Chetan Kumar (eds.), *Peacebuilding as Politics: Cultivating Peace in Fragile Societies* (Boulder and London: Lynne Rienner, 2001); Thomas Franck, "A Holistic Approach to Building Peace," in Olara Otunnu and Michael Doyle (eds.), *Peacemaking and Peacekeeping for the New Century* (Lanham, New York, Boulder, and Oxford: Rowman & Littlefield, 1998); World Bank, *Post-Conflict Reconstruction: The Role of the World Bank* (Washington, D.C.: World Bank, 1998); and I. William Zartman, *Collapsed States: The Disintegration and Restoration of Legitimate Authority* (Boulder and London: Lynne Rienner, 1995).

2

West Africa Since Independence: A Griot's Tale

> The art of eloquence has no secrets for us; without us the names of kings would vanish into oblivion, we are the memory of mankind; by the spoken word we bring to life the deeds and exploits of kings for younger generations.
>
> —D. T. Niane, *Sundiata: An Epic of Old Mali*

West African griots are repositories of their people's histories.[1] These fabled storytellers and troubadours often keep alive the history of their ancestors by passing these tales down to successive generations. The contemporary tale that we tell in this chapter describes the obstacles faced by West African states in establishing political, security, and economic cooperation in Africa's three postindependence decades. The main protagonists of the tale are Nigeria and France and their political rivalry as played out on a West African stage. Côte d'Ivoire, Ghana, and Senegal play lead roles, while Benin, Burkina Faso, Cape Verde, Gambia, Guinea, Guinea-Bissau, Liberia, Niger, Mali, Mauritania, Togo, and Sierra Leone act as the supporting cast in this epic drama set in the background of West Africa's savanna grasslands and dense rainforests.

In the heady postindependence years of the 1960s, leaders like Kwame Nkrumah, Sékou Touré, Abubakar Tafawa Balewa, Félix Houphouët-Boigny, Léopold Sédar Senghor, Modibo Keita, Sylvanus Olympio, and Siaka Stevens bestrode the West African political landscape like titans. These "Founding Fathers" had delivered their countries to independent nationhood and many would remain in power for decades. Most of them did this by de-democratizing political systems and establishing one-party states based on personality cults.[2,3] Parliaments were dissolved or turned into rubber stamps. Civil society groups like trade unions, women's movements, student groups, and farmers associations were often forced to support ruling parties or go out of business. The "rule by plot" saw several

23

leaders using bogus plots to eliminate political rivals. Many of West Africa's postindependence leaders turned out to be emperors without clothes. Military coups, often involving assassinations, toppled potentates like Nkrumah, Balewa, Keita, and Olympio, as West Africa's "men on horseback"—the military—made a dramatic entry onto the political stage.[4] But neither the soldiers nor the politicians were able to rise to the daunting challenge of building nations out of poor states that had been ill prepared for independence by their departing European colonial overlords.

The background provided in this chapter is essential to understanding the subregional dynamics of the three cases of Liberia, Sierra Leone, and Guinea-Bissau that form the core chapters of this study. This chapter is also important for assessing efforts at institutionalizing the military cooperation of the three ECOMOG interventions, an issue addressed in the final chapter of this occasional paper. A historical perspective helps the reader to understand five important aspects of the three ECOMOG interventions: first, Nigeria's image of itself as an aspiring hegemon in West Africa; second, the opposition of francophone ECOWAS states to the Nigerian-led ECOMOG missions in Liberia and Sierra Leone; third, Nigeria's historical rivalry with Ghana, which was also evident in ECOMOG's missions in Liberia and Sierra Leone; fourth, the search for subregional security and military cooperation efforts that preceded the ECOMOG interventions; and fifth, France's neocolonial ambitions in West Africa and its interest in Guinea-Bissau, a member of the francophone currency zone by 1997.

The fifteen states that make up the Economic Community of West African States today—Benin, Burkina Faso, Cape Verde, Côte d'Ivoire, Gambia, Ghana, Guinea, Guinea-Bissau, Liberia, Niger, Nigeria, Mali, Togo, Senegal, and Sierra Leone (Mauritania left the organization in December 2000)—are among the poorest countries in the world.[5] The subregion has a population of almost 200 million and an average per capita income of less than U.S.$500. Only three countries—Nigeria, Ghana, and Côte d'Ivoire—have populations over 15 million, raising serious questions about the economic viability of many of the subregion's ministates. Most ECOWAS members have markets that appear to be too small, and states that appear too poor, to sustain industrial development without harnessing their efforts to the wider subregion.

West Africa is also among the world's most unstable subregions: thirty-seven out of seventy-two successful military coups d'état in Africa (about 50 percent) between 1960 and 1990 occurred in West Africa, a subregion with less than a third of the OAU's members. In the last decade, Liberia and Sierra Leone have been embroiled in protracted civil wars, Guinea-Bissau experienced a brief internecine conflict in the late 1990s, Casamance separatists have continued to battle the Senegalese government as they have done for two decades, the Tuareg problem has simmered in Mali and Niger, and Liberia and Guinea continue to accuse each other of launching cross-border raids against their territories in a conflict also involving Sierra Leonean rebels.

In order to understand the dynamics that drive the West African security complex, it is important to explain the link between security and trade issues that led to the creation of ECOWAS in 1975.[6] It is also vital to understand the historical context of the geostrategic rivalry between Nigeria and France during the era of the Cold War. In stark contrast to France, Britain—the other major imperial power in West Africa—avoided direct military interventions in its former colonies. It is important to remember that ECOWAS was established in 1975 primarily to promote subregional economic integration and not as a security organization. ECOWAS has since had to adapt its institutions to play a conflict management role as a result of the realization that economic integration can only occur under conditions of peace and security.

1960–1970: NOT YET UHURU

This section will examine the first decade of independence in West Africa, assessing the origins of the rivalry between Nigeria and France and the continuing ties between France and its former colonies. This rivalry was particularly evident during Nigeria's civil war from 1967 to 1970. The section also assesses the rivalry between Côte d'Ivoire and Senegal in their battle for preeminence in francophone West Africa.

The Birth of the Francophonie

The acrimonious rivalry between Nigeria and Ghana dominated the first six years of diplomacy in anglophone West Africa. Both countries contributed troops to the UN's peacekeeping mission in Congo, beginning a long history of peacekeeping that would be continued in Lebanon, Liberia, and Sierra Leone. Despite his calls for regional integration in Africa, Kwame Nkrumah dismantled most of the common subregional institutions inherited from colonial rule. His idea of an African High Command, a continental army to promote collective defense, was roundly rejected by other African states. Under Prime Minister Abubakar Tafawa Balewa, Nigeria was considered a "moderate" state as part of the Monrovia Group, which favored a more gradualist approach to African unity. Nkrumah was a key member of the "radical" Casablanca Group, which called for more rapid integration and a nonalignment policy that opposed the establishment of foreign military bases in African countries.[7]

However, the most important obstacle to Nigeria's regional hegemonic ambitions turned out to be not Kwame Nkrumah's Ghana, but rather France. Humiliated by events in Dien Bien Phu, Algeria, and the Suez debacle, postwar France attempted to cling to the illusion of remaining a Great Power through a *politique de grandeur* that involved establishing a sphere of influence in Africa.[8] As former French president François Mitterrand remarked in 1957: "Without Africa, France will no longer have a history in the twenty-first century."[9] Many former French colonies remained heavily dependent on the Mother country after independence. For many of these countries, France was the only source of external aid. Guinea's difficulties in finding other sources of external aid after enfant terrible Sékou Touré cut ties with France in 1958 was a stark reminder of this fact.[10]

By 1963, most of France's African territories had gained political independence. But Paris continued to maintain influence through an intricate network of political, military, economic, and cultural ties. Thirteen African countries tied their Communauté Financière Africaine (CFA) franc to the French franc, giving Paris effective control over the zone's central banks and the French treasury control over their foreign reserves. Cooperation agreements gave France priority access to Africa's strategic minerals.[11] French *coopérants* provided technical assistance to African ministries, sometimes overruling ministers and acting as powers behind the throne.[12] The vast majority of the twenty-one francophone African states supported French policies in Africa, giving the Gallic nation a solid bloc of votes in international forums like the UN and the OAU. France signed military assistance and defense agreements with three West African states: Côte d'Ivoire, Togo, and Upper Volta (now Burkina Faso). In 1962 the Force Interarmées d'Intervention was established with 8,000 French troops deployed to military bases including in Côte d'Ivoire and Senegal. France intervened militarily eight times in the 1960s in Cameroon and Chad, Nigeria's neighbors, as well as in Congo-Brazzaville, Gabon, and Mauritania, to suppress riots and revolts and to prevent a military coup against Gabonese president Leon M'ba in 1964.

But the francophone bloc was neither monolithic nor totally united. Despite these close military and economic ties, there were political differences within the francophone bloc in West Africa. The rivalry between Côte d'Ivoire and Senegal dominated the diplomacy of the 1960s in francophone West Africa. Ivorian leader Félix Houphouët-Boigny saw himself as the leader of the francophone bloc and the interlocutor and diplomatic bridge between Africa and the former metropolis. He sought to use the Conseil de l'Entente, an Ivorian-subsidized economic grouping established with

Dahomey (now Benin), Niger, Upper Volta, and Togo, to isolate alternative poles of influence like Ghana, Guinea, Nigeria, and Senegal.[13] The conseil undertook joint management of railways and harbors and members shared customs revenues. It guaranteed Abidjan cheap labor, particularly from Burkina Faso, and granted other members access to Côte d'Ivoire's important meat and livestock market.

But Houphouët-Boigny's leadership ambitions were challenged by Senegal's Léopold Sédar Senghor. The roots of the rivalry go back to Senghor's support of the continuation of the preindependence French West African Federation, which had been broken up before independence in 1960 at Houphouët-Boigny's instigation. Dakar had been the capital of the federation, which had helped it to attract investment, services, and infrastructure. Houphouët-Boigny distrusted the Senegalese and accused the federation of devouring Ivorian resources, as Abidjan's wealth subsidized other French West African territories. After Senghor established the putative Mali Federation with Mali, Upper Volta, and Dahomey in November 1958, Houphouët-Boigny used his personal friendships, economic muscle, and political prestige to lure Upper Volta and Dahomey away to join his own entente in 1959.[14] Senegal's federation with Mali collapsed in 1960. Senghor created the Senegal River Basin Organization with Guinea, Mali, and Mauritania in 1964 in an effort to counter the entente and to rebuild an institution through which Senegal could exert leadership. Senghor also tried to lure Dahomey and Upper Volta away from the entente and worked assiduously to bring the radical regimes of Guinea and Mali back into the francophone fold.[15] Unlike anglophone states, however, most francophone states retained close ties with their former colonial power and refrained from dismantling the common institutions inherited at independence.

The Nigerian Civil War

During Nigeria's civil war between 1967 and 1970, the rivalry between Nigeria and France was again evident when France set up a loan scheme with Côte d'Ivoire and Gabon to supply arms to secessionist Biafra. French mercenaries were also sent to assist the Biafrans. French president Charles de Gaulle had been particularly angered by Nigeria's severance of diplomatic relations with France in 1961 to protest French atomic tests in the Sahara. Where Côte d'Ivoire and Gabon offered diplomatic recognition to secessionist Biafra, the majority of francophone African states opposed such recognition. Dahomey had agreed to serve as a staging post for Red Cross relief to Biafra in early 1969 before Lagos, fearing that this would become an arms route to Biafra, imposed economic and trade sanctions on

Cotonou, forcing it to rescind the offer.[16] Niger bought arms on behalf of the Nigerian government from countries that refused to sell directly to Lagos.

Hamani Diori, leader of Niger, had a strong economic incentive to assist Nigeria, as his country depended almost entirely on Nigeria's ports, roads, and railways.[17] Nigerian leader General Yakubu Gowon flew to Lomé on 27 May 1968 and promised Togolese leader Gnassingbé Eyadéma U.S.$2 million as a reward for returning a planeload of old Nigerian currency notes, seized in Togo four months earlier, to Lagos. Such diplomatic support proved crucial in efforts to keep Nigeria united.

1970–1979: THE LIMITS OF OIL DIPLOMACY

Nigeria's post–civil war decade saw the country succeed in its attempts to create ECOWAS as an instrument to pursue a leadership role, buy itself security, and expand its markets in West Africa while reducing the dependence of its francophone neighbors on France. But while Nigeria did increase its political influence in West Africa, ECOWAS failed to achieve its economic goals and a rival French-backed francophone organization, the Communauté Économique de l'Afrique de l'Ouest (CEAO), whose members were all part of the CFA franc currency zone, competed with ECOWAS for subregional preeminence. During this period, ECOWAS took its first tentative steps at military cooperation through the signing of a security protocol on nonaggression.

The Roots of Pax Nigeriana

The Nigerian civil war marked a watershed in the country's foreign policy. The civil war and the oil boom of the 1970s provided the rationale and the resources for Nigeria's renewed attempt at regional leadership after a decade of troubles. The experiences of the civil war led to the search for influence over subregional neighbors as well as independence from external powers. The Organization of Petroleum Exporting Countries (OPEC) price hike of 1973 quadrupled oil prices and catapulted Nigeria into the ranks of the nouveaux riches. By 1970, Nigeria's 250,000-strong army was the largest in sub-Saharan Africa, being nearly four times the size of the combined armies of the thirteen independent states in West Africa. By 1974, Nigeria's gross domestic product (GDP) had risen to U.S.$19.7 billion: larger than the combined economies of all of black Africa. Nigeria currently accounts for about 75 percent of West Africa's gross national product (GNP), about 55 percent of its population, and has a 94,500-strong army that dwarfs the combined total of its fourteen neighbors.

Scarred by the experiences of the civil war, Nigeria's leaders acquired a less benign view of external actors in Africa. As General Olusegun Obasanjo, Nigeria's current president and a military commander during the Nigerian civil war, noted: "It was . . . in their [the French] interest to cut Nigeria to size by dismembering her and reducing her influence in francophone Africa."[18] Many of Nigeria's postwar leaders had fought in the civil war and their foreign policy outlook was shaped by these events. Nigeria is geographically surrounded by francophone states: Niger and Chad to the north, Benin to the west, and Cameroon to the east. Its policymakers, therefore, feared encirclement by French-backed states during periods when national security was threatened. Nigerian leaders focused the bulk of their attention on their West African subregion in the post–civil war years. The military support of Biafra by Gabon, Côte d'Ivoire, and France had resulted in Nigeria's leaders concluding that there was an urgent need to loosen French influence in the subregion. As Ibrahim Gambari, Nigeria's foreign minister between 1984 and 1985, put it: "Nigeria considered it necessary to weaken if not break the ties between France and her former colonies in West Africa."[19]

At the African, Caribbean, and Pacific (ACP) Trade Ministers meeting in Lagos in February 1973, Nigerian ambassador Olu Sanu was asked to be Africa's spokesman at the Lomé Convention talks between the ACP and the European Economic Community (EEC), which led to a new agreement in February 1975. Lomé was the first negotiating forum involving francophone and anglophone states and was crucial in increasing the confidence and trust that would lead to the creation of ECOWAS in May 1975. Following the unity that was forged in the Lomé process, francophone states saw that economic cooperation in a larger bloc could bring mutual benefits to West African states, and Nigeria was finally being accepted as a leader on African issues.

Nigeria's post–civil war foreign policy was based on creating a network of enmeshed economic ties with its neighbors. These policies were born out of the need to buy security for Nigeria in order to prevent assistance to any future secessionists, and to benefit economically from these new ties by opening up new markets for Nigeria's goods. The civil war had forced the realization that Nigeria needed to remain on good terms with its neighbors. General Gowon pursued a policy of "checkbook diplomacy" in a bid to dispel the fears of his neighbors about Nigerian domination. After the war, he toured the subregion and, with the self-confidence of an oil-rich shaikh, wrote checks at every stop. Nigeria also sold oil at concessionary rates to francophone states like Côte d'Ivoire, Senegal, and Togo.

Nigeria further demonstrated its leadership ambitions through two peacemaking initiatives with its neighbors in the 1970s. General Gowon mediated a territorial dispute in 1970 between Dahomey and Niger. Seven years later, General Obasanjo also acted as a regional peacemaker, inviting Mathieu Kérékou and Gnassingbé Eyadéma to Lagos and successfully mediating the border dispute between Benin and Togo, leading to the reopening of their common border, which had been closed for two years.

The Creation of ECOWAS

Building on his civil war relationship with Eyadéma, Gowon went to Lomé in April 1972 and signed an agreement to establish a Nigerian-Togolese economic community as an embryonic West African economic community. Professor Adebayo Adedeji, Nigeria's influential minister of economic development, embarked on a tour of West Africa, accompanied by Togolese trade minister Henri Dogo acting as a traveling salesman for the creation of a subregional economic community. The efforts bore fruit in December 1973 when fifteen subregional states met in Lomé to discuss the proposals for an economic community. After several more rounds of meetings, the Economic Community of West African States was finally established with the signing of the Treaty of Lagos on 28 May 1975 by nine francophone states (Côte d'Ivoire, Dahomey, Guinea, Niger, Mauritania, Mali, Togo, Senegal, and Upper Volta), five anglophone states (Gambia, Ghana, Liberia, Nigeria, and Sierra Leone), and one lusophone state (Guinea-Bissau). The treaty was ratified by December 1975 and lusophone Cape Verde joined shortly thereafter.

The main goals of ECOWAS, as enshrined in its five protocols agreed upon at the 1976 summit in Lomé, included: the elimination of customs duties and all quantitative and administrative restrictions to trade; the establishment of a common customs tariff within fifteen years; the abolition of the obstacles to the free movement of persons, labor, and capital; the harmonization of agricultural, industrial, and monetary policies; and the establishment of the Fund for Cooperation, Compensation, and Development to help compensate poorer countries for loss of tariffs.[20] Adebayo Adedeji would later admit that ECOWAS leaders at the time did not even imagine that a security dimension would be a necessary part of the new organization.[21]

ECOWAS's lofty ambitions faced four practical problems. First, ECOWAS contained some of the poorest countries in the world, with an average per capita income of only U.S.$270 in 1974, and many of these countries had little or no industry, energy, cash crops, or minerals. Benin, Gambia, Sierra Leone, and Upper Volta relied on customs duties for 35–50 percent of their government revenues. Second, there were no less than ten currencies within ECOWAS. Only the CFA franc and Liberian dollar were convertible, making intracommunity trade and inward investment difficult.

Third, even accounting for widespread smuggling, intracommunity trade was estimated at only 5–6 percent of total trade, subregional exports remained competitive rather than complementary, and colonial trading patterns remained intact. Finally, there were serious infrastructural difficulties in transportation and communication that would take decades to overcome.

The first few years of ECOWAS's life revealed a lack of political commitment to the organization. Nigeria shouldered about 33 percent of the ECOWAS budget while Côte d'Ivoire and Ghana were assessed at about 13 percent each. By the end of 1978, two-thirds of the secretariat's budget had not been paid and eleven countries had outstanding dues. Nigeria and Côte d'Ivoire often had to bail out the organization with interest-free loans. Lagos subsidized ECOWAS, exchanging political influence for economic losses, and for Nigeria, ECOWAS was as much a political organization as it was an economic one.

The CEAO: A Francophone "Trojan Horse"

French president Georges Pompidou expressed well his country's rivalry with Nigeria, on a state visit to Niger in 1972: "It is . . . appropriate that the French-speaking countries should harmonize their views and coordinate their efforts, *vis-à-vis* English-speaking Africa and Nigeria in particular."[22] Following the historic rapprochement between Houphouët-Boigny and Senghor in December 1971, Côte d'Ivoire and Senegal provided the political leadership for the creation of the Communauté Économique de l'Afrique de l'Ouest in Abidjan in April 1973 with Mali, Mauritania, Niger, and Upper Volta. The creation of the CEAO was a tactical maneuver to strengthen these states' cooperation before ECOWAS's birth. Abidjan was determined to maintain a leadership position in West Africa even as Lagos attempted to expand its own influence. Abidjan and Dakar were also keen to achieve the economies of scale in industrial development needed to be able to compete with Nigeria's manufactured goods.[23] The CEAO was an insurance policy against Nigeria's economic and political dominance of West Africa, leading Lagos to regard it as France's Trojan horse within ECOWAS.

Like ECOWAS, the CEAO aimed to establish a common external tariff, improve transportation and communication links between states, promote industrial development, allow free movement of persons and capital, and increase trade in agricultural and manufactured goods. But the goals of the CEAO sometimes conflicted with those of ECOWAS. The CEAO had no tariffs on agricultural goods but kept them on manufactured goods, and it sought a customs union within twelve years while ECOWAS set a fifteen-year goal.[24] France and its West African clients had found an instrument they could use to forge unity against Nigeria's leadership ambitions in the subregion.

Subregional Military Cooperation

We will next assess efforts at military cooperation in West Africa during the 1970s. Nine West African states experienced twenty-one successful military coups between 1960 and 1980.[25] Nigeria experienced a three-year civil war, while Mali and Upper Volta fought a brief border war in December 1974. Such instability forced subregional states to seek military cooperation agreements. Gambia and Senegal signed a defense agreement in February 1965, while Guinea and Sierra Leone signed a defense pact that enabled Guinea to send troops to protect the regime in Freetown in March 1971. After a military intervention in 1978, involving Ivorian, Senegalese, and Togolese troops in support of Mobutu Sese Seko following an invasion of Zaire's Shaba province, Senegal's Léopold Sédar Senghor called for the creation of an all-African Force Africaine Commune to which France was expected to provide logistical support.

Many African states opposed the proposed force, seeing it as a further effort to legitimize French military interventions in Africa. Mali was especially opposed to the idea and CEAO states instead signed a nonaggression pact in June 1977. Other subregional states signed military pacts during this period: Côte d'Ivoire and Liberia signed a nonaggression pact in May 1977; Guinea and Liberia signed a nonaggression and defense pact in January 1979; and Nigeria and Benin signed a military cooperation pact in April 1979, offering training facilities to Beninois soldiers in Nigeria—the first instance of close military cooperation between Nigeria and a francophone state.

ECOWAS ventured into the military sphere for the first time with the signing of the Protocol on Non-Aggression on 22 April 1978. The protocol requested states to desist from the threat or use of armed force against each other, to refrain from supporting subversion in the subregion, and to refer disputes to the Authority of ECOWAS Heads of State. At another ECOWAS summit in Dakar in May 1979, Senegal and Togo submitted proposals for an ECOWAS defense pact. Spurred on by growing subregional instability, ECOWAS had taken its first tentative steps toward cooperative security.

The Gendarme de l'Afrique

Following de Gaulle's resignation in 1969, there were widespread calls in France's *pré carré* (backyard) for a renegotiation of economic and military agreements signed at independence. Niger abrogated its defense pact with France after a 1974 coup and Dahomey, Mauritania, and Togo requested changes in or cancellations of their defense agreements with France. But Côte d'Ivoire and Senegal kept their previous agreements allowing French military bases on their territories. Under Georges Pompidou's presidency from 1969 to 1974, Paris renegotiated most of its defense accords with African states. But Paris maintained its strong military and economic ties with its former colonies. Valéry Giscard d'Estaing, France's president between 1974 and 1981, drastically increased military and economic assistance to Africa. Between 1977 and 1978, French military assistance to Africa increased from 414 million to 644 million French francs. Nigeria, despite its oil wealth, could not hope to match this sum. France signed military assistance and defense agreements with three of Nigeria's neighbors: Benin, Niger, and Togo. French troops also intervened militarily during the 1970s in Chad, Central African Republic, Djibouti, Mauritania, and Zaire, mostly in support of local leaders.

Côte d'Ivoire, the indisputable leader of the francophone bloc in West Africa, tried to remain a subregional rival to Nigeria in West Africa through its impressive economic performance: between 1960 and 1980, the Ivorian economy grew by an average of 7 percent annually. Côte d'Ivoire developed agro-industry and a varied manufacturing sector including oil refining, plastic products, textiles, and vehicle assembly that by 1980 contributed more to its GNP than agriculture. By 1980, Côte d'Ivoire had the highest per capita income in West Africa at U.S.$1,150.[26]

1980–1990: GULLIVER AND THE GENDARME

During the early 1980s, Nigeria damaged its leadership credentials in West Africa amid a weakening commitment to ECOWAS. This commitment was revived only in 1985. Two expulsions of West African citizens from Nigeria revealed an increasingly lukewarm attitude toward ECOWAS amid the end of the oil boom of the 1970s and increasing indebtedness and domestic economic problems. Nigeria, West Africa's Gulliver, was taking out its troubles on its Lilliputian neighbors. However, ECOWAS signed a Protocol on Mutual Assistance and Defense in 1981, though the negotiation of the protocol revealed persistent subregional tensions and fears of Nigeria's economic and military weight. Trade relations between Nigeria and France continued to grow in the 1980s, while an unprecedented visit to France by Nigerian head of state General Ibrahim Babangida in 1990 suggested the possibility of a rapprochement between the two political rivals in West Africa.

Nigeria and ECOWAS

During the 1980s, rather than providing leadership in pursuit of ECOWAS's integrationist goals, Nigeria still maintained import restrictions, high tariffs, and exchange controls, and was reluctant to open its markets to the manufactures of French multinational companies based in Côte d'Ivoire. ECOWAS remained more a political forum to forge subregional consensus than an economic union providing tangible benefits from increased trade. In January 1983, Nigerian president Shehu Shagari ordered the expulsion from Nigeria of 2 million ECOWAS citizens. Since these individuals had no residence permits, they were declared "illegal aliens." Nigerian leader General Muhammadu Buhari ordered a second enforced exodus of 700,000 "illegal aliens" from ECOWAS countries in April 1985.[27] Both acts undermined the 1979 ECOWAS Protocol on the Free Movement of Persons, which Nigeria had signed.

With these expulsions, Nigeria crassly sacrificed its historic foreign policy goals of promoting economic integration in West Africa and championing political unity in Africa, on the altar of xenophobic nationalism. By expelling nearly 3 million West African citizens in two years, Nigeria went against the very principles it had set out to achieve in its subregion: removing barriers among countries in order to increase the free movement of people, goods, and services, for the mutual benefit of all members. The "Giant of Africa" had revealed itself to be a nasty ogre in the eyes of its neighbors and the world.

A large part of the growing xenophobia in Nigeria's foreign policy was due to its growing economic problems at home, as foreigners were being scapegoated for everything from rampant crime to soaring unemployment. By 1983, Nigeria had accumulated an external debt of U.S.$16 billion amid the corrupt profligacy of the Second Republic. Nigeria's leadership ambitions in West Africa were further damaged by the closing of its borders with its neighbors between April 1984 and February 1986 in an apparent bid to stem smuggling. The action had devastating effects on the economies of Benin, Niger, Togo, and Chad, whose leaders constantly pleaded in vain to have the decision reversed.

Under General Ibrahim Babangida's leadership after August 1985, Nigeria demonstrated a renewed commitment to ECOWAS when it held the chair of the subregional body for an unprecedented three times between 1985 and 1988. Lagos also hosted the 1986 and 1987 ECOWAS summits and contributed U.S.$5 million to the U.S.$15 million cost of building the new ECOWAS secretariat in its new capital of Abuja, a grandiloquent symbol of Nigeria's leadership aspirations.[28]

The ECOWAS Protocol Relating
to Mutual Assistance on Defense

At the ECOWAS summit in Lomé in 1980, Togo, Senegal, and Nigeria pushed strongly for a common defense pact, which Mali, Cape Verde, and Guinea-Bissau all opposed, fearing abuse by the larger states. The Protocol Relating to Mutual Assistance on Defense (MAD) was unveiled at the ECOWAS summit in Freetown on 29 May 1981, with Cape Verde, Guinea-Bissau, and Mali declining to sign. Benin, Togo, Sierra Leone, and Liberia, which had all had border clashes with their neighbors, were among the protocol's strongest supporters. Senegal also strongly supported the agreement. Though remaining wary of Nigeria, both Senegal and Togo felt that Nigeria could potentially play a stabilizing role and act as a deterrent against external aggression in West Africa.[29]

Côte d'Ivoire and Niger were more reluctant to sign the 1981 protocol, fearing the potentially overbearing influence of Nigeria. But Côte d'Ivoire, Senegal, Togo, and Niger had all backed French intervention in Chad and regarded the protocol as a long-term insurance policy in case Paris unilaterally withdrew from its military commitments in Africa. Nigeria regarded the protocol as a further chance to weaken France's grip on its former colonies by making them more dependent on Nigeria in the military sphere, as it had tried to do in the economic sphere through ECOWAS.

The 1981 protocol promised "mutual aid and assistance for defense" in the event of an externally instigated or supported armed threat or aggression against a member state. The protocol also called for an Allied Armed Forces of the Community (AAFC) consisting of standby forces from ECOWAS states and other supporting institutions. But as in the economic sphere, the anglophone/francophone rivalry spilled over into the military sphere. The CEAO states and Togo signed a mutual defense pact, the Accord de Non-Aggression et d'Assistance en Matière de Défense, in 1977. In October 1984, ANAD agreed to set up its own *force de paix* consisting of standby forces from member states that would intervene to stabilize crisis situations. But there were some internal divisions within ANAD: Mali and Mauritania were critical of the continuing close military ties between France and Africa, and several states called for the dismantling of French military bases in Africa. Guinea also did not join ANAD.

Troubles in the *Pré Carré*

In furtherance of its interventionist policy in Africa, France sent troops to Togo in September 1986 to bolster Eyadéma's regime after an internal uprising. But military solutions could not mask serious economic problems in France's former West African colonies. By the 1980s, even France's West African "crown jewels" were experiencing serious economic problems. The collapse of world coffee and cocoa prices led Côte d'Ivoire to seek International Monetary Fund (IMF) assistance in 1980 and, in 1987, its GDP fell by 3.9 percent.[30] By 1989 the country had accumulated a public external debt of U.S.$14.5 billion even as Houphouët-Boigny completed his pharaonic basilica in Yamoussoukro at an estimated cost of U.S.$300 million. Between 1970 and 1984, Senegal's balance of payments deficit soared from U.S.$16 million to U.S.$274 million and its foreign debt increased from U.S.$131 million to U.S.$1.5 billion.[31] Dakar increasingly sought the economic assistance of wealthy Gulf states, using its Muslim identity to host Islamic conferences while building stronger economic and military ties with the United States.[32] Growing economic problems adversely affected the pace of economic integration within the CEAO. Landlocked Burkina Faso, Niger, and Mali voiced old complaints about a disproportionate amount of benefits from the CEAO flowing to Côte d'Ivoire and Senegal. They demanded increased compensation and pursued increasingly protectionist policies.[33]

The Francophonie also experienced military and political divisions in the 1980s. Further cracks appeared in the ranks of francophone West Africa on 25 December 1985, when troops from Burkina Faso and Mali clashed over territorial claims in the mineral-rich Agacher region. Similar clashes had occurred a decade earlier. Members of ANAD met in Abidjan four days after the clashes and sent a Truce Observation Force to the area after securing a cease-fire. Houphouët-Boigny summoned ANAD members to Yamoussoukro for peace talks on 31 January 1986 after the ANAD force had already been withdrawn. The fact that ANAD members rejected mediation efforts and troops from Nigeria again demonstrated their determination to resolve the conflict within the Francophonie family.

On 4 August 1983, Captain Thomas Sankara seized power in Upper Volta before renaming the country Burkina Faso. The new leader established close ties with "radical" regional leaders like Muammar Qaddafi and Jerry Rawlings and talked of exporting his revolution to other African countries. He boycotted Franco-African summits and described francophone states as "African vassals" paying obeisance to the "French sovereign." He criticized the cooperation agreements with Paris as neocolonial. Not since the days of Kwame Nkrumah and Sékou Touré had a leader caused so much unease and aroused such resentment in francophone Africa. Sankara's relations with France and conservative francophone states like Côte d'Ivoire, Mali, Niger, and Togo became extremely strained. French development assistance fell from U.S.$43.5 million in 1983 to U.S.$26.5 million in 1985.[34]

Relations between Ouagadougou and Abidjan particularly suffered following accusations by Sankara that Voltaic laborers were facing discrimination in Côte d'Ivoire. Accusing Abidjan of deriving the bulk of profits from tariffs and duties in the jointly administered Abidjan-Ouagadougou railway, the Burkinabè leader cut these bilateral ties in 1987. Sankara was assassinated in October 1987 with the apparent complicity of his previously loyal lieutenant, Captain Blaise Compaoré, who took over as head of state.[35] Compaoré moved Burkinabè diplomacy back closer to Abidjan and Paris.

France and Nigeria

We conclude this section by assessing changing Franco-Nigerian relations in the 1980s. By 1984, 21 percent of Nigeria's oil exports went to France, making it the largest recipient of Nigerian oil that year. In the same year, Nigeria was France's largest trading partner in black Africa, accounting for 20.3 percent of all French imports from Africa and 8.3 percent of all French exports to Africa. By 1985, 25 percent of the combined assets of all commercial and merchant banks in Nigeria were French; Peugeot sold 70 percent of all cars and light vehicles in Nigeria; and Elf was producing 35 million barrels of oil a year in Nigeria. French net investments in Nigeria totaled U.S.$500 million by 1988, the second largest after Britain; French firms won lucrative construction contracts; and French military manufacturers continued to conduct a profitable trade with the Nigerian army.[36]

But despite this lucrative bilateral trade, Paris was conscious of the importance of maintaining the credibility of its military involvement to its francophone African allies. French military aid to Africa increased from 660 million French francs in 1982 to 800 million French francs in 1984, and in 1990, France still had 6,600 troops in Africa. France also gave diplomatic support to Cameroon in its long-running border dispute with Nigeria over the Bakassi peninsula. By 1990, however, three signs pointed to improving Franco-Nigerian relations. First, France seemed more willing to accommodate Nigeria's interests in countries like Benin and Niger as economic problems increased in its francophone *domaine réservée* (private hunting ground). Second, Nigeria had become the largest market for French investment in black Africa with U.S.$23 billion, and important French political and business interests argued that Nigeria should play a greater role in regional integration. Finally, there was a new generation of French policymakers pushing for a change in African policy, encouraging greater democracy, and a lessening of the francophone African burden on the French treasury.[37]

General Babangida became the first Nigerian leader to pay a state visit to France when he visited Paris from 26 to 28 February 1990. He told his Parisian audience: "the French presence is a historical fact with which Nigeria has not only learnt to live but, over the years, has come to perceive in a positive light."[38] Such sentiments were now being uttered more frequently by both sides as old taboos were shattered and both countries appeared to be slowly accepting their roles in West Africa as complementary rather than competitive. But the continued suspicions about Nigeria's motives and continuing close ties with France meant that institutions like the francophone economic grouping, the West African Monetary and Economic Union (UEMOA), involving Benin, Burkina Faso, Côte d'Ivoire, Guinea-Bissau, Mali, Niger, Senegal, and Togo, continued to frustrate Nigerian-led efforts to create a West African common market.

GOVERNANCE, DEMOCRACY, AND SECURITY IN WEST AFRICA

In concluding this chapter, which began by describing the disappointing performance of West Africa's postindependence leaders, it is important to mention briefly some democratic developments in the subregion after the end of the Cold War. While many states in West Africa are formal democracies in the sense of conducting free and fair elections at regular intervals, democracy throughout the subregion continues to face many tensions that could easily reverse the gains of the past decade.[39] Pressure for greater freedom within states and for cooperation among them competes with troubling signs of antidemocratic behavior like the harassment of opposition parties, civil society groups, and the press, and the conducting of elections of questionable legitimacy in countries like Gambia, Guinea, and Togo.[40]

In the early 1990s, civil society actors in Benin, Mali, and Niger played an instrumental role in democratic transitions.[41] Several traditional leaders and women's organizations were involved in efforts at resolving the Tuareg problem in northern Mali. These efforts clearly demonstrate that the search for durable peace in West Africa is directly related to issues of governance and democratization and that civil society groups are important to such efforts. Aside from the continuing instability in the Mano River basin, involving Liberia, Guinea, and Sierra Leone, civil society groups in Benin, Côte d'Ivoire, Ghana, Guinea-Bissau, Mali, Nigeria, and Senegal continue to play a role in efforts to achieve democratic consolidation after decades of military rule or one-party regimes. In addition to these efforts, governments in West Africa will have to undertake policies to reverse past discrimination in the distribution of positions in state institutions like the military and civil service if future armed conflicts are to be avoided.

Another important source of instability in West Africa is the continuing role of the military and the phenomenon of military regimes during the decade of the 1990s in places like Nigeria, Niger, Gambia, Ghana, and Sierra Leone. Of the fifteen ECOWAS states, only Cape Verde and Senegal have avoided the scourge of military coups d'état. Reforming West African militaries is vital to avoid future coups in Africa's most coup-ridden subregion. It is also important to understand how the military has exercised power in West Africa in ways that have either fueled or successfully managed conflicts.[42]

This griot's tale sadly does not have a happy ending. West Africa's first three postindependence decades have been nothing short of disappointing for the mass of its population. Grinding poverty, military coups d'état, political autocracy, widespread corruption, and foreign meddling have all turned the dreams of an economically integrated and politically united West Africa into a living nightmare for most of its citizens. The end of the Cold War by 1989, the emergence of more democratic governments, and the growing rapprochement between Nigeria and France seemed to offer some hope that bridges could be built across the subregion's political and linguistic fault lines. But the next three chapters demonstrate that such hopes proved to be tragic illusions. Devastating civil conflicts erupted in Liberia, Sierra Leone, and Guinea-Bissau in the 1990s, exposing the subregion's divisions and ushering in an age of plundering warlords, militias, and sobels. These three civil wars have caused untold horror and destruction and have threatened to engulf the entire subregion with their violent flames.

NOTES

1. The title of this chapter is borrowed from Ali Mazrui, "A Griot's Tale," *Africa Report* 39, no. 5 (September/October 1994): 28–33.

2. On one-party states, see James Coleman and Carl Rosberg (eds.), *Political Parties and National Integration in Tropical Africa* (Berkeley, Los Angeles, and London: University of California Press, 1970); and Aristide Zolberg, *Creating Political Order: The Party-State of West Africa* (Chicago: Rand McNally, 1966).

3. On personality cults, see, for example, Robert Jackson and Carl Rosberg, *Personal Rule in Black Africa: Prince, Autocrat, Prophet, Tyrant* (Berkeley and London: University of California Press, 1982); and A. H. M. Kirk-Greene, "His Eternity, His Eccentricity, or His Exemplarity? A Further Contribution to H.E., the African Head of State," *African Affairs* 90 (1991): 163–187.

4. See, for example, Samuel Decalo, *Coups and Army Rule in Africa,* 2nd ed. (New Haven and London: Yale University Press, 1990); and Eboe Hutchful and

Abdoulaye Bathily (eds.), *The Military and Militarism in Africa* (Dakar: CODESRIA, 1998).

5. For historical studies on West Africa's economies, see Samir Amin, *Neo-Colonialism in West Africa* (New York and London: Monthly Review Press, 1973); and Robert Bates, *Markets and States in Tropical Africa* (Berkeley, Los Angeles, and London: University of California Press, 1981).

6. See, for example, Adebayo Adedeji (ed.), *Comprehending and Mastering African Conflicts: The Search for Sustainable Peace and Good Governance* (London and New York: Zed Books, 1999).

7. See Olajide Aluko, *Ghana and Nigeria, 1957–70: A Study of Inter-African Discord* (London: Rex Collings, 1976); A. H. M. Kirk-Greene, "West Africa: Nigeria and Ghana," in Peter Duignan and Robert H. Jackson (eds.), *Politics and Government in African States, 1960–1985* (Stanford: Hoover Institution Press, 1986), p. 30; and W. Scott Thompson, *Ghana's Foreign Policy, 1957–1966* (Princeton: Princeton University Press, 1969).

8. See, for example, John Chipman, *French Power in Africa* (Oxford: Basil Blackwell, 1989).

9. Quoted in Christopher M. Andrew, "France: Adjustment to Change," in Hedley Bull (ed.), *The Expansion of International Society* (Oxford: Clarendon Press, 1984), p. 337.

10. See Ladipo Adamolekun, *Sékou Touré's Guinea: An Experiment in Nation Building* (London: Methuen, 1976); and Claude Rivière, *Guinea: The Mobilization of a People* (Ithaca: Cornell University Press, 1978).

11. See Guy Martin, "Continuity and Change in Franco-African Relations," *Journal of Modern African Studies* 33, no. 1(March 1995): 6.

12. See, for example, Douglas Yates, *The Rentier State in Africa: Oil Rent Dependency and Neocolonialism in the Republic of Gabon* (Trenton, N.J., and Asmara, Eritrea: Africa World Press, 1995).

13. Daniel Bach, "Francophone Regional Organizations and ECOWAS," in Julius Okolo and Stephen Wright (eds.), *West African Regional Cooperation and Development* (Boulder, San Francisco, and Oxford: Westview Press, 1990), p. 54.

14. See Yves Person, "French West Africa and Decolonization," in P. Gifford and W. R. Lewis (eds.), *The Transfer of Power in Africa: Decolonization 1940–1960* (New Haven: Yale University Press, 1982), pp. 141–172.

15. See Yakubu Gowon, *The Economic Community of West African States: A Study of Political and Economic Integration* (Ph.D. thesis, Warwick University, February 1984), pp. 51–68.

16. John Stremlau, *The International Politics of the Nigerian Civil War, 1967–1970* (Princeton: Princeton University Press, 1977), p. 383.

17. See Emeka Nwokedi, "Nigeria and Niger: The Mechanics of Compatibility and Consensus," in Bassey Ate and Bola Akinterinwa (eds.), *Nigeria and Its Immediate Neighbors* (Lagos: Nigerian Institute of International Affairs, 1992), pp. 103–120.

18. Olusegun Obasanjo, *My Command* (London: Heinemann, 1980), p. 152.

19. Ibrahim Gambari, *Political and Comparative Dimensions of Regional Integration: The Case of ECOWAS* (Atlantic Highlands, N.J., and London: Humanities Press International, 1991), p. 48.

20. See Ralph Onwuka, *Development and Integration in Africa: The Case of the Economic Community of West African States* (Ile-Ife, Nigeria: University of Ife Press, 1982).

21. Personal discussions with Adebayo Adedeji, New York, 20 June 2001.

22. Quoted in Gowon, *Economic Community of West African States*, p. 239.

23. Bach, "Francophone Regional Organizations and ECOWAS," p. 57.

24. S. K. B. Asante, "ECOWAS/CEAO: Conflict and Cooperation in West Africa," in R. I. Onwuka and A. Sesay (eds.), *The Future of Regionalism in Africa* (London: Macmillan, 1985), pp. 86–87. See also Daniel Bach, "The Politics of West African Economic Cooperation: CEAO and ECOWAS," *Journal of Modern African Studies* 21, no. 4 (1983).

25. See A. H. M. Kirk-Greene, *"Stay by Your Radios"* (Leiden and Cambridge: African Studies Centre, 1981), pp. 32–35.

26. See Cyril Kofie Daddieh, "Ivory Coast," in Timothy Shaw and Olajide Aluko (eds.), *The Political Economy of African Foreign Policy* (Aldershot: Gower, 1984).

27. See Olajide Aluko, "The Expulsion of Illegal Aliens from Nigeria: A Study in Decision-Making," *African Affairs* 84, no. 337 (October 1985).

28. See Adekeye Adebajo, "Abuja," *Newswatch* 23, no. 23 (3 June 1996).

29. Chipman, *French Power in Africa*, p. 176.

30. See Femi Aribisala, "The Political Economy of Structural Adjustment in Côte d'Ivoire," in Adebayo Olukoshi, Omotayo Olaniyan, and Femi Aribisala (eds.), *Structural Adjustment in West Africa* (Lagos: Nigerian Institute of International Affairs, 1994); and Yves A. Fauré, "Côte d'Ivoire: Analysing the Crisis," in Donal B. Cruise O'Brien, John Dunn, and Richard Rathbone (eds.), *Contemporary West African States* (Cambridge: Cambridge University Press, 1989).

31. See Christian Coulon and Donal B. Cruise O'Brien, "Senegal," in O'Brien, Dunn, and Rathbone, *Contemporary West African States*, p. 154.

32. See Peter Schraeder, "Senegal's Foreign Policy: Challenges of Democratization and Marginalization," *African Affairs* no. 96 (1997).

33. Bach, "Francophone Regional Organisations and ECOWAS," p. 59.

34. Pierre Englebert, *Burkina Faso: Unsteady Statehood in West Africa* (Boulder and Oxford: Westview Press, 1996), p. 152.

35. See the excellent article by the former U.S. ambassador in Ouagadougou, Elliot Skinner, "Sankara and the Burkinabè Revolution: Charisma and Power, Local and External Dimensions," *Journal of Modern African Studies* 26, no. 3 (1988); and Englebert, *Burkina Faso*, pp. 55–64.

36. See L. S. Aminu, "French Economic Penetration of Nigeria: Its Security Implications," in Ate and Akinterinwa, *Nigeria and Its Immediate Neighbors*, pp. 208–210.

37. See Kaye Whiteman, "Two Agendas in Paris," *West Africa* no. 3784 (5–11 March 1990).

38. Quoted in *West Africa* no. 3785 (12–18 March 1990): 403.

39. On African democracy, see, for example, Richard Joseph, "The Reconfiguration of Power in Late Twentieth-Century Africa," in Richard Joseph (ed.), *State, Conflict, and Democracy in Africa* (Boulder and London: Lynne Rienner, 1999), pp. 57–80; and Crawford Young, "The Third Wave of Democratization in Africa: Ambiguities and Contradictions," in Joseph, *State, Conflict, and Democracy in Africa*, pp. 15–38.

40. I thank Chris Landsberg for drawing my attention to these points.

41. See, for example, John F. Clark and David E. Gardinier, *Political Reform in Francophone Africa* (Boulder and Oxford: Westview Press, 1997).

42. See, for example, Jimmy Kandeh, "What Does the Militariat Do When It Rules? Military Regimes: Gambia, Liberia, and Sierra Leone," *Review of African Political Economy* 69 (1996): 387–404.

3

Liberia:
A Banquet for the Warlords

Doe came to redeem us and what did we get? Taylor came as our
redeemer—to get Doe off our backs, and all of these people joined him.
More redeemers. What did they get us?
                                    —Michael Francis, Archbishop of Monrovia

This chapter will briefly trace the roots of Liberia's civil war, between 1989
and 1997, to the country's political autocracy and economic anomie under a
tiny Americo-Liberian oligarchy between 1847 and 1980, as well as under
the brutal regime of Master-Sergeant Samuel Doe between 1980 and 1989.[1]
Doe's regime was supported by the United States as part of its Cold War
strategy in Africa.

The Liberian civil war, which claimed an estimated 200,000 lives,[2]
defied peacekeeping and peace enforcement solutions by ECOMOG due to
three principal obstacles. First, the security environment in Liberia was
exceptionally challenging. When ECOMOG intervened in 1990, the
Liberian state had collapsed, warring factions were splintering and prolifer-
ating, and the most powerful faction, the National Patriotic Front of
Liberia, opposed ECOMOG's intervention, condemning it as a Nigerian-led
attempt to deny the NPFL the political fruits of its military labors. In
response to NPFL leader Charles Taylor's armed resistance, ECOMOG initially chose a coercive strategy and attempted to force him to make peace.

Between 1990 and 1995, the peacekeepers militarily supported an
interim government in Monrovia in which civil society actors were promi-
nently represented. This strategy failed, however, due to the second con-
straint on ECOMOG: its political master, ECOWAS, was hopelessly divided over the intervention. The NPFL was supported by several members of
ECOWAS, who opposed any attempt by ECOMOG to enforce peace, while
several ECOMOG states supported various anti-NPFL factions. Nigeria and
Ghana, ECOMOG's two largest contingents, squabbled over military and

43

diplomatic strategy. Third, the reduced strategic value of Africa after the end of the Cold War, coupled with international opposition to military rule in Nigeria (the key contributor to ECOMOG), resulted in the international community, particularly the United States, failing to provide the necessary logistical and financial support for the intervention.

The war in Liberia ended because of the removal of these three obstacles to peace. Eventually, the growing strength of Taylor's opponents eroded his territorial dominance and provided him with an incentive to regard a peace agreement as a means of winning power. ECOMOG changed its strategy from backing civil society–based interim governments to creating an interim government involving Taylor and other Liberian warlords. ECOWAS itself grew more united over time as leaders changed in key countries and as the war destabilized neighboring states. The rapprochement between Nigeria and Taylor in 1995 and the increased though erratic cooperation of Liberia's warlords in an interim government, resulted in the agreement of key ECOWAS francophone states to contribute troops to ECOMOG. This led international actors like the United States and the European Union finally to commit logistical and financial resources to assist ECOMOG's efforts to end the war.

After providing a brief background to the Liberian civil war, this chapter divides the peace process in Liberia into three distinct phases. The first phase, between May 1990 and August 1994, saw ECOMOG unsure of its mandate and switching uneasily between keeping and enforcing peace while simultaneously attempting to overcome subregional disunity and to negotiate peace. Enforcement actions taken against the NPFL and collaboration with two NPFL foes, the Armed Forces of Liberia (AFL) and the United Liberation Movement of Liberia for Democracy (ULIMO), compromised ECOMOG's neutrality during this phase. This situation deprived the force of the NPFL's cooperation, hindered subregional consensus, and denied the peacekeepers—intervening in an area of low priority to the west—substantial external support. During the second phase of the peace process, between September 1994 and August 1996, Charles Taylor negotiated more seriously with ECOMOG as he lost control of Liberian territory to his rivals and as a regime more conciliatory to Taylor took power in Nigeria. Fierce factional fighting in Monrovia in April and May 1996, however, proved to be a major setback to international peacemaking efforts. The third phase of the peace process, between September 1996 and July 1997, saw the provision of substantial international assistance for ECOMOG to disarm Liberia's fighters, and elections were held in July 1997 in which the most powerful warlord, Charles Taylor, threatened, bought, and charmed his way to power.

After a brief conclusion summarizing the main arguments of the chapter, a postscript considers the durability of the peace that has emerged in Liberia since 1997. Alarming trends concerning Taylor's politicization of the security forces, the use of repressive measures against political opponents and government critics, and continuing appeals to ethnic divisions all raise serious doubts about the prospects for a durable peace in Liberia.

BACKGROUND TO CONFLICT:
DOMESTIC AND EXTERNAL DIMENSIONS

Liberia, a republic of 2.5 million inhabitants on West Africa's coast, was founded in 1847 by freed black American slaves. Despite constituting only 5 percent of the population, this coastal settler elite established an oligarchy that excluded and oppressed the indigenous inhabitants. The 133-year rule of the Americo-Liberian oligarchy created deep-seated resentment and divisions within Liberian society and left historical scars on the oppressed indigenous population that the reforms enacted by Presidents William Tubman and William Tolbert (1944–1980) failed to heal.[3] Amid growing economic problems, Tolbert was faced with unprecedented political challenges from Liberian opposition groups. The spontaneous jubilation of non–Americo-Liberian indigenous people following a coup of 1980 by low-ranking soldiers graphically symbolized the level of hostility that had welled up against the ruling True Whig Party.

The brutality of Master-Sergeant Samuel Doe's regime was heralded by his assassination of Tolbert and thirteen of the Americo-Liberian president's senior officials within a week of taking power. Over the next four years, Doe eliminated potential rivals through assassination or enforced exile. Human rights abuses proliferated against civil society groups, including among them students, journalists, and others who challenged Doe's rule. The Liberian autocrat's crude tactics, typified by the blatantly rigged, U.S.-condoned 1985 elections, closed off peaceful avenues for dissent and resulted in several military challenges to his regime, which culminated in Charles Taylor's 1989 invasion.

Like other Liberian institutions before 1980, the AFL's senior leadership was dominated by Americo-Liberians, creating resentment among the indigenous lower ranks, who did not share in the benefits enjoyed by the officer corps. On assuming power, Doe perpetuated these divisions by filling the most important military positions with fellow members of his ethnic group and purging the army of Gios and Manos. He effectively turned a national institution into a Krahn-dominated instrument of oppression: a reputation that followed the AFL throughout the civil war.

The brutality of Doe's rule and his parochial, ethnic power base deepened ethnic divisions within Liberian society. Krahns, making up only 5 percent of the population, were disproportionately represented in the cabinet, though Doe co-opted some Mandingo elements into the political system. This created enemies among important political groups. Many Americo-Liberians felt alienated by the murder of their former leaders, while Gios and Manos, about 15 percent of the population, felt victimized on several fronts.[4] On 12 November 1985, General Thomas Quiwonkpa, a Gio from Nimba county and former commander of Doe's army, led a failed military coup. Doe executed Quiwonkpa and his fellow putschists and purged the army of Gios. His Krahn-dominated soldiers then took their revenge by going on a rampage in Nimba county, where they burned villages and indiscriminately killed a reported 3,000 Gios and Manos. This single episode, more than any other, set the stage for the exploitation of ethnic rivalries that would eventually culminate in Liberia's civil war. Nimba citizens were purged from the army, while Gio politician Jackson Doe was robbed of probable electoral victory in 1985. The combination of widespread corruption under the Doe regime, the precipitous decline in revenues from Liberia's main exports (rubber, timber, and iron ore), and the cessation of U.S. economic assistance proved disastrous to Doe.

Of Warlords and War Chests

On 24 December 1989, a band of about 168 NPFL fighters crossed into Liberia's Nimba county from Côte d'Ivoire in order to topple Doe's regime. The rebels rallied support among disaffected Nimba citizens, building an ethnic army as they marched toward Monrovia. Ethnic scores were settled as Gio and Mano NPFL fighters killed Krahns and Mandingos, while Krahn AFL soldiers killed Gios and Manos.[5] Liberia's civil war was mainly fought by eight factions. Charles Taylor, an Americo-Liberian, led the 12,500-strong NPFL. He had escaped from a Massachusetts prison in 1985, where he was being held pending possible extradition to Liberia to face charges that he had embezzled U.S.$900,000 while serving as chief of Liberia's General Services Agency under Doe. The nucleus of the NPFL consisted of Gio soldiers and farmers from Nimba county, joined by Burkinabè, Gambian, and Sierra Leonean mercenaries.

Two other splinter groups later emerged from the NPFL. The 6,000-strong Independent National Patriotic Front of Liberia (INPFL) was founded by Prince Yeduo Johnson, who broke away from Taylor in July 1990. A violent and unpredictable warlord prone to public acts of cruelty, Johnson captured Doe in September 1990 and videotaped his grisly torture and murder. The INPFL ceased to exist after 1993 when ECOMOG banished Johnson to Nigeria and many of his fighters joined other factions. The

NPFL Central Revolutionary Council (CRC) was led by Tom Woewiyu, Laveli Supuwood, and Sam Dokie, senior NPFL officials who broke with Taylor in 1994, luring hundreds of combatants away from the NPFL.

The AFL, with about 7,000 soldiers, was the remnant of Doe's Krahn-dominated army. Headed by General Hezekiah Bowen, the AFL was based in Monrovia for most of the war. ULIMO was founded in May 1991 in Sierra Leone by leading Krahn and Mandingo politicians who recruited the bulk of their fighters from the Liberian refugee population in Sierra Leone. ULIMO split into two factions in 1994, with Roosevelt Johnson, a Krahn, heading the 3,800-strong ULIMO-J, while Alhaji Kromah, a Mandingo, headed the 6,800-strong ULIMO-K. The Liberia Peace Council (LPC) emerged in 1993. It had about 2,500 fighters and was headed by George Boley, a prominent Krahn politician who had served as a minister under both Tolbert and Doe. The Lofa Defense Force (LDF) emerged in 1993. It had about 400 fighters and was headed by François Massaquoi, an indigene of Lofa county.

None of the faction leaders spelled out their ideological reasons for waging the war. None provided any coherent plan for fundamentally changing Liberia's political and economic structures and society. All defined their struggle in vague, broad terms that were based more on personal expediency than political ideology. Taylor claimed to be waging the war to remove Doe, but opposed the principle of democratic elections for several years. Anti-NPFL factions claimed to be fighting for the democratic rights of all Liberians, but were essentially ad hoc ethnic armies led by individuals with dubious democratic credentials. The war witnessed widespread human rights abuses and atrocities.[6] Underfed and mostly unpaid fighters, many of them drug-induced children, were often only nominally controlled by their leaders.

One of the main difficulties in efforts to resolve Liberia's civil war was the fact that the country's economic resources provided warlords with the means to enrich themselves and continue to finance their military campaigns. Battles were often fought for control of areas rich in economic resources in a land blessed with diamonds, gold, timber, rubber, and iron ore. Taylor derived an estimated U.S.$75 million annually from these exports, including a reported U.S.$10 million a month from a consortium of North American, Japanese, and European miners, and an estimated U.S.$300,000 a month from foreign timber firms.[7,8] ULIMO-K was keen to restore the Mandingos' diamond trading links with Sierra Leone, from which they had been excluded in March 1991. ULIMO-J was involved in diamond mining in Bomi county, while the LPC exported rubber from Buchanan port.[9] In 1995 alone, between U.S.$300 million and U.S.$500 million worth of diamonds and gold, U.S.$53 million worth of timber, and

U.S.$27 million worth of rubber were exported to markets in Europe and Southeast Asia by Liberia's warlords.[10]

The Subregional Actors

In postindependence West Africa, institutions are notoriously weak and leaders notoriously strong, and a change of regime can radically and suddenly alter foreign policy alliances.[11] Often, an intricate network of personal relationships and shifting alliances determined the policies of individual states toward the Liberian conflict.

NPFL rebels entered Liberia through Côte d'Ivoire in 1989. They had received training in guerrilla warfare in Burkinabè and Libyan military camps, and both countries supplied Charles Taylor with arms during the war. These actions stemmed from personal networks and relationships. Ivorian leader Félix Houphouët-Boigny had never forgiven Doe for executing Benedict Tolbert, the husband of his adopted daughter and son of the murdered Liberian president, during the bloody 1980 coup. For much of the Liberian civil war, the NPFL enjoyed access into Liberia through Côte d'Ivoire, and Ivorian-based commercial interests benefited from NPFL mineral and timber concessions.[12] Burkina Faso lent several hundred of its soldiers to Taylor in the early stages of Liberia's war.[13] Burkinabè leader Blaise Compaoré had obtained Taylor's release from a Ghanaian jail a few years earlier and later introduced him to Libyan leader Muammar Qaddafi, who sought to punish Doe for closing down the Libyan embassy in Liberia in 1981 and for supporting U.S. anti-Libyan policies.[14]

Nigeria provided 80 percent of ECOMOG's troops and 90 percent of its funding during much of the war, giving it the lead in determining ECOMOG's policies. Abuja had several reasons for its involvement in Liberia. Some Nigerian citizens had been killed by NPFL fighters in Monrovia in early 1990 and Nigerians were held hostage by Taylor's forces. Historically, Nigeria's military leaders have been eager to forge a Pax Nigeriana, portraying their country as the indispensable power in West Africa.[15] They were concerned about the impact of the civil war on the stability of the subregion and on ECOWAS, an economic integration scheme launched with strong Nigerian leadership in 1975 (see Chapter 2). Nigeria remained involved in Liberia in part because its political generals personally benefited from revenues written off as ECOMOG expenses, while the ECOMOG mission helped General Sani Abacha, Nigeria's leader between 1993 and 1998, ward off the threat of severe international sanctions against his regime. General Ibrahim Babangida, Nigeria's leader between 1985 and 1993, furnished arms to Doe at the start of the conflict, creating in Taylor's mind a lasting distrust of Nigeria.

Several ECOWAS states also had their own interests in supporting ECOMOG. A few NPFL fighters had been involved in the unsuccessful Gambian coup of 1981. NPFL ally Burkina Faso sheltered Gambian dissidents, and the unsuccessful 1981 coup in Gambia was widely believed to have been sponsored by Libya, another strong supporter of the NPFL. Guinea and Sierra Leone, as two of the three states most directly affected by the spillover of refugees from the war, also had reason to support the ECOMOG intervention: by August 1990, Guinea hosted 225,000 refugees and Sierra Leone 69,000. Furthermore, the NPFL had Sierra Leonean dissidents within its ranks who aimed to destabilize Sierra Leone. Guinean and Sierra Leonean soldiers fought alongside ULIMO against the NPFL and its Sierra Leonean allies, the RUF, during the war, while Alhaji Kromah, the ULIMO-K chief, enjoyed close political ties with Guinea.

Liberia's Historical Godfather:
The United States

The United States, historical godfather and Cold War patron of Liberia, was the only non-African power that could have provided an alternative to the ECOMOG intervention. But the Liberian war occurred at the end of the Cold War, when the United States perceived little strategic interest in Africa and was preoccupied with the annexation of Kuwait by Iraq.[16] Concerned about Libya's links with the NPFL, the United States sent military advisers to AFL positions in Nimba county at the start of the conflict, but congressional complaints soon led to their speedy withdrawal. Thereafter, Washington limited itself to supporting the ECOWAS peace plan, and contributed U.S.$500 million in humanitarian assistance to Liberia during the civil war. But the United States distanced itself from ECOMOG, and President George Bush ordered his officials to avoid a high-profile role in Liberia.[17] Washington evacuated its citizens from Liberia and ignored widespread calls from Liberians and some of its European allies to stage a military intervention. The sudden withdrawal of U.S. assistance to Doe had a destabilizing effect on Liberia, leaving a security vacuum that Charles Taylor's invasion attempted to exploit.

Next we will examine in detail the fourteen peace agreements of the Liberian civil war, starting with the nine accords reached between 1990 and 1994, continuing with the five accords signed between 1994 and 1996, and concluding with the implementation of the 1996 Abuja II agreement between 1996 and 1997. These three sections will focus especially on the domestic, subregional, and external obstacles to implementing the fourteen peace agreements.

THE PEACE AGREEMENTS: MAY 1990–AUGUST 1994

Between May 1990 and August 1994, Liberia's parties signed nine peace agreements and implemented none of them. Barriers to settlement included the unwillingness of Taylor to share power; the mutual suspicions of rival warlords and their fears of disarmament if others reneged on the deal; and significantly, the lucrative bounties from economic resources that were derived from areas under the warlords' control. Subregional actors remained divided on the best approach for achieving peace and were compromised by their support for rival Liberian factions. International donors, considering Liberia an area of little strategic interest and wary of Nigeria's military regime, failed to commit the resources needed to implement the accords.

The Nigerian-led ECOMOG was robbed of some of its legitimacy at its creation by the dissent of key francophone states, particularly Côte d'Ivoire and Burkina Faso, but also Senegal, Niger, Mali, and Togo. ECOMOG's legitimacy was also weakened by the refusal of the NPFL to recognize the peacekeepers' authority to intervene militarily in Liberia. Even judged by the terms of ECOWAS's own charter and defense protocols, ECOMOG was on shaky legal foundations, with no specific clauses allowing for military intervention in a member state's internal conflict.[18] ECOMOG justified the intervention largely on humanitarian grounds and by citing the destabilizing effect of the civil war on the entire subregion.[19] UN and OAU diplomatic and eventually military support served to bolster ECOMOG's international legitimacy, as did the addition of Senegalese and Malian military contingents. But the continued opposition of Burkina Faso and the NPFL to the peacekeepers, coupled with ECOMOG's collaboration with anti-NPFL factions, continued to deprive the intervention of universal legitimacy and support.

ECOMOG's efforts were further hampered by noncompliance. The chief "spoiler" was Charles Taylor, leader of the NPFL, which attacked ECOMOG peacekeepers as they arrived in Monrovia in 1990 and which again invaded Monrovia in 1992. ECOMOG initially supported members of Liberia's civil society and provided arms to anti-NPFL factions. The peacekeepers launched attacks against the NPFL in October 1990 and January 1993, blockading its ports, capturing its territory, and attempting to cut off its economic resources. But ECOMOG simply lacked the means and was unwilling to prosecute a guerrilla war against the NPFL. Besides, successful coercion would have required not only military capability bolstered by external logistical support, but also subregional consensus and the willingness of Taylor's allies to abandon him. Neither was forthcoming.

ECOMOG lacked the capacity to confront the factions militarily and, diplomatically divided, grew increasingly unwilling to undertake enforcement actions. There were unsuccessful efforts to seal Liberia's porous borders to prevent arms flows, but there were no attempts to stop European and Asian commercial firms from paying Liberian warlords for illicit exports of minerals and timber. Subregional efforts to secure an economic embargo at the UN Security Council were scuttled by France and several other states whose companies benefited from this illicit trade.[20] ECOWAS threatened economic sanctions against the NPFL in 1992, but ECOMOG obtained the support of neither Burkina Faso and Libya nor foreign firms and governments to stop the flow of arms and resources to Liberia's factions.

The UN and the OAU joined the peace process hoping to gain the confidence of the NPFL by reducing Nigeria's dominance of ECOMOG. The subregional force was diversified to include francophone contingents from Senegal and Mali, OAU peacekeepers from Uganda and Tanzania, and extra-regional UN peacekeepers. However, the role of the UN and the OAU did not go much further than the contribution of less than 3,000 troops and the legitimization of ECOMOG's actions. The establishment of a buffer zone on the border with Sierra Leone was intended to build confidence between the NPFL and ULIMO to encourage them to implement the Yamoussoukro accords of 1991. But the warlords still refused to make peace, Burkina Faso and Libya still refused to stop arming Taylor, and the international community still refused to provide substantial support to ECOMOG. The United States was wary of being too closely associated with brutal military regimes in Nigeria and withheld logistical support from ECOMOG's dominant contingent.

From Banjul to Lomé, May 1990–February 1991

As NPFL rebels marched toward Monrovia in May 1990, an ECOWAS summit in Banjul established a five-member Standing Mediation Committee (SMC) with a mandate to mediate the Liberian civil war. Nigeria, Ghana, Gambia, Mali, and Togo were elected as the first members. Meanwhile, Liberia's Inter-Faith Mediation Committee, composed of religious leaders, organized peace talks at the U.S. embassy in Freetown between 12 and 16 June 1990. The NPFL failed to send representatives, insisting that Doe resign before any talks could be held. At another ECOWAS meeting in Freetown on 12 July 1990, the NPFL rejected a compromise proposal for an interim government in which Doe would not participate. NPFL representatives initially agreed to a regional peacekeeping force that excluded Nigeria, but rejected the proposal after consulting with Taylor.[21]

ECOWAS's Standing Mediation Committee met in Banjul on 6 and 7

August 1990. By that time, nearly 500,000 Liberian refugees had flooded into neighboring Guinea, Côte d'Ivoire, and Sierra Leone. At least 5,000 people had been killed in Liberia, and 3,000 Nigerian, Ghanaian, and Sierra Leonean citizens were being held hostage by the NPFL. The August meeting produced a plan, crafted largely by Liberia's civil society groups in Freetown, to establish a peacekeeping force, ECOMOG, with a mandate to supervise a cease-fire and, following Doe's resignation, to establish an interim government and organize elections after twelve months. None of the faction leaders would be allowed to join the interim government. A U.S.$50 million special emergency fund was proposed to finance ECO-MOG (each contingent was also asked to cover its cost for the first month until ECOWAS took over the funding) and to provide for the immediate humanitarian needs of Liberians. ECOWAS, the OAU, and other members of the international community were asked to contribute to the fund.[22] The UN and the OAU pledged the support of their organizations to ECOMOG, but the two francophone members of the SMC, Mali and Togo, as well as Côte d'Ivoire, declined to contribute troops to ECOMOG.

ECOMOG initially deployed 3,000 soldiers from Nigeria, Ghana, Guinea, Sierra Leone, and Gambia. The troops arrived in Monrovia on 24 August 1990. The force immediately confronted the key problem in its mandate: it had been conceived as a peacekeeping operation, but there was no peace to keep. ECOMOG came under immediate fire from the NPFL and soon concluded that it would need to use force to implement the Banjul plan. Within a month, ECOMOG's leaders deployed 3,000 more troops, mostly Nigerian, changed its mandate from peacekeeping to peace enforcement, and ordered its soldiers to establish a buffer zone to protect Monrovia from NPFL attacks. ECOMOG expelled the NPFL from the capital but compromised its stated neutrality by fighting alongside the INPFL and the AFL. Tension developed between Nigeria and Ghana following the embarrassing capture of Doe at ECOMOG headquarters and his subsequent killing in September 1990. ECOMOG's Ghanaian force commander General Arnold Quainoo was replaced by the "no-nonsense" Nigerian commander General Joshua Dogonyaro, an ally of General Babangida.[23] Accra complained that it had not been consulted on this change, and started attaching conditions to the use of its troops and insisting that it be informed before any changes were made to ECOMOG's mandate.[24]

The peacekeepers still lacked francophone support in November 1990 by the time the first extraordinary ECOWAS summit was held in the Malian capital of Bamako. Mali would soon announce its decision to contribute officers to ECOMOG, in part to dilute the anglophone dominance of the force. ECOMOG's decision to establish an Interim Government of National Unity (IGNU), headed by Amos Sawyer, the exiled head of the

Association for Constitutional Democracy in Liberia (ACDL), caused further friction with the francophone states that had not given their consent, and Taylor predictably dismissed the IGNU as a puppet of ECOMOG. The NPFL chieftain attended the ECOWAS summit in Bamako, where Compaoré reportedly convinced him to sign a peace agreement.[25] Bamako called for a cease-fire, a cessation of arms purchases, the creation by ECOMOG of a permanent buffer zone to separate the belligerents, and the election of an interim government, followed by the disarmament of the factions by ECOMOG.[26] The full ECOWAS authority finally endorsed the Banjul peace plan in Bamako. At another SMC meeting in Togo from 12 to 13 February 1991, the NPFL, the INPFL, and the IGNU signed the Lomé agreement to implement Bamako. A stalemate, however, soon developed: the NPFL insisted on a new interim government before disarmament, while the IGNU insisted on disarmament before the installation of another interim government. This issue remained a major obstacle to the implementation of every peace agreement during Liberia's civil war.

From Yamoussoukro to Cotonou, June 1991–June 1993

Four rounds of negotiations took place in the Ivorian town of Yamoussoukro between June and October 1991 in a bid to resolve the continuing deadlock. The use of francophone capitals as mediation sites, the selection of a new Committee of Five that included Côte d'Ivoire, Senegal, and Togo, and the election of Senegal's Abdou Diouf as ECOWAS chairman in July 1991, all confirmed the ascendancy of the Francophonie in subregional mediation. A division of labor seemed to be emerging within ECOWAS: the francophones took the lead in mediation and left military operations largely to the anglophones.

Despite signs of growing subregional unity, the implementation of Yamoussoukro was further complicated by continuing divisions within ECOWAS and a lack of international support for ECOMOG. Ghana, unlike Nigeria, was prepared to tolerate a Taylor presidency and wanted its troops to engage strictly in peacekeeping functions and avoid a peace enforcement role. The United States forcefully pushed the Yamoussoukro peace process while denying ECOMOG substantial military support and accusing its peacekeepers of supporting anti-NPFL factions. The UN and the OAU continued to lend moral rather than material support to the subregional effort.

The main requirements of the Yamoussoukro agreement included the deployment of ECOMOG to all parts of Liberia; the encampment and disarming of factions under ECOMOG's supervision; the creation of a buffer zone on the Liberia–Sierra Leone border; the monitoring of all airfields and seaports by ECOMOG to stem the flow of arms; and an expansion of ECO-

MOG, with Senegal promising to contribute troops to the mission. Attainment of these objectives was expected within two months. Yamoussoukro also called for the creation of an interim government, an elections commission, and an ad hoc supreme court to oversee elections within six months.[27]

Having signed and broken two previous accords, Charles Taylor continued to act as a "spoiler." He called for the introduction of UN troops into Liberia and a reduction of ECOMOG troops from 6,000 to 1,500. Taylor sought to increase the military costs of intervention to ECOMOG while preventing his own total diplomatic isolation. Regarding militarily-weak Sierra Leone as ECOMOG's Achilles' heel, he encouraged NPFL elements, led by a group of Sierra Leoneans dubbed the Revolutionary United Front, to enter Sierra Leone on 23 March 1991 to destabilize the government and expand his own economic base through revenues derived from Sierra Leonean diamonds (see Chapter 4). By taking the war to Sierra Leone, Taylor also hoped to splinter the ECOMOG coalition and force Sierra Leone to withdraw from the war. He sought to expose ECOMOG's rationale for intervening in Liberia as flawed by showing that the force could neither keep the peace nor prevent the war from spreading to the subregion.

Although Taylor partly achieved his goals, he also suffered military reversals when ULIMO engaged with his troops, backed by Nigeria, Sierra Leone, and Guinea, in western Liberia. He failed to convert his early military successes into diplomatic capital, and no state recognized his National Patriotic Reconstruction Assembly Government (NPRAG) in Gbarnga, though several government-backed foreign firms conducted business with him. Taylor refused to disarm until ULIMO had halted its advances, and his support for Yamoussoukro was largely based on his expectation that ECOMOG's creation of a buffer zone between Liberia and Sierra Leone would ease ULIMO's military pressure on the NPFL.

The next ECOWAS conference on Liberia took place in Geneva from 6 to 7 April 1992. The meeting set new timetables for the deployment of ECOMOG and the completion of disarmament, and acceded to Taylor's request to maintain a personal security unit of company strength.[28] Although by this time officials had been appointed to Liberia's election commission and supreme court, ECOMOG was unable to establish a buffer zone between Sierra Leone and Liberia due to continued fighting between the NPFL and ULIMO.

In early 1992, as part of the implementation of Yamoussoukro, 1,500 Senegalese troops arrived in Liberia. Building on the excellent personal relationship between Presidents George Bush and Abdou Diouf, and cemented by Senegal's contribution of troops to the U.S.-led Gulf War in 1991, the United States contributed U.S.$15 million to the Senegalese contingent's logistical needs.[29] Washington continued, however, to withhold substantial support from other ECOMOG contingents. Although Taylor had first suggested that Senegalese troops join an expanded ECOMOG in order to dilute its anglophone dominance, he would soon complain that "the US is using the Senegalese for their [sic] surrogate activities in Liberia."[30]

ECOMOG deployed its peacekeepers to the Liberian countryside but faced many difficulties: ULIMO incursions into NPFL areas forced the peacekeepers to withdraw from the Liberia–Sierra Leone border zone; ECOMOG's freedom of movement was restricted; and its soldiers' heavy weapons were barred from rebel areas. On 28 May 1992, six Senegalese troops were killed by NPFL commandos in the Lofa village of Vahun in northern Liberia, and 500 ECOMOG peacekeepers were thereafter held hostage by the NPFL for one week.

By the end of 1992, ULIMO had managed to gain control of about 20 percent of Liberian territory. Taylor responded by staging a military offensive in the hope of either defeating ECOMOG or inflicting enough casualties to force its withdrawal from Liberia. On 15 October 1992, the NPFL launched "Operation Octopus," a full-scale attack on Monrovia. The offensive caught ECOMOG by surprise and exposed the weaknesses of its intelligence capabilities. It was not until a week later that ECOMOG counterattacked, bombing NPFL positions from the air and sea. Units of the AFL and ULIMO again fought alongside ECOMOG to defend Monrovia, raising renewed doubts about its stated neutrality. By the time ECOMOG declared a unilateral cease-fire on 10 November, 3,000 people had died in the fighting.

By the middle of January 1993, the Senegalese contingent had withdrawn from Liberia, citing pressing domestic problems.[31] The loss of a respected francophone state reduced ECOMOG's credibility as a subregional force. ECOMOG field commander General Adetunji Olurin rushed to Abuja, where he used his personal relationship with Nigerian leader General Babangida to secure the soldiers needed to launch a credible counteroffensive against the NPFL.[32] ECOMOG's estimated strength was thereafter increased to 16,000 troops, of which 12,000 were Nigerian. This marked the zenith of Nigeria's dominance of the ECOMOG force. In the next three months ECOMOG seized NPFL strongholds in the country. The loss of strategic NPFL assets was a serious blow to Charles Taylor, reducing his access to arms and cutting into his profits from iron ore, rubber, and timber exports. Elsewhere in Liberia, the proliferation of factions intensified. ULIMO seized control of most of northwest Liberia from a distracted NPFL, but lost several towns in Lofa county to the Lofa Defense Force. The Liberia Peace Council was also waging war against the NPFL for control of southeastern Liberia.

ECOMOG's enforcement actions again brought out tensions between

Nigeria and Ghana regarding their respective military approaches. As Eboe Hutchful noted:

> The Ghanaians were constantly perplexed by the *modus operandi* of the Nigerians, who they found "very, very unconventional" in the administration of their forces. Ghanaian officers were critical in private of what they perceived as the patronage relationship between Nigerian officers and soldiers, the involvement of Nigerian soldiers in various corrupt and illicit businesses, and command practices that compromised discipline and operational security.[33]

The Nigerians were also accused of failing to involve other contingent commanders in planning for military operations, an accusation repeated during the ECOMOG intervention in Sierra Leone a few years later.[34] For their part, the Nigerians justified their secrecy by insisting that the largest contingent should naturally determine military planning, and by citing past security breaches after they had confided military plans to other contingents.[35]

From Cotonou to Akosombo, July 1993–August 1994

The next efforts to end Liberia's civil war took the form of peace talks sponsored by the UN, in cooperation with ECOWAS and the OAU, in Geneva from 10 to 17 July 1993. These talks produced the Cotonou agreement, named after the Beninois capital where the accord was signed on 25 July. Under Cotonou, ECOMOG was to expand its force to include UN and OAU peacekeepers; establish a cease-fire by 1 August 1993; set up a five-member executive Council of State; install a Liberian National Transitional Government (LNTG) by the end of August 1993; hold presidential elections in seven months; and establish buffer zones on Liberia's borders with Guinea, Côte d'Ivoire, and Sierra Leone.

The most detailed peace agreement of the Liberian civil war, Cotonou specified the supervisory and monitoring roles of ECOMOG and the UN, the prohibitions on the parties, acts that constituted cease-fire violations, and the most far-reaching details on the structure and mandate of an interim government. A joint cease-fire monitoring committee, to be chaired by a UN Observer Mission in Liberia (UNOMIL) and involving ECOMOG and representatives of the armed factions, was established to investigate and resolve cease-fire violations. The Cotonou agreement explicitly gave ECOMOG peace enforcement powers with the approval of a UN-chaired cease-fire violations committee. The accord was signed barely two months after ECOMOG's capture of the key NPFL-controlled port of Buchanan. NPFL control of Liberian territory had shrunk from 95 percent in 1990 to 50 percent, and it faced continuing challenges from ULIMO, the LPC, and the LDF. ECOMOG had effectively bombed Charles Taylor to the negotiating table.

Concomitant with the installation of a transitional government in Monrovia on 7 March 1994, ECOMOG started deploying its troops to the Liberian countryside accompanied by 1,500 OAU troops from Tanzania and Uganda and 368 unarmed UN military observers. ECOMOG, however, had not received the logistical and financial support it had consistently requested from the international community and was deployed in less than 15 percent of the country.[36] Continued fighting in the countryside hampered ECOMOG's disarmament efforts and by August 1994, only 3,612 of an estimated 33,000 combatants had been disarmed. Several ambushes of OAU and ECOMOG soldiers by Liberia's factions forced the UN to withdraw its observers to Monrovia and reduce UNOMIL's peacekeepers from 368 to 90.

Tensions between ECOMOG and UNOMIL further hampered implementation of the Cotonou accord. ECOMOG soldiers often complained that UNOMIL withheld its vehicles and helicopters from their use. UN personnel were paid much higher stipends than ECOMOG's, fueling further discord.[37] Four other areas of disagreement emerged between ECOMOG and the UN. First, ECOMOG wanted UNOMIL to have a passive rather than a lead role in disarmament, observing rather than directing the process. Second, ECOMOG officials were angered by what they regarded as UN Special Representative Trevor Gordon-Somers's unilateral disarmament negotiations with the parties. Third, in contrast to UNOMIL's chief military observer, Kenyan general Daniel Opande, ECOMOG's field commander, Nigerian general John Inienger, preferred a hard-line approach toward disarming the NPFL. Finally, ECOMOG criticized UNOMIL for failing to consult it before deploying troops, while UNOMIL complained that ECOMOG was incapable of protecting its military and civilian personnel.[38]

Aside from these military difficulties, there were political obstacles to the implementation of the Cotonou accord. Professor David Kpomakpor, the IGNU nominee and a law professor, was installed as chairman of the Council of State in March 1994. The council also included representatives of the NPFL and ULIMO. But the LNTG was unable to extend its authority beyond Monrovia and remained entirely dependent on foreign donors for its financial survival. Council members sharply disagreed over appointments to public corporations and agencies, as the warlords struggled for their share of the limited spoils.

Liberia's warlords signed Cotonou as they had signed previous peace agreements, largely for tactical reasons. Charles Taylor agreed not because of a sincere commitment to implementing the accord, but largely due to external political pressure from ECOWAS members and internal military pressure from ULIMO, the LPC, and the LDF, which had significantly reduced his control of Liberian territory. ECOMOG's military offensive had also weakened Taylor's economic base. The IGNU signed the peace deal in the hope that it would bring an end to the war and result in a settlement that would give civilians a significant role in a new political order. Liberia's politicians realized that most of their country lay under the control of the warlords and regarded the signing of peace agreements and the ECOMOG presence as necessary diplomatic and military tools to pressure the warlords into giving up territory and agreeing to an interim government.

As for the other Liberian factions, ULIMO, the LPC, and the LDF hoped to obtain a share of political power in a future government through the conquest of territory, which would then provide them with some leverage during peace negotiations. ULIMO's presence at the Cotonou talks in 1993, after its exclusion from Yamoussoukro in 1991, was a clear sign to other factions that gaining territory was the most viable way of winning a place at the negotiating table. New factions had much to lose and nothing to gain from the successful implementation of Cotonou. The failure of Cotonou was in their interest, as the failure of Yamoussoukro had been in ULIMO's interest.

THE PEACE AGREEMENTS:
SEPTEMBER 1994–AUGUST 1996

From Akosombo to Accra, September 1994–January 1995

In September 1994, barely a month after becoming ECOWAS chairman, Ghanaian president Jerry Rawlings summoned the leaders of Liberia's three largest factions, Taylor, Kromah, and General Bowen, to Akosombo. The meeting produced an agreement calling for a new five-member Council of State on which the three warlords would sit along with one representative jointly nominated by Taylor and Kromah, with the remaining seat occupied by a nominee of the civilian Liberian National Conference (LNC). This agreement marked the start of ECOMOG's strategy of appeasing the warlords to win their compliance in recognition of the peacekeepers' inability to impose peace on Liberia. It also led to the marginalization in the peace process of Liberia's civil society groups and to a termination of ECOMOG's support for an interim government led by civil society representatives.

Akosombo gave joint responsibility for disarmament, monitoring of

Liberia's borders, and arms searches to ECOMOG, the UN, and the warlord-dominated LNTG. The transitional government was granted the right "to use the necessary force available to compel compliance . . . in collaboration with ECOMOG." The agreement also gave the LNTG responsibility for restructuring the Liberian army with the assistance of ECOWAS, the UN, and "friendly governments." Akosombo was a warlords' agreement. Charles Taylor had long argued that the leaders of the warring factions should be directly represented on the Council of State, and that the LNTG be allowed to supervise disarmament: Akosombo fulfilled both of these wishes. But Akosombo was a stillborn agreement. At the time of its signing, fighting was raging throughout Liberia and rival factions had militarily expelled two of its three signatories from their headquarters: Taylor from Gbarnga and Kromah from Tubmanburg. The exclusion of the LPC, the LDF, ULIMO-J, and the CRC-NPFL from the Akosombo agreement, despite their control of large swathes of Liberia, meant that the accord bore no resemblance to the military and political realities in Liberia.

Rawlings amended the agreement in response to mounting criticism from within Liberia and the subregion, especially from Nigeria. Whereas Accra believed that if the warlords could run the government, disarmament would automatically follow, Abuja believed that if the warlords could be convinced to disarm, an effective interim government would follow. ECOWAS foreign ministers met in Accra on 22 November 1994 to renegotiate the Akosombo agreement. Three weeks of discussions in Accra led to agreement on a five-member Council of State. Seats were to be divided between the NPFL; ULIMO-K; the coalition of anti-NPFL factions (the AFL, the CRC-NPFL, the LDF, the LPC, and ULIMO-J) founded in September 1994; the LNC, consisting largely of civil society representatives; and a fifth member elected by the electoral college of the LNTG. The AFL and other security forces were to be restructured, with ECOMOG and UN assistance, to include all factions. The warlords signed the Accra agreement on 21 December 1994. Like twelve other peace agreements before it, Accra was never implemented. The cease-fire was consistently flouted as fighting raged in the southeast between the NPFL and the LPC and in central Liberia between the NPFL and ULIMO-J. The amorphous anti-NPFL coalition never agreed on its candidate for the Council of State.

The Road to Abuja, June–August 1995

On 2 June 1995, an unexpected breakthrough occurred between Nigeria and Charles Taylor that would prove decisive in ending Liberia's civil war. Coaxed by Compaoré and Rawlings, the NPFL warlord spent four days with Nigerian leader General Sani Abacha in a rapprochement between

ECOMOG's dominant force and Liberia's strongest faction. Abacha was less secure within the Nigerian army than his predecessor, General Babangida, and was forced to focus more attention on domestic issues. He depersonalized the rivalry between Taylor and Babangida, and was more pragmatic in seeking a solution to the conflict. As Nigeria no longer opposed his ambitions and the NPFL had lost territory to rival factions, Taylor became more amenable to a peace deal.

On the eve of an ECOWAS meeting in August 1995, Rawlings met with Abacha in Abuja. The two leaders decided to break the diplomatic impasse in Liberia by convincing the anti-NPFL coalition's nominee, Tom Woewiyu, to relinquish his council seat for LPC leader George Boley.[39] All the warlords attended the meeting, as did civil society representatives from the Liberia Women Initiative and the Inter-Faith Mediation Committee of Liberia, groups that were fast losing influence over ECOMOG to Liberia's warlords. During this meeting, Nigeria's abrasive foreign minister, Tom Ikimi, called for a council that could provide strong and effective leadership and would be able to control the whole territory of Liberia.[40]

Nigeria gradually acceded to Ghana's position that only the inclusion of the warlords in the government would bring peace to Liberia. During a meeting of ECOWAS leaders in Abuja on 18 and 19 August 1995, Taylor, Kromah, and Boley were nominated to an extended six-member Council of State and asked to suggest candidates for council chairman.[41] Along with the three powerful warlords, there were three civilians on the Council of State: its chairman, Wilton Sankawulo, a former literature professor, Chief Tamba Tailor, an aged traditional leader, and LNC representative Oscar Quiah. As only Quiah had intimate experience of Liberian politics, the civic groups feared the warlords would dominate the council. Quiah was also considered close to George Boley, one of the warlords on the council.[42]

Ministerial posts were shared on an inclusive basis, with faction leaders Roosevelt Johnson, Hezekiah Bowen, Tom Woewiyu, and François Massaquoi obtaining cabinet posts. Positions to the supreme court, autonomous agencies, and public corporations were also divided among the armed factions and civilians. Abuja was a lavish banquet to whet the appetite of Liberia's avaricious warlords. It was a desperate attempt to buy peace by offering the faction leaders the spoils of office. The rationale was that political power could be exchanged for military peace. It was the same idea behind the hastily arranged Akosombo agreement from which Accra had learned the lesson of not consulting closely with Abuja before making important decisions. The Abuja agreement was signed on 19 August 1995. Abuja returned sole authority for military enforcement action to ECOMOG, and removed the role that Akosombo had assigned to the LNTG. A cease-fire was to come into effect on 26 August 1995. ECOMOG and UNOMIL would then deploy throughout the country. The disarmament and demobilization of the belligerents was expected to be completed by January 1996.

Despite the failure of a dozen previous peace agreements, there was widespread optimism, for three reasons, that the Abuja agreement would finally end Liberia's war. First, Nigeria and the NPFL had made peace, removing a major obstacle that had frustrated earlier peacemaking efforts. Second, all the warlords were directly involved in the council for the first time and were therefore thought to have a direct stake in keeping the peace. Finally, there was war-weariness among the 33,000 faction fighters, some of whom had started voluntarily disarming to ECOMOG even before the Abuja agreement had been signed.

From Abuja I to Abuja II, September 1995–September 1996

The implementation of Abuja, however, like that of previous agreements, proved more difficult than its negotiation. On 27 October 1995, a donor conference on assistance to Liberia was held in New York. The conference sought support for humanitarian assistance, disarmament and demobilization, recovery and rehabilitation, and assistance to ECOMOG. However, the low priority that Western policymakers accorded to Liberia ensured that only U.S.$145.7 million was pledged for Liberia's reconstruction, even as the international community pledged U.S.$6 billion for the reconstruction of Bosnia.[43] ECOWAS chairman Jerry Rawlings had asked for U.S.$195 million for ECOMOG's and UNOMIL's disarmament and demobilization tasks alone.[44] Two months after the donor conference, ECOMOG's logistical shortcomings were again glaringly exposed when ULIMO-J combatants attacked its troops in the western Liberian town of Tubmanburg, killing sixteen Nigerian peacekeepers, wounding seventy-eight others, and capturing some of ECOMOG's heavy weapons and other equipment.

The warlords used the Council of State as a platform for the presidential campaign and there were increasing complaints about Sankawulo's weak and ineffectual leadership. Without an army or popular support, he was constantly being outmaneuvered by the warlords. The faction leaders also tried to increase their own authority by arguing, in contravention of Abuja, that they were part of a collective executive presidency and were therefore responsible for disarming fighters and approving ECOMOG's deployment plans.[45]

Such behavior eventually led Taylor and Kromah to attempt to exploit a split within the leadership of ULIMO-J by sending elements of the national police, backed by NPFL and ULIMO-K fighters, to arrest Roosevelt Johnson on 6 April 1996. Johnson predictably refused to surrender, resulting in street battles between NPFL and ULIMO-K forces on the one hand and a Krahn alliance of ULIMO-J elements supported by the AFL and the LPC on the other. After two months of fighting in Monrovia, 3,000 people had died.[46]

OAU leaders meeting in Yaoundé in July 1996 responded to these events by warning that "should the ECOWAS assessment of the Liberian peace process . . . turn out to be negative, the OAU will help sponsor a draft resolution in the UN Security Council for the imposition of severe sanctions . . . including the possibility of the setting up of a war crimes tribunal to try the leadership of the Liberian factions on the gross violations of the human rights of Liberians."[47] Although the resolution reflected growing regional frustration with the Liberian conflict, as long as the warlords remained in the interim government and as long as ECOMOG's peacemaking strategy required continued cooperation with them, its implied threat remained unconvincing.

In recognition of the precarious situation then prevailing in Liberia, ECOWAS decided to postpone elections from August 1996 to May 1997. Following the horrific fighting in Monrovia in April and May 1996, the United States finally decided to separate its displeasure with the domestic politics of Nigeria's military regime from its support for ECOWAS's multilateral peacekeeping effort.[48] The United States, followed shortly after by the European Union, promised to provide logistical support to all of ECOMOG's contingents for the first time since its deployment. Disarmament, demobilization, and the repatriation of Liberian refugees were now expected to occur by January 1997. The ECOWAS heads of state designated Ruth Perry, a former Liberian senator and leading member of the Liberia Women Initiative, as the new council chairperson. This agreement came to be known as Abuja II.

The implementation schedule of the new agreement was divided into five stages, with three assessment meetings and two ECOWAS foreign ministerial meetings scheduled for Monrovia between October 1996 and April 1997. As part of Abuja II, it was determined that sanctions, including travel and residence restrictions, freezing of business activities and assets, and exclusion from the electoral process, could be recommended against Liberia's factions by ECOWAS foreign ministers. For repeated noncompliance, ECOWAS could invoke the OAU 1996 summit resolution threatening a war crimes tribunal. ECOWAS leaders also adopted a code of conduct for the Council of State that gave ECOWAS the power to replace erring members.[49] These sanctions revealed ECOWAS's determination to monitor the implementation of the peace agreement more closely and to take punitive measures against "spoilers." But success still depended on the cooperation of the warlords and greater unity among ECOWAS members, some of whom continued to support individual warlords.

IMPLEMENTING ABUJA II: SEPTEMBER 1996–JULY 1997

Disarming the Factions

ECOMOG's commitment to disarming Liberia's factions was aided tremendously by the rapprochement between Nigeria and Taylor, an increasingly consensual subregional approach to peacemaking, and newfound international assistance. During the mayhem in Monrovia in April and May 1996, the United States helped to create the International Contact Group on Liberia to identify how international actors could assist Liberia and ECOMOG. Between August and December 1996, the United States provided the logistical support it had long denied ECOMOG's peacekeepers, releasing U.S.$40 million for, among other things, helicopters, communication equipment, uniforms, and medical equipment. Instrumental in convincing the United States to support ECOMOG was a seasoned African American career diplomat, Howard Jeter, the U.S. presidential envoy to Liberia and current ambassador to Nigeria.[50]

This assistance, along with the arrival of 119 trucks, and also helicopters and communication equipment from EU states, gave the peacekeepers the logistical support to deploy confidently to the countryside for the first time since the start of their mission. It was also crucial that Liberia's warlords continued to cooperate with ECOMOG. The Dutch minister for development cooperation, Jan Pronk, launched a fundraising process in October 1996 that culminated in three donor conferences that eventually provided vital funds to support Liberia's disarmament, demobilization, and electoral process.[51]

By November 1996, ECOMOG's Nigerian force commander, General Victor Malu, had deployed his troops to disarmament sites all over Liberia. Malu, who had served as ECOMOG chief of staff between 1992 and 1993, was widely praised for his dynamic leadership of the mission. The fact that he had the ear of General Sani Abacha and enjoyed the respect of all the warlords and the Liberian public was helpful in maintaining Nigeria's commitment to Liberia. The disarmament process started on schedule on 22 November. Fighters were given food rations and provided transportation to chosen destinations in exchange for the surrender of a serviceable weapon or a hundred rounds of ammunition. Despite the scale of the disarmament exercise, many of the weapons surrendered in the early stages were unserviceable. The second Abuja accord did not provide even small assistance packages for former combatants, who complained about the meager food rations. But despite these difficulties, the warlords largely cooperated with disarmament. There were, however, reports of arms caches being buried in the Liberian countryside by the factions.[52]

According to UN figures, by 9 February 1997, 24,500 of the estimated

33,000 fighters, 74 percent, had been disarmed and demobilized. These included 4,306 child fighters and 250 adult female fighters. Over 9,570 weapons and 1.2 million pieces of ammunition were also surrendered, while ECOMOG's cordon-and-search operations around the country yielded another 122,162 pieces of ammunition and 917 weapons.[53] Most roadblocks were cleared and manned by ECOMOG soldiers. With the arrival between February and April 1997 of 650 Malian, 500 Ghanaian, 320 Burkinabè, 321 Nigerien, and 250 Beninois peacekeepers, along with a 35-member medical team from Côte d'Ivoire, ECOMOG's troop strength grew from 7,500 to 10,500, with an additional 1,000 Nigerian troops also sent to Liberia. The arrival of new national contingents diversified the force's composition to include six francophone and four anglophone states, though Nigeria still had 7,000 of the 10,500 troops. But for the first time since its arrival in Liberia, ECOMOG's francophone contingents outnumbered their anglophone counterparts.

The 19 July 1997 Election

On 7 April 1997, a month behind schedule, Liberia's independent elections commission and supreme court were installed in Monrovia. Three weeks later, an ECOWAS foreign minister delegation met with the elections commission and Liberia's political parties to discuss the draft electoral law, the electoral timetable, and the elections commission's budget. During the meeting, the delegation reduced the commission's proposed budget from U.S.$9.5 million to U.S.$5.4 million and decided that ECOWAS should assume greater responsibility for the physical and logistical aspects of the electoral process, including transportation and the procurement of electoral matériel.[54]

ECOWAS's assertiveness reflected the tension that pervaded the electoral preparations. Following tense bilateral relations between the United States and the military junta in Abuja, Nigeria was keen not to allow external actors to steal the glory for ending the Liberian war. A minimum U.S.$100,000 levy was imposed on ECOWAS members to help pay for the elections in a bid to raise U.S.$1.5 million on top of the U.S.$5.4 million earlier approved for the electoral process. Between January and August 1997, the United States contributed U.S.$25 million to support Liberia's electoral and reconstruction efforts. ECOWAS and the UN established a joint electoral coordination mechanism, which met regularly with Liberia's elections commission to discuss operational and other issues related to electoral preparations.

On 21 May 1997, the ECOWAS heads of state held an extraordinary summit in Abuja. The meeting postponed Liberia's elections from May to

July 1997 and approved the new Liberian electoral law, which was based in part on the country's 1985 constitution, with its six-year presidential term.[55] Only about 75,000 refugees returned home to participate in Liberia's elections, leaving over 550,000 disenfranchised refugees, a fifth of the population, in neighboring countries. Many of these refugees still felt it was unsafe to return to Liberia. However, based on the scale of Taylor's electoral victory, their participation would not have made much difference to the eventual outcome of the presidential election.

On 19 July, elections were held in Liberia, with ECOMOG providing security at the 1,864 voting stations, and 500 international observers from the UN, the EU, the OAU, the Carter Center, and Friends of Liberia observing the poll.[56] The Liberian Elections Observer Network (LEON), a coalition of civil society groups, also had 1,300 observers who monitored the poll. Final results were announced on 24 July, with Charles Taylor scoring a landslide victory. He won 75.3 percent of the presidential vote, while his closest rival, Ellen Johnson-Sirleaf, won 9.5 percent. Taylor's National Patriotic Party (NPP) also won 21 out of 26 Senate seats and 49 of the 64 seats in the House of Representatives. An impressive 85 percent of the 750,000 registered voters turned out to cast their ballots on polling day. ECOWAS and the UN declared the election "free and fair." There were some logistical and technical deficiencies: voter education had been inadequate, no census was conducted, and ballot secrecy was sometimes compromised by assistance given to illiterate voters. But after seven years of civil war, some of these difficulties were to be expected in the first Liberian election in twelve years.

Two reasons account for Taylor's spectacular victory. First, Liberians saw Taylor as a guarantor of peace and stability and feared a return to war if he lost. During the campaign, Taylor had repeatedly told journalists that he could not imagine himself losing the election and that the issue of accepting electoral defeat was irrelevant. Second, with an estimated U.S.$450 million in earnings from natural resources in areas he controlled during the war, Taylor had an electoral war chest that his rivals simply could not match. This enabled him to reach more voters through private radio stations and newspapers as well as allowing him to distribute largesse to voters.

On 2 August 1995, Charles Taylor was inaugurated as Liberia's twenty-first president, finally achieving his long-held ambition at tremendous cost to the country. It was clear, however, that there were difficult times ahead: the new government was inheriting an empty national treasury with only U.S.$17,000, a domestic debt of U.S.$200 million, and an external debt of U.S.$3 billion.[57] Taylor's electoral victory still left many skeptics wondering whether a ruthless warlord and former jailbird could successfully transform himself into an enlightened statesman and attract the international assistance necessary to revive Liberia's economic and political fortunes.

CONCLUSION

The failure to implement thirteen major peace agreements in Liberia for six years can best be explained through an assessment of complex interactions at the domestic, subregional, and extra-subregional levels. Domestically, peace was rendered difficult by the proliferation of armed factions and the manipulation of ethnic rivalries by power-seeking warlords, a situation exacerbated by the refusal of the strongest faction, the NPFL, to share power with other groups. Mutual suspicions and fears rendered the factions unwilling to commit to disarmament. Economic profits derived from territory under their control proved a powerful disincentive to ending the war. At the subregional level, ECOWAS disagreed on how to resolve the conflict. Burkina Faso and Côte d'Ivoire supported the NPFL militarily for much of the war, while complaining about Nigeria's ambitions to dominate West Africa; Guinea and Sierra Leone backed ULIMO; Nigeria provided military assistance to the AFL and the LPC; and Ghana and Nigeria disagreed on fundamental diplomatic and military issues. While ECOWAS lacked political unity, allowing the warlords to exploit subregional divisions, ECOMOG lacked the military tools and was unwilling to engage the warlords in a protracted guerrilla war.

At the extra-subregional level, international actors largely ignored subregional efforts to resolve the conflict. The United States, Liberia's Cold War patron, channeled its support largely toward humanitarian relief. Washington criticized ECOMOG for lack of impartiality and its deteriorating diplomatic relations with Abuja after annulled Nigerian elections by its military in 1993 and continued repressive military rule resulted in inconsistent support for ECOMOG. The UN had less than 100 unarmed military observers in Liberia for most of the war, while the OAU's 1,500 peacekeepers withdrew after a year, following the failure of the international community to deliver on promised logistical support.

By 1997 most of these difficulties were finally resolved. At the domestic level, the warlords largely cooperated with ECOMOG in disarming their fighters. The most powerful, Charles Taylor, was confident of winning power through elections. At the subregional level, Nigeria made peace with Taylor and no longer supported his enemies, resulting in Burkina Faso and Côte d'Ivoire contributing troops to ECOMOG. At the extra-subregional level, the United States and the European Union provided crucial logistical support to the West African peacekeepers, enabling ECOMOG to disarm the factions. In the end, contingencies and personal relations between ECOWAS leaders and Liberian warlords, rather than any structured plans, led to the end of the war in Liberia.

ECOMOG's strategy was largely improvised, building on acquired experience, and only the decision to appease the warlords by granting them political power eventually terminated the conflict. The proliferation and strength of military factions that successfully challenged NPFL control over Liberian territory led Taylor to negotiate more seriously. The changed and ultimately successful Nigerian policy of rapprochement with the NPFL was crucial to ending the war, but was itself possible only after a change of regime in Abuja in 1993.

POSTSCRIPT: POSTWAR OR PREWAR LIBERIA?

President Charles Taylor's first four years in office have been financially difficult and marred by controversy over human rights violations.[58] After the 1997 elections, the UN established its first, small peacebuilding support office in Liberia (UN Office in Liberia [UNOL]) to coordinate postconflict programs of various UN agencies, support the rehabilitation of demobilized soldiers, and promote international assistance for Liberia's reconstruction efforts. The head of the UN office, Felix Downes-Thomas, has been criticized by Liberian civil society groups, opposition parties, and sections of the national media for being too close to Taylor, for not supporting UN human rights efforts, and for interpreting the UN mandate too narrowly. These domestic actors complained that they had had no contact with Downes-Thomas and regarded him as an apologist for the Taylor regime.[59] As an internal UN report of July 2001 admitted, the UN peacebuilding office was poorly resourced and its mandate was weak and not politically intrusive due to the initial reluctance of the UN Security Council to establish the office. The Liberian government had accepted the office as the lesser evil to a continued ECOMOG presence in the full knowledge that the UN would not interfere with its running of the country.[60]

Taylor has been unable to attract much foreign assistance to rebuild his shattered country. Liberia's National Reconstruction Program (NRP) sought U.S.$433 million over the first two postelection years to revive government institutions, provide essential social services, rehabilitate public infrastructure, repatriate and resettle refugees and internally displaced persons, and reintegrate demobilized fighters into society. The program talked of "transparency," "accountability," and "broad-based participation."[61] But the reality of postwar Liberia has scarcely matched these noble objectives.

Though Taylor at first embarked on a policy of national reconciliation by inviting members of rival parties to join his cabinet, he soon cracked down on opposition and attempted to institutionalize his dominance of the Liberian state. Former Taylor ally and later opponent Sam Dokie and members of his family were murdered in November 1997 after being arrested by Taylor's security forces. The suspects were acquitted in April 1998 as a result of an apparent lack of evidence. Liberia's journalists and human rights activists have been harassed and jailed for criticizing the government. Two radio stations were shut down in March 2000, while four newspapers were closed down and several journalists for the *News* were arrested in February 2001. Taylor now controls most of Liberia's media through his private radio stations and newspapers. In November 2000, 300 armed men vandalized the office of the Center for Democratic Empowerment (CEDE) in Monrovia and injured its directors, Amos Sawyer and Commany Wesseh, forcing both into exile shortly afterward. Members of the Catholic Justice and Peace Commission, including its director James Verdier and his predecessor Samuel Kofi Woods, as well as the deputy director of Liberia Democracy Watch, Augustine Toure, have complained about threats on their lives.

Liberia's security situation remains precarious four years after the end of the war. Armed robbery, looting of food aid, and banditry have thrived in rural Liberia. Crime and insecurity plague Monrovia. The mobilization of armed ethnic groups in support of the agendas of rival warlords during the civil war has led to continuing political problems in postwar Liberia. Following intense fighting in Monrovia, a shooting incident involving Taylor's security men and his former Krahn minister of rural development, Roosevelt Johnson, at the U.S. embassy in Monrovia in September 1998 led to fifty-two deaths and the evacuation of Johnson from Liberia. There were reports of the harassment of Krahns in Monrovia by Taylor's security forces following this incident, forcing over 4,000 Krahns to flee to Côte d'Ivoire.[62] Another disturbing trend involves reports of Mandingos being violently attacked by Lomas in Lofa county and by Gios and Manos in Nimba county. These clashes are related to disputes over land and resources as refugees return to areas abandoned during the civil war. By June 1998, arsonists had burned six mosques throughout the country. Liberia's ethnic and religious powderkegs can be reignited, with disastrous results, if these conflicts are not carefully managed.

Following the election of 1997, instability on Liberia's borders soured relations between Taylor and ECOMOG, which, along with the United States and others, criticized Taylor's continued military support for RUF rebels who were fighting ECOMOG in Sierra Leone. Taylor, in turn, accused ECOMOG of supporting some of his rivals in Sierra Leone;

refused ECOMOG jets permission to use Liberian airfields for missions into Sierra Leone; criticized ECOWAS and UN sanctions against the Armed Forces Ruling Council (AFRC)/RUF military junta in Freetown; and publicly opposed the Nigerian-led intervention in Freetown to restore the elected government of Ahmed Tejan Kabbah in February 1998. By the end of 1998, ECOMOG finally withdrew its peacekeepers from Liberia.

Following ECOMOG's departure, insecurity has continued along Liberia's borders with Guinea and Sierra Leone. After 200,000 Sierra Leonean refugees flooded into Liberia in September 1997 following fighting in that country, Taylor sent troops to guard his border with Sierra Leone. The Liberian president is particularly sensitive about his border areas as ULIMO launched its invasion against the NPFL from Sierra Leone, and as Taylor himself invaded Liberia from Côte d'Ivoire. In an outbreak of violence that could signify the start of Liberia's second civil war in a decade and reverse ECOMOG's gains, Liberian dissidents invaded the towns of Voinjama and Kolahun, both in Lofa county, in April and August 1999. These attacks were launched from Guinea by the Liberians United for Reconciliation and Democracy, who are thought to be mostly Mandingo and Krahn fighters of the former ULIMO-K and ULIMO-J militias. ULIMO-K leader Alhaji Kromah had close ties to Conakry during Liberia's seven-year civil war. Former ULIMO-J leader Roosevelt Johnson had left Liberia after intense fighting with Taylor's security forces in 1998.

Shortly before May 1999, Taylor-supported RUF rebels had launched attacks into Guinea, destroying property and lives.[63] In September 1999, two Guinean villages on the border with Liberia were attacked by Guinean rebels believed to be backed by Taylor.[64] The acrimonious relationship between Taylor and the Guinean leader, Lansana Conté, dates back to 1990, before the ECOMOG intervention, when Conté threatened to invade Liberia unilaterally following the NPFL invasion.[65] In March 2001, Taylor announced the expulsion of the Guinean and Sierra Leonean ambassadors from Monrovia, accusing them of aiding rebels to attack Liberia. He had withdrawn his own ambassador from Conakry three months earlier. The relationship between Liberia and Guinea worsened following renewed attacks into Lofa county by LURD rebels between July and November 2000, forcing thousands of refugees to flee the area. Guinea issued inflammatory statements against Liberian and Sierra Leonean refugees, which led to xenophobic attacks against nationals of the two countries. Like Taylor, General Conté, who once enjoyed close ties with France, has scarcely been a paragon of democratic leadership: he has conducted deeply flawed elections and jailed his political rivals. By April 2001, heavy fighting raged between Taylor's army and Guinean-backed Liberian rebels near the Lofa towns of Foya and Kolahun and was spreading into Nimba county.

Having already deployed troops in Lofa county, Taylor was forced to mobilize 15,000 former NPFL fighters to repel the rebels. The fighting made it impossible for ECOWAS to implement a plan to deploy 1,700 troops along the borders of Liberia, Sierra Leone, and Guinea. Taylor's claims that his army was bringing the situation in Lofa county under control rang especially hollow when suspected LURD rebels killed François Massaquoi, his minister for youth and sports and former leader of the LDF faction, shooting down his helicopter as it attempted to land in Lofa county. Daniel Chea, Liberia's defense minister, warned that his troops would pursue the rebels across the border into Guinea, threatening a further escalation of the conflict.

A particularly disturbing aspect of postwar Liberia is Taylor's failure to restructure the AFL and other security forces, with the assistance of ECOMOG and the UN, as envisaged in the Accra agreement of 1994. After his election in 1997, Taylor refused to allow the peacekeepers a role in restructuring and training his security forces. He ordered the demobilization and retirement of 2,628 soldiers from the AFL, including many Krahn officers, in January 1998. Taylor has included thousands of his former NPFL fighters in the new Liberian army and has created the notorious Anti-Terrorist Unit as a private army.[66] The restructuring process has been criticized as partisan and lacking in transparency.

Taylor's decision to fill his security forces with loyal lieutenants is hardly unique in contemporary African politics, where leaders in Burundi, Rwanda, Côte d'Ivoire, Togo, and Zaire have followed tradition in placing kinsmen in strategic military positions. The fragile state of postwar Liberia and the continuing sources of insecurity, however, suggest that Taylor is repeating Doe's fatal mistake: by filling the army with ethnic loyalists and by using it as a tool against political opponents, Taylor has created conditions for the mobilization of ethnic groups to protect their own people against a partisan army. The institutionalization of violence that was a hallmark of the Doe regime and that became a way of life during Liberia's brutal civil war seems to be continuing into the Taylor era.[67] Liberia's security forces have historically served as an instrument of partisan rule, first defending the interests of the Americo-Liberian oligarchy, then keeping the autocratic regime of Doe in power, and now attempting to ensure the survival of Taylor's regime.

Most of Taylor's opponents view the state apparatus as an extension of his own personal power: the dispensation of justice is not perceived to be neutral. As the Liberian president continues to use state power to silence his critics and aims to remove all opposition to his rule prior to the next elections scheduled for 2003, he has created a situation similar to that produced by Doe's fraudulent election of 1985, where opponents were left with no legitimate way of challenging Doe except through violence. All of Taylor's main political rivals now live outside the country. On 12 November 1998, Taylor accused thirty-two people, including self-exiled former warlords Alhaji Kromah, Roosevelt Johnson, George Boley, and Ellen Johnson-Sirleaf of involvement in a plot to overthrow his government. Following a court trial in Liberia, many of the suspects were convicted, some in absentia, and several were jailed.

Having waged a guerrilla campaign for seven years, Taylor still has the psychology of a warlord. He has failed to transform himself from warlord into statesman. Good governance in a democratic setting has been far more difficult than the unencumbered autocracy of warlord politics. During the civil war, Taylor briefly lost his headquarters in Gbarnga to his enemies, saw other factions gang up against him, witnessed Nigeria, Sierra Leone, and Guinea providing assistance to rival factions, and heard calls by several Nigerian generals for his assassination. He is still profoundly scarred by these experiences. Having himself led an ultimately successful rebellion into Liberia based on the exploitation of ethnic grievances, and having witnessed Doe's grisly end, Taylor is deeply aware of his own vulnerability in Liberia's political cesspit. His paranoia and obsession with security are not altogether surprising. Within days after the assassination of Congolese leader Laurent Kabila by one of his bodyguards in January 2001, Taylor replaced his own personal security detail.[68] As the Liberian leader candidly admitted, "Once you are in, because of the chaos created from outside, you become undemocratic in the preservation of power. It is almost like the survival of the fittest."[69] Having amassed so much illicit wealth and gathered so many enemies in his bloody ascent to power, Taylor, like Doe before him, is determined to retain his position to prevent any vindictive rival from probing his past practices.

The lack of security, the collapse of public infrastructure, and the absence of the rule of law in Liberia have made donors stingy and deterred foreign investors. South African and Canadian firms are involved in prospecting for Liberian minerals, but such interest has been rare. Taylor has maintained close political relations with Burkina Faso and Libya and sought to court Taiwanese and French investors. But traditional trading partners like the United States, Japan, and Germany continue to stay away. Liberian diamonds are still being smuggled out of the country and there are reports of lucrative contracts being awarded to Taylor's close political associates.[70] The Liberian president has asked the National Assembly to grant him the sole power to conclude commercial contracts over exploiting "strategic commodities," the clearest sign of the former warlord's determination to use the trappings of sovereignty to continue to plunder his country's resources. A donor conference for Liberia's reconstruction sheld in

Paris in April 1998 led to pledges of U.S.$200 million. But these funds were made conditional on progress on security and human rights and never arrived. Four years after a devastating civil war, Liberia's shattered infrastructure has not been revived even as a new war in the north causes further damage.

Amid these domestic difficulties, Taylor faces unprecedented external pressure. In March 2001, the UN Security Council, led by the United States and Britain, demanded that Liberia halt the importation of Sierra Leonean diamonds, end Liberian support for the RUF, and pressure the rebels to allow the UN Mission in Sierra Leone (UNAMSIL) access to rebel-controlled territory. Liberia's support for the rebels reportedly included the training of RUF rebels in Liberia, strategy meetings with the RUF in Monrovia, and supply of military assistance to the RUF from Liberia. These allegations were documented by a Panel of Experts on Sierra Leone Diamonds and Arms established by the UN Security Council in a report of 20 December 2000.[71] Taylor made frantic efforts to comply with the Security Council's requests by grounding all Liberian aircraft, inviting international monitoring of Liberia's diamond trade, calling for the deployment of UN monitors along Liberia's land and sea borders, and announcing the expulsion of former RUF commander Sam Bockarie from, and the closure of the RUF office in, Monrovia.

But there were still reports of continuing collaboration between Taylor and the RUF, and Bockarie's expulsion, which was vociferously supported by Liberia's religious and civic groups, could not be independently verified.[72] Deciding that Taylor's efforts lacked conviction, the UN Security Council on 7 May 2001 imposed a ban on the export of diamonds from Liberia as well as travel sanctions on senior government officials and their spouses. The council also tightened an existing arms embargo by prohibiting the sale or supply of arms and related matériel to Liberia and banning the provision of military training to the government. These sanctions, which many of Liberia's civil society groups and opposition politicians supported on the basis that they would hurt the leadership in Liberia more than the people, are to be reassessed every fourteen months.

The UN Security Council delayed the imposition of sanctions for three months at the urging of most ECOWAS states, with the notable exceptions of Guinea and Sierra Leone. The sanctions debate between the Security Council and ECOWAS reflected a continuing difference of approach between the two bodies. Most ECOWAS states argued against what they saw as a policy of sticks without carrots, and criticized the Security Council's policy for being contradictory. The council sought to punish Taylor for supporting the RUF while simultaneously seeking Taylor's assistance in gaining the RUF's compliance to implement the Lomé peace plan in Sierra Leone.[73] ECOWAS's own policy may not be entirely free of contradictions. Nigerian president Olusegun Obasanjo has actively courted Charles Taylor since taking office and has worked closely with him in negotiating the Lomé agreement to end Sierra Leone's war (see Chapter 4). But while Obasanjo told a visiting UN Security Council mission in October 2000 that he believed that Taylor was behind the destabilization of the subregion, he and many of his colleagues seem to believe that the former warlord can still be transformed into a responsible statesman through diplomatic means.[74] ECOWAS leaders, several of whom have themselves demonstrated undemocratic and destabilizing behavior, also doubtless fear the precedent of the UN Security Council imposing sanctions on Liberia for bad behavior.

In order for the UN sanctions to be effective, it is important that the Security Council secure ECOWAS's cooperation for this approach. The diamond sanctions may not be watertight, since Liberian gems can easily be smuggled through third countries and since no effective enforcement mechanism exists on the ground. The travel sanctions and arms embargo will also need the support of ECOWAS states to be implemented. But the sanctions have clearly rattled Taylor. He has accused their main architects, Britain and the United States, of attempting to overthrow his regime. He has also mounted an effective public relations campaign in which he has blamed UN sanctions for all the ills of his regime: from lack of international assistance to inflation to the continuing war in Lofa county.[75] More devastating economic sanctions on Liberia's U.S.$13 million annual timber trade were blocked in the UN Security Council by France and China, which together import about 45 percent of Liberia's timber.[76]

Taylor currently faces the greatest challenge to the survival of his regime. Liberia's total government revenue for 2000 is estimated to have been only U.S.$85 million, even as the Liberian president announced that U.S.$15 million of this sum had been diverted to the war effort in Lofa county.[77] Meanwhile, civil service salaries in Liberia went unpaid for almost a year. The situation in postwar Liberia parallels that in prewar Liberia: widespread insecurity, a weak economy, patronage-fueled corruption, government harassment of the press and civic groups, interethnic clashes, trumped-up coup plots, and external financial sanctions. The current cycle of violence, which began with Master-Sergeant Samuel Doe's bloody coup of 1980, has certainly not been broken by Taylor's 1997 electoral victory.

NOTES

1. This chapter is adapted from an earlier paper written as part of a Stanford Center for International Security and Cooperation/IPA project on "The Implementation of Peace Agreements," funded by the Ford Foundation.

2. On the estimated loss of life, see Final Report of the Secretary-General on the UN Observer Mission in Liberia, S/1997/712, 12 September 1997, p. 5.

3. See G. E. Saigbe Boley, *Liberia: The Rise and Fall of the First Republic* (New York: St. Martin's Press, 1983); Gus Liebenow, *The Evolution of Privilege* (Ithaca: Cornell University Press, 1969); Eghosa Osaghae, *Ethnicity, Class, and the Struggle for State Power in Liberia* (Dakar: CODESRIA, 1996); and Amos Sawyer, *The Emergence of Autocracy in Liberia: Tragedy and Challenge* (San Francisco: ICS Press, 1992).

4. The figure for Gios and Manos, like figures for other ethnic groups, is an estimate based on the 1974 Liberian census.

5. For accounts of the Liberian civil war, see Adekeye Adebajo, *Liberia's Civil War: Nigeria, ECOMOG, and Regional Security in West Africa* (Boulder and London: Lynne Rienner, forthcoming 2002); Abiodun Alao, John Mackinlay, and Funmi Olonisakin, *Peacekeepers, Politicians, and Warlords: The Liberian Peace Process* (Tokyo, New York, and Paris: UN University Press, 1999); Stephen Ellis, *The Mask of Anarchy* (London: Hurst, 1999); Karl Magyar and Earl Conteh-Morgan (eds.), *Peacekeeping in Africa: ECOMOG in Liberia* (Hampshire, London, and New York: Macmillan and St. Martin's Press, 1998); Klaas Van Walraven, *The Pretence of Peace-keeping: ECOMOG, West Africa, and Liberia (1990–1998)* (The Hague: Netherlands Institute of International Relations, 1999); and Margaret Vogt (ed.), *The Liberian Crisis and ECOMOG: A Bold Attempt at Regional Peacekeeping* (Lagos: Gabumo Press, 1993).

6. See Human Rights Watch/Africa, "Waging War to Keep the Peace: The ECOMOG Intervention and Human Rights," vol. 5, no. 6 (June 1993); Human Rights Watch/Africa, "Liberia: Emerging from Destruction," vol. 9, no. 7 (November 1997); and the UN Secretary-General's Reports to the Security Council on Liberia.

7. On the mining consortium, see William Reno, "The Business of War in Liberia," *Current History,* May 1996, p. 115.

8. On the timber consortium, see "Liberia: Sparking Fires in West Africa," *Africa Confidential* 32, no. 10 (17 May 1991): 3.

9. William Reno, *Warlord Politics and African States* (Boulder and London: Lynne Rienner, 1998), pp. 104–105.

10. Philippa Atkinson, *The War Economy in Liberia: A Political Analysis* (London: Overseas Development Institute, 1997), p. 9.

11. See Henry Bienen, *Armed Forces, Conflict, and Change in Africa* (Boulder, San Francisco, and London: Westview Press, 1989); Samuel Decalo, *Coups and Army Rule in Africa,* 2nd ed. (New Haven and London: Yale University Press, 1990); and William Foltz and Henry Bienen (eds.), *Arms and the African: Military Influences on Africa's International Relations* (New Haven and London: Yale University Press, 1985).

12. Paul Richards, "Rebellion in Liberia and Sierra Leone: A Crisis of Youth?" in Oliver Furley (ed.), *Conflict in Africa* (New York and London: Tauris Academic Studies, 1995), p. 143.

13. Emmanuel Kwezi Aning, "Managing Regional Security in West Africa: ECOWAS, ECOMOG, and Liberia" (working paper no. 94.2, Centre for Development Research, Copenhagen, February 1994), p. 12.

14. Stephen Ellis, "Liberia 1989–1994: A Study of Ethnic and Spiritual Violence," *African Affairs* 94, no. 375 (April 1995): 181.

15. See, for example, Joseph Garba, *Diplomatic Soldiering: Nigerian Foreign Policy, 1975–1979* (Ibadan: Spectrum Books, 1987); Yakubu Gowon, *The*

Economic Community of West African States: A Study of Political and Economic Integration (Ph.D. thesis, Warwick University, February 1984); and Olusegun Obasanjo, *Not My Will* (Ibadan: University Press, 1990).

16. On U.S. policy toward Liberia, see Herman Cohen, *Intervening in Africa: Superpower Peacemaking in a Troubled Continent* (Hampshire, London, and New York: Macmillan and St. Martin's Press, 2000); Katherine Harris, *African and American Values: Liberia and West Africa* (Lanham, New York, and London: University Press of America, 1985); Mark Huband, *The Liberian Civil War* (London and Portland: Frank Cass, 1998); Tunji Lardner, "An African Tragedy," *Africa Report* 35, no. 5 (November/December 1990): 14–16; Reed Kramer, "Liberia: A Casualty of the Cold War's End?" *CSIS Africa Notes* no. 174 (July 1995); and Gus Liebenow, *Liberia: The Quest for Democracy* (Bloomington and Indianapolis: Indiana University Press, 1987).

17. Personal interview with Herman Cohen, former U.S. assistant secretary of state for African affairs, Washington, D.C., July 1997.

18. See the ECOWAS charter of 1975 and security protocols of 1979 and 1981.

19. See Adekeye Adebajo and Chris Landsberg, "The Heirs of Nkrumah: Africa's New Interventionists," *Pugwash Occasional Paper* 2, no. 1 (January 2001): 75–77; Abass Bundu, "The Case Against Intervention," *West Africa* no. 4156 (30 June–6 July 1997); and David Wippmann, "Enforcing the Peace: ECOWAS and the Liberian Civil War," in Lori Fisler Damrosch (ed.), *Enforcing Restraint: Collective Intervention in Internal Conflicts* (New York: Council on Foreign Relations, 1993), pp. 157–203.

20. Wippmann, "Enforcing the Peace," p. 174. See also David Cortright and George A. Lopez (eds.), *The Sanctions Decade: Assessing UN Strategies in the 1990s* (Boulder and London: Lynne Rienner, 2000), pp. 187–193.

21. Personal interview with Omar Sey, foreign minister of Gambia 1987–1994, Baghdad, 14 December 1997.

22. See First Session of the ECOWAS Standing Mediation Committee, Final Communiqué, Banjul, 6–7 August 1990.

23. See Nkem Agetua, *Operation Liberty: The Story of Major-General Joshua Nimyel Dogonyaro* (Lagos: Hona Communications, 1992).

24. M. A. Vogt, "The Problems and Challenges of Peace-Making: From Peace-Keeping to Peace-Enforcement," in Vogt, *Liberian Crisis and ECOMOG*, p. 168.

25. Personal interview with Prosper Vokouma, foreign minister of Burkina Faso 1989–1991, Ouagadougou, 22 July 1999.

26. See First Extraordinary Session of the Authority of Heads of State and Government, Final Communiqué, Bamako, 27–28 November 1990.

27. See Second Meeting of the ECOWAS Committee of Five, Final Communiqué, Yamoussoukro, 16–17 September 1991; and Third Meeting of the ECOWAS Committee of Five, Final Communiqué, Yamoussoukro, 29–30 October 1991.

28. See Informal Consultative Group Meeting of the ECOWAS Committee of Five on Liberia, Final Communiqué, Geneva, 6–7 April 1992.

29. Discussion of Senegal's role based on a personal interview with General Mamadou Seck, former chief of staff of the Senegalese army, Washington, D.C., 21 July 1997. See also Peter Schraeder, "Senegal's Foreign Policy: Challenges of Democratization and Marginalization," *African Affairs* 96 (1997).

30. Quoted in "Taylor Explains," excerpts of a BBC interview, *West Africa* no. 3892 (20–26 April 1992): 674.

31. See Lindsay Barrett, "Why Senegal Withdrew," *West Africa* no. 3931 (25–31 January 1993); and Robert Mortimer, "Senegal's Role in ECOMOG: The Francophone Dimension," *Journal of Modern African Studies* 34, no. 2 (1996).

32. Personal interview with General Adetunji Olurin, ECOMOG field commander 1992–1993, Lagos, 9 August 1999.

33. Eboe Hutchful, "Peacekeeping Under Conditions of Resource Stringency: Ghana's Army in Liberia," in Jakkie Cilliers and Greg Mills (eds.), *From Peacekeeping to Complex Emergencies: Peace Support Missions in Africa* (Johannesburg and Pretoria: South African Institute of International Affairs, and Institute for Security Studies, 1999), p. 107.

34. Ibid., p. 108.

35. I thank Augustine Toure, Ruth Young Forbes Civil Society Fellow at the IPA, for drawing my attention to this point.

36. For further details on ECOMOG's logistical shortcomings, see Herbert Howe, "Lessons of Liberia: ECOMOG and Regional Peacekeeping," *International Security* 21, no. 3 (Winter 1996/1997); and Cyril Iweze, "Nigeria in Liberia: The Military Operations of ECOMOG," in M. A. Vogt and A. E. Ekoko (eds.), *Nigeria in International Peacekeeping, 1960–1992* (Lagos and Oxford: Malthouse Press, 1993).

37. Personal interview with Trevor Gordon-Somers, UNDP, New York, May 1997.

38. See "Liberia: Problematic Peacekeeping," *Africa Confidential* 35, no. 5 (4 March 1994); Clement Adibe, "The Liberian Conflict and the ECOWAS-UN Partnership," *Third World Quarterly* 18, no. 3 (1997); Binaifir Nowrojee, "Joining Forces: UN and Regional Peacekeeping, Lessons from Liberia," *Harvard Human Rights Journal* 18 (Spring 1995); and Funmi Olonisakin, "UN Co-operation with Regional Organizations in Peacekeeping: The Experience of ECOMOG and UNOMIL in Liberia," *International Peacekeeping* 3, no. 3 (Autumn 1996).

39. Ben Asante, "Straightjacket Deal," *West Africa* no. 4067 (18–24 September 1995): 1477.

40. Economic Community of West African States Consultative Meeting on the Liberia Peace Process, Final Report, ECW/MINFA/CTTE9/VI/2, Abuja, 16–19 August 1995, p. 8.

41. Ibid., p. 10.

42. I thank Augustine Toure for drawing my attention to this point.

43. See Adekeye Adebajo, "Rich Man's War, Poor Man's War," *The World Today* (August/September 1996).

44. James Butty, "International Aid at Last," *West Africa* no. 4073 (6–12 November 1995): 1717.

45. Seventh Meeting of ECOWAS Committee of Nine Foreign Ministers, Final Report (Restricted), ECW/MINFA/CTTE9/VII/2/Rev.1, Accra, 7 May 1996, p. 7.

46. For a detailed account of the events in Monrovia, see Seventeenth Progress Report of the Secretary-General on the UN Observer Mission in Liberia, S/1996/362, 21 May 1996.

47. Quoted in Kaye Whiteman, "The OAU Summit," *West Africa* no. 4109 (22–28 July 1996): 1139.

48. Personal interview with Ambassador Howard Jeter, U.S. presidential envoy to Liberia, Washington, D.C., 3 April 1997.

49. See Fourth Meeting of ECOWAS Heads of State and Government of the Committee of Nine, Final Communiqué, Abuja, 17 August 1996, pp. 4–7.

50. See Howard Jeter, "ECOMOG: An American Perspective on a Successful Peacekeeping Operation," in *Militaries, Democracies, and Security in Sub-Saharan Africa* (papers presented at a conference in Nigeria, 1–4 December 1997), pp. 175–189.

51. See Klaas Van Walraven, *The Netherlands and Liberia: Dutch Policies and Interventions with Respect to the Liberian Civil War* (The Hague: Netherlands Institute of International Relations, 1999).

52. For further details, see Victor Tanner, "Liberia: Railroading Peace," *Review of African Political Economy* 25 (March 1998).

53. Twenty-second Progress Report of the Secretary-General on the UN Observer Mission in Liberia, S/1997/237, 19 March 1997, pp. 3–4.

54. Ibid., p. 2.

55. See Independent Elections Commission, *Special Elections Law for the 1997 Elections* (Monrovia: Sabanoh Press, 1997).

56. See Terrence Lyons, *Voting for Peace: Post Conflict Elections in Liberia* (Washington, D.C.: Brookings Institution, 1998).

57. *Economist Intelligence Unit,* "Liberia," 4th Quarter 1997, pp. 1–10.

58. See Jon Lee Anderson, "The Devil They Know," *New Yorker,* 27 July 1998; and Baffour Ankomah, "Knives Out for Taylor," *New African,* September 1998.

59. Report of the Joint Review Mission on the UN postconflict peacebuilding offices, UN Department of Political Affairs/UNDP, 20 July 2001, p. 14.

60. Ibid., p. 11.

61. See Norwood Langley, "The National Reconstruction Program in Liberia," in *State Rebuilding After State Collapse: Security, Democracy, and Development in Post-War Liberia,* Report of the Strategic Planning Workshop on Liberia, 19 June 1998 (London: Center for Democracy and Development, 1998).

62. *Economist Intelligence Unit,* "Liberia," 1st Quarter 1999, p. 8.

63. Meeting of ECOWAS Ministers of Foreign Affairs, Final Communiqué, Lomé, 24–25 May 1999, p. 5.

64. *Economist Intelligence Unit,* "Liberia," 4th Quarter 1999, pp. 36–40, and 2nd Quarter 1999, p. 36.

65. Personal interview with Professor Amos Sawyer, president of Liberia 1990–1994, Monrovia, 14 July 1999.

66. "Liberia: Taylorland Under Siege," *Africa Confidential* 40, no. 4 (19 February 1999): 7.

67 Amos Sawyer, "Foundations for Reconstruction in Liberia: Challenges and Responses," in *State Rebuilding After State Collapse,* p. 69.

68. Jeffrey Bartholet, "Liberia's Charles Taylor: Inside the Mind of a Tyrant," *Newsweek,* 14 May 2001, p. 31.

69. Charles Taylor (interview), "The West Wants to Suffocate Liberia," *West Africa* no. 4251 (6–12 November 2000): 11.

70. On diamond smuggling, see *Economist Intelligence Unit,* "Liberia," 3rd Quarter 1998, p. 11.

71. See Report of the Panel of Experts Appointed Pursuant to Security Council Resolution 1306 (2000), para. 19, in Relation to Sierra Leone, S/2000/1195, 20 December 2000, pp. 32–34.

72. On collaboration between Taylor and the RUF, see First Report of the Secretary-General Pursuant to Security Council Resolution 1343 (2001) Regarding Liberia, S/2001/424, 30 April 2001, p. 3.

73. Ibid., p. 6.

74. On the alleged culpability of Taylor, see Report of the Security Council Mission to Sierra Leone, S/2000/992, 16 October 2000, p. 8.

75. Report of the Secretary-General in Pursuance of Paragraph 13(a) of Resolution 1343 (2001) Concerning Liberia, S/2001/939, 5 October 2001, p. 6.

76. *Economist Intelligence Unit,* "Liberia," March 2001, p. 49.

77. Ibid., p. 42.

4

Sierra Leone:
A Feast for the Sobels

We are always preaching the ministry of reconciliation. No matter what those guys [the soldiers and rebels] may have done, there is room on the side of the Lord to forgive them and to bring them back on the road that they are supposed to be on.

—Reverend Fornah Usman, Wesleyan minister, Makeni

This chapter will examine the roots of the civil war in Sierra Leone, which erupted in March 1991, tracing the outbreak of violence to the political misrule of Siaka Stevens (1968–1985) and General Joseph Momoh (1985–1992), and the deteriorating economic conditions and collapse of the country's diamond revenues and other sources of income exacerbated by the excesses of a corrupt elite. This situation combined with worsening socioeconomic inequalities between a corpulent urban elite and impoverished unemployed youths in the countryside who had limited access to education and employment and were thus denied the opportunity of social mobility. A potent cocktail of political autocracy and socioeconomic decay produced a mass of disaffected youths in the countryside, many of whom formed the core of Revolutionary United Front rebels, willingly joined the rebellion, or were forcibly recruited to the RUF. Numbers of these youths saw the war as a chance to plunder, mine diamonds, and perhaps replace the ruling class in Freetown. They were often joined in their quest for riches by poorly paid government soldiers from the same impoverished socioeconomic stratum. Using a broader definition than is usually found in the literature on Sierra Leone, we refer here to the alliance between government soldiers and rebels that was formalized during the military junta of 1997–1998 as "sobels."

This chapter also examines the political and economic objectives and military strategy of the principal actors involved in Sierra Leone's civil war. The bulk of the chapter assesses the international military and diplomatic efforts, involving members of ECOWAS, the UN, the OAU, and the Commonwealth, to build peace in Sierra Leone between 1991 and 2001 through the tools of peacemaking, peacekeeping, and peace enforcement. Of particular interest here will be ECOMOG's military role and the international community's peacemaking efforts, which resulted in three peace agreements in Abidjan, Conakry, and Lomé between 1996 and 1999. We will explain why both ECOMOG and international mediators failed to achieve their military and diplomatic objectives. The role of more controversial external actors such as International Alert, Executive Outcomes, and Sandline International will be very briefly discussed. We will also examine the role of Sierra Leonean civil society groups—particularly women's and religious groups—in promoting peace and democratization during the course of the civil war.

The chapter will focus particularly on the factors that prolonged the war at three interdependent levels. These include: domestically, the profits from diamonds, the rampaging brutality of the RUF, and the inability of successive military and civilian governments in Freetown to defeat the guerrillas militarily; subregionally, the divisions within ECOWAS and in particular the support given to the rebels by several subregional states and opposition within ECOWAS to Nigeria's hegemonic ambitions; and extraregionally, the lack of external support and concern for Sierra Leone, a country that was viewed as strategically insignificant by powerful members of the UN Security Council, with the notable exception of Britain. Sierra Leone's former colonial power was the only permanent member of the UN Security Council to demonstrate a sustained interest in the country. Britain was instrumental in the successful establishment of a UN peacekeeping mission in Sierra Leone (UNAMSIL) in 1999 and sent a small contingent to Freetown to support the UN mission. UNAMSIL has, however, suffered from logistical, political, and administrative problems, while the RUF refused to cooperate with the UN and attacked its peacekeepers. All these factors hampered the military efforts of ECOMOG and the UN as well as the implementation of the three peace agreements designed to end the war in Sierra Leone. Recent events have seen more cooperation by the RUF with the UN's disarmament efforts, and parliamentary and presidential elections are planned for May 2002.

THE ROOTS OF A CIVIL WAR

Sierra Leone achieved independence from Britain in April 1961. The country was ruled successively until 1967 by the Margai brothers, Milton and Albert, under the Sierra Leone People's Party (SLPP). The ruling SLPP lost the election of 1967 to the All People's Congress (APC), which was headed by the charismatic and cunning Siaka Stevens. Stevens ran a populist campaign in which he mobilized rural communities against the corrupt urban elite and rural chiefs. A military coup d'état prevented Stevens from taking power until a countercoup in 1968 handed power to the APC. Stevens established a staggeringly corrupt patrimonial system in which he doled out patronage to loyal clients to ensure political support. Sierra Leone was transformed into a de facto one-party state by 1973 (and a de jure one-party state by 1978) and parliament became a rubber stamp for Stevens's decrees. The army was weakened after several military coup attempts, and Stevens ensured that its senior officers were all APC loyalists.[1]

Stevens's seventeen-year rule saw a diminishing of the role of civil society in the political life of Sierra Leone as he brought trade unions, agricultural cooperatives, and business and professional organizations under the sway of the government. But courageous groups within civil society continued to oppose the APC regime. Students at the elite Fourah Bay College received widespread support after demonstrating against rigged elections in 1977. Sierra Leone's irrepressible press also remained vibrant under difficult circumstances and was critical of government corruption.

Stevens's governance failures were exacerbated by an economic crisis brought about by political corruption and a difficult international economic climate. A rapacious Sierra Leonean political class and a parasitic Lebanese business clique combined to loot the country's diamond revenues, even as agricultural production collapsed. Foreign firms abandoned Sierra Leone's diamond and iron ore mines by 1982, to be replaced by a motley crew of adventurist rogues and shady Israeli firms. When Stevens came to power in 1968, Sierra Leone was earning about U.S.$200 million a year from its diamonds. By the time he left power, only about U.S.$100,000 of diamond revenues was entering government coffers annually.[2] A lavish OAU summit in Freetown consumed the equivalent of a year of government spending, while the profligate Stevens's personal wealth was estimated by one analyst at U.S.$500 million.[3] The tripling of international oil prices in 1973 and 1979 had coincided with a decline in revenues for Sierra Leone's main exports: diamonds, iron ore, coffee, and cocoa.

In 1985, Stevens handed over the reins of power to his loyal army chief, General Joseph Momoh, who inherited a divided APC, a weak army, and an economic crisis. The downward economic spiral continued under Momoh: between 1984 and 1992, official diamond exports declined as a percentage of total exports from 31 to 21 percent, and 33 to 50 percent of diamonds were thought to be smuggled out of the country.[4] Between 1980 and 1987, state spending on health and education declined by 60 percent, and by 1988, Momoh was unable to pay arrears on the country's debt even as inflation reached triple digits.[5] These governance failures mirrored those faced by Master-Sergeant Samuel Doe on the eve of Liberia's civil war in 1989 with similarly catastrophic results.

Sierra Leone's civil war erupted in March 1991 when RUF rebels, consisting of Sierra Leonean fighters who, with Liberian members of the National Patriotic Front of Liberia, had received military training in guerrilla warfare in Libya and Burkina Faso, invaded diamond-rich southeastern Sierra Leone from Liberia. The RUF force consisted of about 300 fighters, including "special forces" of Charles Taylor's NPFL. Mercenaries from Burkina Faso also joined the invasion force as they had the NPFL invasion of Liberia in December 1989 (see Chapter 3).[6] Taylor had three main motives for backing the rebels: to force the withdrawal of Sierra Leone from ECOMOG, to help install his RUF allies in power in Freetown, and to profit from the diamond trade in Sierra Leone.

ECOMOG's involvement in Sierra Leone was inextricably linked to its eight-year peacekeeping efforts in neighboring Liberia. The RUF invasion from Liberia resulted in several hundred Nigerian, Ghanaian, and Guinean troops being sent to Sierra Leone to assist their fellow ECOMOG member. Both Guinea and Nigeria had formal defense pacts with Sierra Leone, and Abuja and the government in Freetown were involved in recruiting (largely from the Liberian refugee population in Sierra Leone), arming, and training fighters of the Liberian faction, the United Liberation Movement of Liberia for Democracy, to fight the RUF.[7] Freetown had been the staging post for ECOMOG's intervention in Liberia in August 1990 and remained the rear base for Nigerian soldiers in Liberia and the base for Nigeria's Alpha jets used in bombing NPFL positions in Liberia. Taylor had promised that Sierra Leone would "taste war" for its support of ECOMOG's efforts in Liberia. The Liberian warlord lived up to this promise by assisting the invasion of Sierra Leone and by supporting his RUF allies against ECOMOG throughout the war.

The Sierra Leonean civil war was fought between successive civilian and military governments in Freetown in alliance with civil defense groups including local hunters, the *kamajors,* against the RUF. Corporal Foday Sankoh, a former itinerant army photographer who had been jailed in 1971 for his role in an alleged coup plot and dismissed from the army, led the RUF. The relationship between Sankoh and Charles Taylor was cemented by their trade in diamonds and arms. RUF rebels and rogue military officers and units in Sierra Leone's army controlled a diamond trade worth an estimated U.S.$250 million per year, spawning the phenomenon of the "sobel": soldiers by day, rebels by night.[8] The economic fruits to be derived from the conflict reduced incentives for the factions to reach a negotiated settlement to the war.

The following three sections divide the international military and diplomatic involvement in Sierra Leone into distinct phases. The first phase, from 1991 to 1997, saw Nigerian, Ghanaian, and Guinean troops providing security to successive regimes in Freetown against an RUF onslaught. This section also assesses the establishment of an elected government in Freetown and the signing of a peace agreement in Abidjan in 1996. The second phase, from 1997 to 1999, saw a large ECOMOG presence in Sierra Leone following an army coup in May 1997. This section analyzes the complex diplomacy within ECOWAS during efforts to restore constitutional rule in Sierra Leone, and also briefly assesses the British role in Sierra Leone. The third section, which covers events between 1999 and 2001, examines the change of policy in Nigeria under the regimes of General Abdulsalam Abubakar and President Olusegun Obasanjo. These changes eventually led to the phased withdrawal of Nigerian soldiers from Sierra Leone and the subsuming of the remaining peacekeepers under a more internationally diverse UN force. This final section will assess the problems and prospects of the UN peacekeeping mission in Sierra Leone.

THE ROAD TO ABIDJAN: 1991–1997

The RUF Invasion and Its Aftermath

The RUF invaded Sierra Leone from Liberia in March 1991 and conducted a guerrilla war with the government while terrorizing and looting the countryside. This unlikely coalition of rebels, rabble-rousers, and renegades, led by a roving photographer, plunged the country into a protracted decade-long civil war. In stark contrast to the 1989 NPFL invasion of Liberia (see Chapter 3), the RUF rebels failed to rally local support for their cause. Their brutal methods, including beatings, torture, execution, and mutilation, alienated the rural population. As Yusuf Bangura noted: "The vast majority of rural and urban Sierra Leoneans detest the RUF. Indeed, how rational is a movement whose methods of revolutionary struggle have simply served to alienate the bulk of society from its so-called revolutionary agenda?"[9] While attempting to replicate the NPFL invasion, RUF leader Foday Sankoh proved less successful than Charles Taylor in mobilizing antigovernment sentiment against Joseph Momoh's regime in the traditionally antigovernment eastern Kailahun and southern Pujehun districts.[10] Taylor had successfully mobilized support in anti-Doe areas of Nimba county.

The ill-equipped, poorly trained, and logistically deficient Sierra Leone Army (SLA) was, however, unable to defeat the rebel threat, and the RUF was firmly ensconced in the Sierra Leonean countryside by July 1991. The army felt that its military and financial needs were being neglected by Momoh's regime, and staged a coup on 29 April 1992.[11] A military junta was formed in Freetown, the National Provisional Ruling Council (NPRC), under the leadership of twenty-seven-year-old Captain Valentine Strasser, a former ECOMOG soldier in Liberia. The NPRC at first tried to negotiate a peace deal with the RUF involving a broad-based government, but the NPFL, under military pressure from ULIMO near the Sierra Leone border, is said to have encouraged Sankoh to reject the deal.[12] Sankoh also accused Nigeria and Ghana of encouraging Strasser to pursue the military option.[13]

By October 1992, the RUF, which maintained bases in Liberia during the war, was threatening the diamond-rich Kono district.[14] Following significant military advances against the RUF in 1992 and 1993 that sent the rebels reeling toward the Gola forest reserves, the undisciplined army became distracted by the commercial diamond-mining activities of some of its officers and deserting recruits. The RUF also changed its military tactics, abandoning permanent settlements for several bush camps where it trained and indoctrinated new recruits. The rebels then embarked by November 1994 on hit-and-run attacks in all areas of the country and established new forward camps.[15] To fund its war, the RUF sold diamonds in Liberia and Guinea in exchange for arms.[16]

By the end of 1994, Nigerian troops were stationed in Freetown as well as the Gondama refugee camp near Bo. Sierra Leone's army had almost quintupled in size from 3,000 in 1991 to 14,000 by 1994, but many of the new recruits were ill trained and their loyalty was suspect.[17] In March and April 1995, the RUF attacked the suburbs of Freetown and threatened the capital. Strasser called in a few hundred mercenaries from Executive Outcomes, a private South African security firm, to help train and provide logistical support to his army and *kamajor* militias, and to recapture rutile and aluminum mines from the RUF. The rebels were quickly repelled and the mines reconquered by August 1995. During this period, the military consumed 75 percent of government spending and the economic situation facing the regime was dire: in 1991, exports of minerals (rutile, diamonds, bauxite, and gold) was U.S.$134 million; four years later, this figure had declined to U.S.$900,000.[18,19] The government could neither service its debt nor balance its budget and had to sack a third of all civil servants as a condition for continuing to receive international financial assistance.

From Military Rule to Democratic Elections

In January 1996, thirty-two-year-old Brigadier-General Julius Maada Bio, the chief of defense staff and deputy head of the NPRC, toppled Strasser in a palace coup after the latter had reneged on a prior pledge not to run for the presidency. Strasser was believed to have been tricked into running for the presidency by some of his more ambitious colleagues.[20] The extent of Nigeria's increasing influence on the political situation in Sierra Leone was reflected by the fact that, prior to the event, Bio had informed Nigeria's chief of defense staff, General Abdulsalam Abubakar, that he would stage the coup. Abubakar had passed on the information to Nigerian head of state General Sani Abacha, who assured Bio that Nigerian troops based in Sierra Leone would do nothing to foil his plan.[21] Abacha had been particularly angered by Strasser's decision to vote to censure Nigeria at the Commonwealth summit in Auckland in November 1995 after the hanging of Ken Saro-Wiwa and eight other environmental activists by the Abacha regime. After his successful coup, Bio formed close ties with three West African leaders with military backgrounds: Nigeria's General Sani Abacha, Ghana's Jerry Rawlings, and Guinea's Lansana Conté. Abacha and Rawlings even encouraged Bio to hold on to power and not to rush to hold elections.[22]

But enormous domestic and international pressure eventually forced Bio to hold elections in February 1996. James Jonah, the head of Sierra Leone's electoral commission and former UN Undersecretary-General for Political Affairs, played an important role in keeping the process on track. The Sierra Leone Women's Movement for Peace (SLWMP) also deserves special praise for its peace marches and courageous support of democratic elections in the face of opposition by the military during the National Consultative Conference (Bintumani II) in February 1996.[23] The British and U.S. ambassadors in Freetown, Ian McCluney and John Hirsch, also maintained pressure on the soldiers to return to their barracks.[24] A month later, the military held elections in which Ahmed Tejan Kabbah, a former senior UN official and standard bearer of the SLPP, became president. Though many Sierra Leoneans enthusiastically took part in the polls, parts of the countryside, particularly in the north and the east, were too unstable to conduct elections.

The new regime experienced at least three coup attempts in its first ten months in office and Kabbah struggled to maintain the confidence of Sierra Leoneans, many of whom criticized him for being a weak and indecisive leader.[25] While sometimes valid, this criticism often ignored the difficulties faced by a president who lost control of the diamond-rich area of his country to rebels and lacked an effective and loyal army to challenge them. Kabbah foiled yet another military coup attempt in September 1996 with help from Nigerian soldiers based in Freetown. Nigerian soldiers helped investigate the coup plot and their numbers were increased in the capital following this incident.

The Abidjan Accord

Despite the government's difficulties, the military pressure from the merce-
nary-backed coalition of military and *kamajors,* which by October 1996
had expelled the RUF from several key positions in the southeast, including
Kailahun, eventually resulted in a peace agreement between Kabbah and
the RUF. The Abidjan accord of 30 November 1996 was brokered by Côte
d'Ivoire and called for the establishment of a Neutral Monitoring Group
(NMG) to disarm the factions, the withdrawal of Executive Outcomes, and
the repatriation of all foreign troops from Sierra Leone. Under the accord,
the RUF was to be transformed into a political party, and a general amnesty
for war crimes was granted to its members.[26] The negotiations were difficult, and Sankoh often expressed his open distrust of Berhanu Dinka, the
UN Special Envoy who was active in mediation efforts. The RUF was
encouraged in its recalcitrance by Akyaaba Addai-Sebo, a Ghanaian member
of London-based International Alert and a friend of Charles Taylor who did
all he could to sabotage peace talks.

The Abidjan accord was, however, a personal triumph for Ivorian foreign minister Amara Essy, who had worked tirelessly for nearly a year to
bring both sides together. Essy was credited with convincing the notoriously recalcitrant RUF leader Foday Sankoh to leave his bush camp for the
comfort of Abidjan. But Essy was regarded by some observers as favoring
the RUF, a perception fueled by his reported closeness to Addai-Sebo.[27]
The Ivorians were also accused of providing the RUF with a base in
Danané that also reportedly served as an arms supply route for the rebels.[28]
The fact that Côte d'Ivoire, and not ECOWAS, was the only West African
moral guarantor of the agreement, along with the UN, the Commonwealth,
and the OAU, stoked up the historical subregional rivalry between Abidjan
and Abuja. This rivalry dated back to Côte d'Ivoire's recognition of, and
provision of military assistance to, secessionist Biafra during the Nigerian
civil war of 1967 to 1970. Abidjan, with the support of Paris, had led several exclusively francophone economic and political groupings against what
it saw as Nigeria's efforts to dominate the West African subregion through
ECOWAS (see Chapter 2). Abidjan had also supported the NPFL against
ECOMOG in Liberia.

Sankoh's detention under house arrest in Nigeria, where he had reportedly gone to negotiate an arms deal in March 1997, became a further source
of conflict between Abidjan and Abuja. Sankoh, whose forces were running
out of arms, had been directed to Nigeria by Steve Bio, a Sierra Leonean
businessman. Sankoh had left for Lagos without informing his Ivorian
hosts.[29] The Ivorians were enraged that the RUF leader had been arrested
without consulting them, especially since Sankoh was under their protec-

tion, having resided in Abidjan before his arrest in Lagos. The Ivorians were also aggrieved that the Nigerians sent Sankoh to Sierra Leonean custody in July 1999 without consulting them.[30]

FROM CONAKRY TO LOMÉ: 1997–1999

The Sobel Coup

Under pressure from the IMF to cut costs and in partial fulfillment of the Abidjan accord, Kabbah expelled Executive Outcomes from Sierra Leone in January 1997. Kabbah had never liked the presence of the South African mercenary outfit in his country.[31] At about the same time, Nigerian troops took over the task of providing personal bodyguards for Kabbah. There were about 900 Nigerian troops in Sierra Leone at this time. Some elements in the SLA were feeling increasingly threatened by Kabbah's reliance on the *kamajors,* and on 25 May 1997 they staged a coup against Kabbah's regime, springing Major Johnny Paul Koromah, a putschist from the foiled September 1996 coup, from jail to lead the new Armed Forces Ruling Council. Kabbah fled to exile in Conakry and asked Nigeria to restore him to power in Freetown. The AFRC invited the RUF, against which it had supposedly been waging a war for the last six years, to partner in the new regime.[32] During the 1997 coup, Nigerian troops suffered dozens of casualties, some of them were captured by the rebels, and the rest were forced to withdraw to the outskirts of the capital.

Nigerian head of state General Sani Abacha, the ECOWAS chairman at the time, attempted at first to reverse the coup through diplomatic rather than military means. He convened several meetings of the Committee of Four (Nigeria, Ghana, Guinea, and Côte d'Ivoire). This committee was later transformed into the Committee of Five when Liberia asked to join, and by 1999 had become the Committee of Seven after Togo and Burkina Faso also joined. ECOWAS imposed sanctions on the junta in Freetown, which Nigerian, Ghanaian, and Guinean troops were asked to implement.[33] The international community refused to recognize the military regime in Sierra Leone: the Commonwealth invited President Kabbah to attend its summit in Edinburgh in 1997 as Sierra Leone's legitimate leader, and the OAU condemned the coup and barred the junta from its summits.

In the face of increasing pressure, the mercurial Koromah broke off talks with ECOWAS in July 1997, complaining that he would not be stampeded into a return to civilian government. One month later, ECOWAS foreign ministers recommended that the peacekeepers in Freetown be known as ECOMOG II. The subregional force tightened the blockade around

Freetown, barring all ships and aircraft, while Nigeria launched bombing raids from air and sea on rebel positions. In October 1997, the UN Security Council imposed an embargo on the sale and supply of oil and arms to Sierra Leone. The resolution had been largely drafted by Britain, the only permanent member of the UN Security Council with a sustained interest in Sierra Leone.

In the same month, further talks were held in Guinea between representatives of the junta and ECOWAS. There were complaints about Nigerian foreign minister Tom Ikimi's unilateral negotiating style and his failure to consult with other members of the ECOWAS Committee of Seven. Ikimi reportedly told the AFRC that they should either surrender power or they would be flushed out of Freetown. He told them he was not there to negotiate but to reach a timetable for their departure.[34] Nigeria's foreign minister also irritated Kabbah's officials, whose role he often downplayed during these talks.[35] This meeting nevertheless resulted in the Conakry agreement of 23 October, which called for Kabbah's reinstatement by 22 April 1998. Koromah at first gave his consent to the deal, but soon continued to talk of staying in power until 2001. Clashes continued between Nigerian troops and the junta on the outskirts of Freetown, as did Nigerian aerial and naval bombardments of rebel positions. At an ECOWAS extraordinary summit in Lomé in December 1997, a few ECOWAS states, led by Senegal, expressed unease at what they regarded as Nigeria's unilateral actions, saying that ECOMOG was there to enforce the embargo and not to employ force against the junta.[36] As in Liberia, Ghana also expressed unease at the prospect of a domineering Nigerian hegemon.

The Nigerian Response

On 6 February 1998, fighting erupted between ECOMOG and the junta in eastern Freetown, with Nigeria accusing Koromah's soldiers of attacking its troops. Others argued that Nigeria was just waiting for an excuse to avenge its losses from the May 1997 fighting and had planned this attack in advance. The UN Security Council called for a cease-fire even as Nigerian reinforcements streamed across the Mano River from Liberia. Employing heavy weaponry, the Nigerian troops flushed the rebels out of Freetown and restored Kabbah to power by 10 March 1998. Questions have since been raised as to why the Nigerian troops allowed the AFRC/RUF leadership to escape from Freetown. It is likely that the Nigerians were seeking to minimize civilian casualties in populated areas as well as human rights abuses and destruction by the cornered rebels.[37] General Maxwell Khobe, a veteran of the ECOMOG mission in Liberia, led the Nigerian military effort and was rewarded by being appointed chief of defense staff of Sierra Leone's army by Kabbah. As commander of the ECOMOG task force, Khobe was also tasked to reform the Sierra Leonean army. He performed these dual roles until his death by illness in April 2000.[38]

The international media later reported that in a bid to restore Kabbah to power, Sandline International, a private security firm under a former British army colonel, Tim Spicer, with ties to the British diamond-mining firm Branch Energy, had shipped weapons to ECOMOG's allies, the *kamajors*, with the knowledge of Peter Penfold, the British high commissioner (ambassador) in Freetown (but not, apparently, with the knowledge of other senior figures in Westminster). This action violated the UN Security Council's arms embargo crafted a few weeks before by Britain.[39] Senior British officials were later cleared by a parliamentary investigation, but the "Sandline affair" damaged Penfold's standing in the British Foreign and Commonwealth Office. Though Sandline had also reportedly provided some transport to ECOMOG, despite the British media brouhaha, its role in this operation was negligible. As President Kabbah later noted, it was Nigerian troops and not Sandline that had restored constitutional rule in Freetown.

Nigeria's unilateral intervention, without recourse to ECOWAS or the UN, elicited sharp reactions from some of its neighbors. Burkina Faso's leader, Blaise Compaoré, a close ally of Charles Taylor and the RUF, publicly questioned Nigeria's motives, asking: "just what might be the intentions of those who have employed force for the restoration of President Kabbah[?]"[40] Senegal's Sud-Quotidien newspaper questioned Nigeria's "eternal quest for leadership" and criticized its "opportunism" in transforming ECOMOG in Liberia into ECOMOG II in Sierra Leone.[41]

ECOWAS defense ministers and army chiefs of staff met in Accra in May 1998, where Nigeria's chief of staff, General Abdulsalam Abubakar, who would become the country's leader barely a month later following Abacha's sudden death, called on other ECOWAS states to diversify ECOMOG by sending troops to Sierra Leone. With many ECOWAS states facing logistical and financial constraints and political problems at home, no states came forward to meet this offer. It is important to note that while Nigeria faced criticisms in its subregion for its military actions in Sierra Leone, many of its critics refused to contribute the troops that could have diversified the force and diluted Nigeria's preponderant strength. Benin, Côte d'Ivoire, Gambia, and Niger all promised troops to ECOMOG that never arrived.

It is also important to remember that some states, including Burkina Faso and Liberia, had their own political axes to grind in Sierra Leone since they had a clear preference for an RUF victory that they saw Nigeria as obstructing. It was sometimes easier for ECOWAS states and the wider international community to criticize from the sidelines and let Nigeria bear the financial and military burden, while doing nothing to lighten this weight. As Nigerian president Olusegun Obasanjo noted during an address to the UN General Assembly in 1999:

> The time has come . . . for the Security Council to assume its full responsibility, specifically in Sierra Leone and other flash points in Africa. For too long, the burden of preserving international peace and security in West Africa has been left almost entirely to a few states in our subregion. . . . Nigeria's continual burden in Sierra Leone is unacceptably draining Nigeria financially. For our economy to take off, this bleeding has to stop.[42]

After Abacha's death in June 1998, relations briefly improved between the Abubakar regime in Abuja and Abidjan. At a time when Nigeria had not yet appointed a foreign minister, Abubakar invited Côte d'Ivoire to chair an ECOWAS meeting of the Committee of Seven on Sierra Leone in Abidjan in December 1998. ECOWAS foreign ministers called on Liberia and Côte d'Ivoire to put pressure on Sankoh and Kabbah to resolve the crisis. Relations between Abidjan and Abuja, however, turned sour again after Ivorian foreign minister Amara Essy went to Freetown on 10 January 1999 following another rebel invasion (discussed below) and met with Kabbah. Nigeria's foreign minister, Ignatus Olisemeka, pointedly noted that he saw no reason why the Ivorians should adopt such a high-profile diplomatic role when they had no troops in Sierra Leone. The statement particularly rankled Essy, who regarded it as a sign of ingratitude on the part of the Nigerians. These subregional differences are crucial in understanding some of the problems of peacemaking in Sierra Leone. Historical suspicions and antagonisms often led to a failure by ECOWAS to coordinate diplomatic and military strategies and created divisions that Sierra Leone's rebels and their subregional backers sought to exploit.

The Politics of ECOMOG

ECOMOG's ill-equipped peacekeepers were unable to defeat the AFRC/RUF alliance in a guerrilla war in the densely forested countryside for which their conventional armies were not trained. As in Liberia, ECOMOG troops in Sierra Leone still lacked not only helicopters and gunships, but also sufficient trucks, tanks, ambulances, communication equipment, spare parts, uniforms, medical supplies, and office equipment. Much of ECOMOG's old and worn-out equipment from Liberia was simply transferred to Sierra Leone. In June 1998, the UN provided 50 unarmed military observers to support ECOMOG's 13,000 peacekeepers. But there was strong resentment among ECOMOG soldiers against the better-paid and better-resourced UN military observers. As one ECOMOG officer wryly put it: "They [UN observers] are here on picnic and holiday. I wish we could open the beaches for them to sun-tan and enjoy their dollars."[43] Nearly 12,000 of ECOMOG's 13,000 troops, about 90 percent, came from Nigeria, while the Ghanaians and Guineans each had about 600 troops in Sierra Leone, and the Malians contributed a 500-strong contingent.[44]

Military problems that arose during the Liberia mission were also evident in Sierra Leone. Some of the Nigerian troops spent two to three years in the field before being rotated. They were paid in quarterly installments and their stipends often arrived late.[45] There were also complaints that Nigeria dominated most of the positions in ECOMOG's High Command and other contingents called for a restructuring of the command. ECOMOG's force commander was Nigerian as was the chief of staff, the chief military information officer, the chief military public information officer, the chief of logistics, the chief naval officer, and the chief air force officer. Two deputy force commanders came from Ghana and Guinea, while the chief of operations was Ghanaian.

While acknowledging the inevitability of Nigerian dominance due to its provision of 90 percent of the peacekeeping force, Guinea's ECOMOG deputy force commander, Colonel Ibrahim Jalloh, insisted that Nigeria still had to share command posts as well as give others a role in military and political decisionmaking.[46] The Nigerian military top brass in ECOMOG seemed totally impervious to these criticisms and often compared the Nigerian dominance of the force to the U.S. role in NATO. ECOMOG force commander General Felix Mujakpero noted in July 1999: "When Nigeria has about 90 percent of the fighting force, I don't know how another country can come and command the troops."[47] The specter of Nigeria as a bullying hegemon continued to haunt multilateral peacekeeping efforts in Sierra Leone, as it had done in Liberia.

Other operational problems seen in Liberia were also evident in Sierra Leone. Both anglophone and francophone countries failed to provide bilingual officers, and communication between national contingents was therefore often difficult. Nigerian officers in Freetown were particularly angered that the Ghanaians did not fight during the rebel attack on the capital in 1999, withdrawing Ghanaian troops from Freetown to Lungi airport, a maneuver that explained the lack of Ghana's military casualties.[48] According to Nigerian ECOMOG officers in Freetown, the Ghanaians also refused to follow orders to capture Waterloo from the rebels, on the basis that ECOMOG was in Sierra Leone for peacekeeping and not war fighting.[49] This reflected a difference in military approach between Abuja and Accra that was also evident in Liberia.

Brigadier H. W. K. Agbevey, ECOMOG's Ghanaian deputy force commander, admitted that instructions from the Nigerian force commander had to be cleared first with Accra. Agbevey complained that Nigeria controlled most of the fuel for ECOMOG that Nigeria supplied, and that the Nigerians did not let any other contingents near the logistics department.[50] Similar problems arose with other contingents. Nigeria helped to deploy the Malian contingent to Sierra Leone, which was based in Port Loko. But after sustaining some casualties in March 1999, the Malians withdrew to Lungi with the Ghanaians, who were perceived by Nigerian officers as attempting to turn the Malians against the Nigerian contingent.[51]

Explaining Pax Nigeriana

Since there has been much debate and many misperceptions about Nigeria's motives for intervening in Sierra Leone, it is important to explore this issue. Nigeria became involved in Sierra Leone for three main reasons: first, the ECOMOG mission helped Nigerian leader General Sani Abacha to ward off the threat of severe international sanctions against his regime; second, some of Nigeria's generals personally benefited from revenues written off as ECOMOG expenses; and third, the mission represented Nigeria's historic quest for hegemony in its own subregion. General Abacha was attempting to break his diplomatic isolation by demonstrating his regime's indispensability to peacekeeping in a region of the world in which the West was keen to avoid being drawn into humanitarian interventions and was thankful for Nigeria's sacrifices. By restoring democracy to Sierra Leone, Abacha and his generals could continue to divert millions of dollars from government coffers to private bank accounts while billing them as ECOMOG expenses. The staggering levels of corruption under the Abacha regime, involving billions of dollars, were exposed by the two subsequent regimes.

Nigeria's generals were also pursuing their historic quest for Pax Nigeriana. Since 1960, Nigeria's search for continental leadership has involved a rivalry for subregional leadership with France, which culminated in the creation of Nigerian-led ECOWAS in 1975; a strong contribution to regional peacekeeping in Congo, Chad, and Somalia; and the provision of military and diplomatic support to liberation movements in southern Africa.[52] Many of Nigeria's military leaders regarded their country as a "big brother" and "Giant of Africa," providing security and attempting to spread prosperity as the public goods of a benevolent hegemon.[53] As General One Mohammed, ECOMOG's Nigerian chief of staff in Sierra Leone, noted: "We had to put out the fire in order to stop it from extending to our own houses."[54]

Nigeria also intervened in Sierra Leone to restore Kabbah in power in 1998 due to General Abacha's need to break his diplomatic isolation, marked by limited sanctions imposed on Nigeria by the United States, the Commonwealth, and the European Union. The entire international community was opposed to the coup in Freetown, and the British high commissioner in Sierra Leone particularly encouraged the ousting of the military regime and lent support to the efforts of Sandline International.

Abacha, whose soldiers had successfully helped disarm Liberia's factions and who as ECOWAS chairman had played a prominent part in Liberia's July 1997 elections, was keen to portray himself as a promoter of peace and democracy in his subregion, despite the ironies involved in restoring democracy in Sierra Leone while retarding democracy in Nigeria. Abacha also had commercial interests with the Kabbah regime: Sierra Leone's oil refinery had been sold to the Nigerian National Petroleum Corporation (NNPC). But it is important to note that Abacha sought to restore a democratic government in Freetown to curry favor with the international community and bolster his country's image as well as his own. Otherwise the Nigerian leader could simply have cut a deal to protect his economic interests with his fellow military brass hats in Sierra Leone who had toppled Kabbah. Nigeria had, after all, continued to support two military leaders in Sierra Leone between 1992 and 1996.

The "Mother Country": Britain in Sierra Leone

The most important extra-regional actor in Sierra Leone was Britain, the former colonial power. London had historical commercial ties with Freetown, and British companies like diamond-mining Branch Energy, Golden Prospects, West African Fisheries, Marine Protection Services, J&S Franklin, Barclays, and Standard Chartered banks all operated in Sierra Leone. Branch Energy's subsidiary, Branch Mining, with ties to Executive Outcomes, had helped the Kabbah government to service its debts, while Executive Outcomes officials maintained contacts with British government officials in Freetown.[55,56]

But Britain lent mostly diplomatic and humanitarian assistance to subregional peacekeeping efforts and desisted from playing a direct military role in Sierra Leone except for a brief and limited military intervention in Freetown in 1999. A small British contingent was dispatched to Freetown and remained outside the UN chain of command. The presence of the force, however, inspired great confidence in many Sierra Leoneans, who regarded the British as the most professional force in the country. The force was also a great source of confidence to the comparatively ragtag UN force in any future defense of Freetown from rebel attack (discussed below).

Peacemaking efforts in Sierra Leone, however, were often overshadowed by the rivalry between Britain and Nigeria. At the Commonwealth Ministerial Action Group meeting in London on 2 March 1998, Tony Lloyd, Britain's minister of state for Africa, declared Nigeria's military operation to oust the junta in Freetown as illegal because it lacked prior UN Security Council authorization.[57] There was a strong feeling among many Nigerian ECOMOG officers in Freetown that Britain had not done enough to support ECOMOG and simply wanted Nigeria to do most of the fighting and dying, while London trumpeted the apparently large sums it was pouring into Sierra Leone.[58]

According to this view, Nigerian military force effectively protected British political interests in Sierra Leone. As General Theophilus Danjuma, Nigeria's defense minister, put it: "The British have a very good propaganda machinery. They make a lot of noise and have succeeded in replacing us in the armed forces headquarters in Freetown, but they are doing very little elsewhere."[59] Other African critics of the British role in Sierra Leone contrasted the speed with which Britain contributed contingents to the Australian- and U.S.-led UN and NATO peacekeeping missions in East Timor and Kosovo, with what they saw as London's lackluster military response in Sierra Leone, where it contributed 23 peacekeepers to the 7,000-strong UN force by May 1999.

Britain's high commissioner in Freetown, Peter Penfold, consistently urged a hard-line military approach against the RUF and strongly backed the Kabbah government.[60] Britain was eventually forced to agree to a rapprochement with the RUF following Nigeria's decision to withdraw the bulk of its troops from Sierra Leone in 1999. Britain hurriedly contributed about U.S.$15 million to ECOMOG following the announcement of the withdrawal of Nigerian troops. During the civil war, London also led the International Contact Group of donor and regional states, which attempted to mobilize funds for Sierra Leone's reconstruction efforts. More recently Britain, along with the World Bank, has financially supported the disarmament and demobilization program in Sierra Leone. But in July 1999, Penfold admitted that he was told not to request any more British funding in some areas due to the pressing needs in Kosovo.[61]

A common complaint of the ECOMOG officers in Sierra Leone was that donors were often divisive in their assistance to ECOMOG forces. Canada, for example, was said to have given generators to Ghana but not to other contingents. Ottawa was said to have donated medicines to Ghana and Nigeria, but left out the Guineans and Malians. France provided forty military transport vehicles to Guinea's ECOMOG contingent, but not to others. The U.S. firm Pacific Architects and Engineers (PA&E), which was responsible for providing ECOMOG with helicopter support and servicing of equipment, was criticized by ECOMOG officers for providing bad service and for refusing to release helicopters during times of crisis.[62] Similar criticisms were leveled at PA&E by ECOMOG soldiers in Liberia.

The 1999 Rebel Invasion and Its Aftermath

During the 6 January 1999 rebel invasion of Freetown, Nigerian jets bombed rebel positions in the capital and its soldiers shelled the outskirts of eastern Freetown. ECOMOG eventually forced the rebels to withdraw from Freetown after more than six weeks with the loss of 3,000 civilian lives and massive destruction of the city by arsonist rebels. About 100 Nigerian soldiers died in this attack and 100 were missing in action. Overall Nigerian casualties in Sierra Leone were about 250, over 300 were missing in action, and 170 had been killed in road accidents and other noncombat-related incidents.[63] The fatalities incurred during the rebel invasion led to brutal reprisals by some Nigerian soldiers who, in an operation code-named "Death Before Dishonor," committed human rights abuses against rebel suspects and sympathizers, including beatings and summary executions. These were captured by a Sierra Leonean photojournalist, Sorious Samura, in a documentary titled *Cry Freetown,* which gained international publicity following its airing on CNN in early 2000.

Following the 1999 Nigerian counteroffensive in Freetown, Burkinabè leader Blaise Compaoré was again in the forefront of critics of ECOMOG, complaining that Nigeria's soldiers "conduct themselves quite simply as an army of occupation. . . . ECOMOG is going well beyond the mandate that was entrusted to it."[64] While Nigerian troops employed excessive and condemnable military force against civilians, they argued that they had no choice but to defend themselves, and to protect Freetown from the AFRC and rebel attack. They noted that their brutal reprisals had a contemporary precedent in the savage reprisals by U.S. soldiers following the death of eighteen of their colleagues in the UN operation in Somalia in 1993, during which an estimated 1,000 Somalis were killed by U.S. forces.[65]

Relations between Nigerian peacekeepers and Sierra Leonean civilians were ambiguous. While many Sierra Leoneans regarded the peacekeepers as heroes who prevented the takeover of their state by marauding, savage RUF rebels, others contended that ECOMOG was an imperial army of occupation who plundered their resources, impregnated their women, and failed to guarantee the security of their capital. Some people simultaneously held these two views of ECOMOG. Many Nigerian peacekeepers regarded their Sierra Leonean hosts as not showing sufficient gratitude for their sacrifices. ECOMOG's Nigerian soldiers felt appreciated mainly after the restoration of Kabbah to power in March 1998, but this did not last long.

They complained bitterly about how the very people they had come to save had often betrayed them.

Several Nigerian officers cited one incident during the rebel invasion of Freetown in 1999 when some Freetown residents, thought to be rebel collaborators, led rebels to a home where Nigerian officers were hiding. The officers were subsequently captured and executed by the rebels. Some Nigerian soldiers reportedly escaped death during the rebel invasion by claiming that they were Ghanaians.[66] Nigerian officers also regarded the Sierra Leonean press in Freetown as hostile toward them. Many Freetowners criticized the ECOMOG-imposed curfew as punishing them in their own country. But many Sierra Leoneans also continued to support the Nigerian peacekeepers, reacting with alarm when the Nigerians started withdrawing from Sierra Leone in 1999, and saying that they had more faith in ECOMOG than in the UN.[67]

The mild-mannered Nigerian ECOMOG force commander General Timothy Shelpidi, who had commanded ECOMOG since October 1998, was widely vilified for not doing more to protect Freetown from the rebels. Shelpidi was also accused of lacking prior peacekeeping experience and for not maintaining firmer control over his troops. Some Nigerian officers were reportedly out of Sierra Leone at the time of the attack and several of the Nigerian officers on the ground abandoned their troops during the fighting.[68] Shelpidi was also condemned for his frequent assurances on the eve of the invasion that Freetown was safe from rebel attack. He had earlier annoyed Sierra Leoneans by reminding them that his soldiers were not mercenaries and that Nigeria and not Sierra Leone was paying for their peacekeeping costs. But there was another, so far unreported, side to this story. Shelpidi's lack of direct access to Aso Rock in Abuja, which previous ECOMOG commanders in Liberia, including Generals Joshua Dogonyaro, Adetunji Olurin, and Victor Malu, had enjoyed, limited his ability to secure speedy reinforcements from the Nigerian defense ministry. Shelpidi had warned of the rebel threat several weeks in advance but received five additional battalions only after the rebel invasion.[69]

The no-nonsense Nigerian general Felix Mujakpero took over as ECOMOG force commander in March 1999. Mujakpero moved to extend ECOMOG's security cordon around Freetown and Lungi airport, but the rebels continued to control large swathes of the northern and eastern provinces, including the biggest prize: the diamond fields in Kono. General Gabriel Kpambe replaced Mujakpero as force commander shortly after Olusegun Obasanjo assumed the presidency in May 1999, reportedly due to the new Nigerian president's unease with Mujakpero, who had been involved in the military tribunal that had jailed Obasanjo in 1995 under the regime of General Abacha.

Shortly after being installed as Nigeria's president, Obasanjo asked the ECOMOG High Command to make contingency plans for the phased withdrawal of Nigerian troops from Sierra Leone.[70] Nigeria, ECOMOG's military and financial bulwark, was signaling that it had done enough in Sierra Leone. With enormous domestic problems, the new civilian regime was not prepared to continue the sacrifices, involving reported costs of U.S.$1 million a day and hundreds of fatalities, that the former military junta incurred. There was a realization in Abuja that Nigeria and its logistically handicapped peacekeepers could not continue to do most of the spending and dying in Sierra Leone while the international community simply sat on its hands. The scene was set for yet another effort to try to break the military stalemate through diplomatic talks in the Togolese capital of Lomé.

FROM ECOMOG TO UNAMSIL: 1999–2001

The Lomé Accord

A cease-fire agreement was signed on 18 May 1999 between Kabbah and the RUF. A suspended death sentence was still hanging over Sankoh's head, even after he had been handed over to Sierra Leonean authorities by Nigeria in July. In the tortuous six weeks of negotiations in Lomé between May and July 1999 guided by a facilitation committee, Kokou Koffigoh, Togo's foreign minister, and Francis Okelo, the Special Representative of the UN Secretary-General in Sierra Leone, were instrumental to the mediation efforts.[71] During the talks, the RUF demanded to be included in a four-year transitional government. As they had done during peace talks in Abidjan and Conakry, the rebels also demanded a blanket amnesty for war crimes, the departure of foreign troops from Sierra Leone, and the establishment of a neutral peacekeeping force.[72] Though the rebel delegation was officially a joint RUF-AFRC team, it was clear that the RUF played the dominant role and that there was a split between AFRC leader Johnny Paul Koromah, who was not present at the talks, and Foday Sankoh.[73]

Sierra Leonean civic groups also played an important part in the peace negotiations, with the Inter-Religious Council of Sierra Leone (IRCSL) deserving special mention as the most effective domestic facilitator in Lomé. Established in April 1997 by Christian and Muslim leaders, some of the IRCSL's members had earned the confidence of both government and rebels during the 1996 Abidjan peace negotiations in which they had participated. The IRCSL had also led a successful civil disobedience campaign, urging workers to stay at home during Koromah's military junta of 1997–1998. During the rebel attack on Freetown in 1999, many churches and mosques were burned and several priests were abducted. UN Special Representative Francis Okelo had turned to the IRCSL for help in bringing Kabbah and Sankoh together before Lomé. After consulting with traditional chiefs, parliamentarians, and other groups, the IRCSL met separately with Kabbah and Sankoh and convinced the government to accept a neutral venue for the peace talks. The religious leaders then traveled to Monrovia in April 1999 to convince President Charles Taylor to take part in peace talks. At the peace talks in Lomé, not only did the RUF invite the IRCSL to take part in its internal consultations, but council members shuttled between both parties to break negotiating deadlocks.[74]

A notable absentee in Lomé was Côte d'Ivoire, which had brokered the 1996 Abidjan peace accord. There was a feeling in Abidjan that Togo's leader, Gnassingbé Eyadéma, who was under international sanctions and was facing criticisms for his repression of his domestic opposition before and after flawed elections in June 1998, was keen to use the talks to boost his own international and domestic standing.[75] The Ivorians regarded the Lomé peace accord as an effort to supersede the Abidjan agreement of 1996.[76] Tension had also been created about Abidjan's role in the peace process after Kabbah accused Côte d'Ivoire of backing the RUF and insisting that the talks be held in Lomé and not Abidjan. The RUF had wanted the talks held in Abidjan or Ouagadougou, but Kabbah felt that the Ivorians and Burkinabès were too close to the rebels. Togo, whose leader was at the time the chairman of ECOWAS, had emerged as a consensus venue.[77] Subregional leaders played a crucial role in brokering the deal: Charles Taylor, Olusegun Obasanjo, and to a lesser extent Blaise Compaoré pressured Sankoh to sign the agreement.[78] The fact that Eyadéma's son was married to Sankoh's daughter (which was revealed later) was also helpful.[79]

Like members of Liberia's interim government in 1995, Kabbah had a weak hand to play: once Nigeria, the backbone of ECOMOG and the Freetown regime's de facto army, signified its intention to withdraw, Kabbah's military options were vastly diminished. U.S. pressure on Kabbah from Reverend Jesse Jackson, the Special Envoy for the Promotion of Democracy in Africa, to reach a deal with the RUF was also significant. Ismail Rashid described well the mediocrity of Kabbah's circumstances: "Refusal to negotiate would mean accepting *de facto* partition of the country, the potential loss of regional and international sympathy and support, and continued instability and violence—especially since all parties were beginning to conclude that the war was unwinnable."[80]

The Lomé agreement was signed on 7 July 1999 between Kabbah's government and the RUF-AFRC, and included the UN, the OAU, the Commonwealth, and Togo as moral guarantors. Representatives of Benin, Burkina Faso, Ghana, Guinea, Liberia, Libya, Mali, Nigeria, Britain, and the United States were also present. The agreement formally lifted the death sentence over Sankoh, called for the RUF to be transformed into a political party, provided for cabinet posts for the RUF in a government of national unity, gave Sankoh the vice presidency as well as the chairmanship of a Commission for the Management of Strategic Resources, and called for the establishment of a Council of Elders and Religious Leaders to mediate political disputes. The AFRC's Johnny Paul Koromah was later appointed chairman of the Commission for the Consolidation of Peace to monitor implementation of the agreement.

As with Abidjan and Conakry, a controversial amnesty was offered for war crimes. The UN was asked to contribute troops to help oversee disarmament and staff to help conduct elections, while an ECOWAS-chaired joint implementation committee was to meet every three months to oversee the agreement's implementation. This committee was also charged with monitoring the repatriation and resettlement of 500,000 Sierra Leonean refugees from Guinea and Liberia.[81] At the time of the signing of the Lomé peace accord, there were still 1 million internally displaced Sierra Leoneans.

There are eerie parallels between the Lomé peace accord in Sierra Leone and that of Abuja in 1995, which eventually ended the civil war in Liberia. Both accords were basically efforts to appease local warlords by giving them political power in exchange for military peace. Both were an open invitation for warlords to enjoy the spoils of office in a giant jumble sale of the national wares. Where Abuja had been a banquet for Liberia's warlords, Lomé was a feast for Sierra Leone's sobels. In both cases, few alternatives existed once ECOMOG, and in particular Nigeria, had made it clear that it was no longer willing to continue to sacrifice men and money. With the military option removed, Liberian and Sierra Leonean politicians were forced to seek a political solution, which inevitably left them at the mercy of wealthy, armed warlords who had looted their countries' resources. Transitional governments of national unity in both countries have been little more than a fractious collection of avaricious warlords and ambitious politicians who have used their positions to campaign for national elections. The big question after Lomé was whether Sankoh could replicate Charles Taylor's spectacular "shotgun" electoral victory of 1997 (see Chapter 3) by employing similar tactics of threatening a return to war in the event of a loss at the ballot box.

Farewell to ECOMOG

On 19 August 1999, Nigeria's President Obasanjo wrote to UN Secretary-General Kofi Annan informing him of Nigeria's intention to withdraw

2,000 of its peacekeepers from Sierra Leone every month. The Nigerian president, however, offered to subsume some of Nigeria's 12,000 troops under a new UN mission.[82] Obasanjo began the phased withdrawal on 31 August and suspended the process only after a plea by Kabbah and Annan not to leave a security vacuum in Sierra Leone. But with the realization that Obasanjo was not bluffing when he announced the withdrawal of Nigerian troops from Sierra Leone, Annan was forced to suggest to the Security Council that a UN peacekeeping mission in Sierra Leone, with a robust enforcement mandate under Chapter 7 of the UN Charter, take over from ECOMOG under an Indian UN Force Commander, General Vijay Jetley.[83] The UN Security Council balked at authorizing a Chapter 7 enforcement mandate in Sierra Leone, although it had done so in the cases of Kosovo and East Timor. Since August 1998, a UN Observer Mission in Sierra Leone (UNOMSIL) had worked alongside ECOMOG. But with only about 50 peacekeepers, UNOMSIL played only a minimal role in Sierra Leone.

Obasanjo rejected a UN proposal that ECOMOG continue to protect Freetown and undertake enforcement actions against rogue elements. He realized that ECOMOG, in being saddled with these dangerous tasks, would remain a useful scapegoat if things went wrong in Sierra Leone. As the UN was widely criticized for failing to protect "safe havens" in Bosnia and civilians in Rwanda, critics would have been able to blame any failings in Sierra Leone on ECOMOG rather than the UN. There is profound resentment among many Nigerians that their sacrifices in money and men have not been properly appreciated and acknowledged, particularly by a Western media and a human rights lobby that seem to delight in disparaging Nigerian peacekeepers as no more than murderers and mercenaries.

UNAMSIL's Baptism of Fire

In order to fill the void left by the departure of Nigerian peacekeepers, the 13,000-strong UN Mission in Sierra Leone was established at a proposed annual cost of U.S.$476 million. Oluyemi Adeniji, a Nigerian diplomat who had served as the UN Special Representative in the Central African Republic, was appointed as the UN Special Representative to Sierra Leone, compensating Nigeria for not gaining the UN Force Commander position that Obasanjo had wanted. Adeniji was forceful in his condemnation of the violations of the peace agreement, and often criticized the prickly Sankoh's undermining of the UN's efforts in Sierra Leone, though many Sierra Leoneans still complained that Adeniji was too eager to appease Sankoh.

UNAMSIL's core contingents consisted of Nigerian, Indian, Jordanian, Kenyan, Bangladeshi, Guinean, Ghanaian, and Zambian battalions. But the peacekeepers soon faced tremendous problems, as Foday Sankoh employed "spoiler" tactics to frustrate the UN. Sankoh complained that RUF members were not being appointed to government positions as agreed at Lomé.[84] The RUF continued to fight the AFRC and Civil Defense Force (CDF) in the countryside, prevented the deployment of UN peacekeepers to the diamond-rich eastern provinces, and from May 2000 attacked UN peacekeepers, holding them hostage and seizing their heavy weapons and vehicles.[85] There were continuing reports of rampaging rebels in the volatile countryside executing people, raping women, abducting children, looting property, burning villages, and stealing food. Thousands of children kidnapped by rebels still remain missing. Many have been used as sex slaves or cannon fodder by rebel commanders.

UNAMSIL also experienced its own internal problems. A UN assessment mission sent to Sierra Leone in June 2000 found serious managerial problems in UNAMSIL and a lack of common understanding of the mandate and rules of engagement. The mission also noted that some of UNAMSIL's military units lacked proper training and equipment.[86] There were constant reports of tension between the UN's political and military leadership even before a confidential report written by General Jetley was published in the international press in September 2000.[87] In the report, the Indian UN Force Commander accused senior Nigerian military and political officials of attempting to sabotage the UN mission in Sierra Leone by colluding with the RUF rebels to prolong the conflict in order to benefit from the country's illicit diamond trade. No evidence was provided for the allegations. Tremendous political damage was done to UNAMSIL by this incident: Nigeria refused to put its peacekeepers under Jetley's command and India subsequently announced the withdrawal of its entire 3,000-strong contingent from Sierra Leone in September 2000. India was followed by Jordan. As of September 2001, there were 16,664 UN peacekeepers from thirty-one countries in Sierra Leone.[88] Bangladesh and Pakistan had the largest contingents in UNAMSIL.

Aside from its political and military problems, UNAMSIL also unsurprisingly failed to fulfill important parts of its mandate on schedule. The disarmament process in Sierra Leone has been fraught with difficulties. Of the estimated 45,000 fighters, only 24,042 had entered demobilization camps by 15 May 2000, many without weapons, and most were rearmed as part of the government effort to wage war on the RUF.[89] The payment of the U.S.$150 remittance to demobilized fighters was slow, and there remained a U.S.$20 million shortfall in international contributions to Sierra Leone's disarmament program in March 2000.[90]

Following UNAMSIL's humiliation by the RUF in May 2000, there were a few encouraging signs of international resolve in Sierra Leone. UNAMSIL responded more forcefully against the RUF in July 2000 by freeing some of its hostages in Kailahun, recapturing the strategic town of Masiaka from the rebels, and clearing illegal checkpoints from the Occra hills.[91] A brief British military intervention between May and June 2000 helped stabilize the situation in Freetown and its environs, and a small British contingent remained in the capital to build a new Sierra Leone army. Following the difficulties with the RUF, ECOWAS agreed to send a 3,000-strong rapid reaction force, consisting largely of Nigerians, to bolster UNAMSIL. The United States has since trained Nigerian, Ghanaian, and Senegalese troops for the UN mission in Sierra Leone.

Another African "Poor Man's War"

The International Contact Group continued to hold periodic meetings in a bid to mobilize funds for Sierra Leone. In recognition of the role of the illicit diamond trade in fueling this conflict, the UN Security Council prohibited the global importation of rough diamonds from Sierra Leone in July 2000 until a certification scheme was put in place for official diamond exports three months later. At a UN hearing in the same month, Washington and London strongly criticized Liberia and Burkina Faso for their role in diamond smuggling and gunrunning in support of RUF rebels in Sierra Leone. The Security Council imposed sanctions on Liberia's diamond exports and a travel ban on its officials in May 2001, even in the face of opposition from several ECOWAS states whose cooperation is essential to implementing most of the sanctions (see Chapter 3).

Many observers have noted that disproportionate international attention has been focused on the tragedies in Kosovo and East Timor, while Africa's civil wars have been left to fester. A donor conference for the reconstruction of the Balkans in 2000 saw pledges of U.S.$1.8 billion, in stark contrast to the paltry U.S.$150 million pledged for Sierra Leone. As Oluyemi Adeniji noted: "The international community has to realize that there can be no double standard. Whatever the cause of the conflict in Africa, human suffering is universal."[92]

Recognizing the importance of a long-term strategy for the survival of Sierra Leone's civilian government and keen to devise an "exit strategy," two external peacekeepers have promoted security-sector reform in Sierra Leone.[93] Nigeria helped to train officers for a new 8,500-strong Sierra Leonean army at the Nigerian Defense Academy. Britain is currently playing the lead role in training the army and police in Sierra Leone. Alpha Konaré, Mali's energetic ECOWAS chairman between 2000 and 2001, tried to maintain the diplomatic momentum by convening meetings of ECOWAS's joint implementation committee (which met less regularly than was foreseen at Lomé) and special ECOWAS summits.

By the end of June 2001, there appeared some glimmers of hope that peace might yet come to Sierra Leone.[94] UNAMSIL's troop strength grew to 12,718 (and later to 17,000) and its peacekeepers were deployed in Freetown as well as in Lunsar, Makeni, Magburaka, and Mano Junction. UN peacekeepers also began patrolling Kamakwie, Kabala, Kailahun, Buedu, and significantly diamond-rich Koidu. Despite some clashes between the RUF and the CDF in the diamond-producing Kono district, and between RUF rebels and Guinean soldiers on the Guinea–Sierra Leone border in May 2001, disarmament of the factions was completed by January 2002. Parliamentary and presidential elections are planned for May 2002. But despite this steady progress, the security situation in Sierra Leone still remains fragile and external donors remain wary about investing in an uncertain peace. With Liberia's Taylor and Guinea's Conté seemingly bent on continuing their personal vendetta through armed clashes waged by local proxies, this volcanic conflict could yet spew its deadly lava and poisonous gases onto Sierra Leone.

CONCLUSION

This chapter has traced the roots of the civil war in Sierra Leone to the political misrule and economic decline of the postindependence era, which created the conditions for a rebel group, backed by two subregional states, to attempt to topple the government in Freetown. Due to its brutal methods and lack of a coherent political ideology, the RUF was unable to rally political support for its cause and a decade-long military stalemate ensued that several external actors tried to break. Under these difficult conditions, Sierra Leone's civil society groups strove courageously to play a role in ending military rule and facilitating peace negotiations between the government and the rebels.

We have examined the reasons for Sierra Leone's decade-long civil war at three interdependent levels: domestic, subregional, and extra-regional. At the domestic level, a combination of avaricious warlords and militias as well as inept politicians and soldiers totally dependent on external military support, led to political and military deadlock. This allowed the rebels to plunder the country's diamond fields in order to continue the war and to enrich the RUF's leadership and their subregional allies. At the subregional level, a divided ECOWAS saw different members supporting either successive governments in Freetown or rebels in the countryside. Several ECOWAS states complained loudly about Nigeria's military dominance and unilateral actions. Nigeria, under a democratically elected government by 1999, was frustrated by the costs of the protracted war and withdrew most of its peacekeepers from Sierra Leone. This led to the subsuming of some troops from ECOMOG, the poorly equipped Nigerian-led peacekeeping force, under UN command.

Both ECOMOG missions in Liberia and Sierra Leone were undertaken for different reasons by domestically powerful military rulers, Generals Ibrahim Babangida and Sani Abacha. Babangida, who was keen on creating a historical legacy, sought to achieve military glory for himself and his country through the intervention and at first tried to protect his ally, Samuel Doe, before quickly withdrawing support for him. Abacha sought to break out of his diplomatic isolation while simultaneously believing that Nigeria should live up to its subregional commitments. Nigeria had signed a military agreement with the Kabbah government pledging to provide it with military assistance. Both ECOMOG interventions in Sierra Leone and Liberia were born primarily out of the desire of two strong-willed Nigerian autocrats to further their own personal ambitions while burnishing Nigeria's leadership aspirations in West Africa.

Finally, the resolution of Sierra Leone's civil war was complicated at the extra-regional level by the fact that the international community starved ECOMOG and Sierra Leone of the resources and attention that could have made peacemaking, peacekeeping, and peacebuilding efforts more effective. Tensions and divisions within the UN peacekeeping force eventually led to the withdrawal of important Indian and Jordanian contingents from Sierra Leone. More effective and logistically rich Western armies, still reeling from difficult experiences in Somalia (1993) and Rwanda (1994), refused to risk the lives of their peacekeepers in what they considered a politically dangerous and strategically insignificant country off the Atlantic coast of West Africa.[95]

NOTES

1. For a background of pre- and postwar Sierra Leone, see Ibrahim Abdullah and Patrick Muana, "The Revolutionary United Front of Sierra Leone: A Revolt of the Lumpenproletariat," in Christopher Clapham (ed.), *African Guerrillas* (Oxford, Kampala, and Bloomington: James Currey, Fountain, and Indiana University Press, 1998), pp. 172–193; Yusuf Bangura, "Understanding the Political and Cultural Dynamics of the Sierra Leone War: A Critique of Paul Richards's *Fighting for the Rainforest*," in *African Development* 22, nos. 2–3 (1997) (special issue on "Youth Culture and Political Violence: The Sierra Leone Civil War"); Fred Hayward, "Sierra Leone: State Consolidation, Fragmentation, and Decay," in Donal B. Cruise O'Brien, John Dunn, and Richard Rathbone (eds.), *Contemporary West African States* (Cambridge: Cambridge University Press, 1989), pp. 165–180; William Reno, *Warlord Politics and African States* (Boulder and London: Lynne Rienner, 1998); and Paul Richards, *Fighting for the Rainforest: War, Youth, and Resources*

in Sierra Leone (Oxford and New Hampshire: James Currey and Heinemann, 1996).

2. Reno, *Warlord Politics and African States,* p. 116.

3. Ibid.

4. Richards, *Fighting for the Rainforest,* p. 45.

5. Reno, *Warlord Politics and African States,* pp. 116–118.

6. Ibid., p. 124; and Richards, *Fighting for the Rainforest,* p. 4.

7. Abdullah and Muana, "Revolutionary United Front of Sierra Leone," p. 178.

8. Reno, *Warlord Politics and African States,* pp. 126–127.

9. Bangura, "Political and Cultural Dynamics of the Sierra Leone War," p. 129.

10. Abduallah and Muana, "Revolutionary United Front of Sierra Leone," p. 178; and Richards, *Fighting for the Rainforest,* p. 22.

11. See A. B. Zack-Williams and Steve Riley, "Sierra Leone: The Coup and Its Consequences," *Review of African Political Economy* no. 56 (1993): 91–98.

12. Abdullah and Muana, "Revolutionary United Front of Sierra Leone," p. 181.

13. Richards, *Fighting for the Rainforest,* p. 5.

14. Abdullah and Muana, "Revolutionary United Front of Sierra Leone," p. 182.

15. Richards, *Fighting for the Rainforest,* p. 6.

16. Abdullah and Muana, "Revolutionary United Front of Sierra Leone," p. 183.

17. Reno, *Warlord Politics and African States,* p. 125.

18. On military budget, see ibid., p. 126.

19. On mineral exports, see ibid., p. 127.

20. Personal interview with James Jonah, former finance minister of Sierra Leone, New York, 2 July 2001.

21. Personal interview with General Julius Maada Bio, former head of state of Sierra Leone, Washington, D.C., 19 January 2001.

22. Ibid.

23. See Yasmin Jusu-Sheriff, "Sierra Leonean Women and the Peace Process," in David Lord (ed.), *Paying the Price: The Sierra Leone Peace Process, Accord* no. 9 (2000): 46–49.

24. For an insider's account, see John Hirsch, *Sierra Leone: Diamonds and the Struggle for Democracy* (Boulder and London: Lynne Rienner, 2001), pp. 44–47.

25. Reno, *Warlord Politics and African States,* p. 137.

26. See Report of the Secretary-General on Sierra Leone, 26 January 1997, pp. 2–4.

27. James Jonah, "Security Co-operation Between the ECOWAS and the United Nations" (paper presented at the IPA/ECOWAS seminar, Abuja, 27–29 September 2001), p. 23.

28. I thank Kathryn Jones at the UN Department of Political Affairs for drawing my attention to these allegations.

29. I thank Maes Kouamé, chief of the Division of African Conflicts in the Ivorian foreign ministry, for providing me with this information during an interview on 9 July 1999.

30. Ibid.

31. Personal interview with James Jonah.

32. See David Keen, "War and Peace: What's the Difference?" *International Peacekeeping* 7, no. 4 (Winter 2000): 1–22.

33. For assessments of ECOMOG's role in Sierra Leone, see Colonel Festus Aboagye, *ECOMOG: A Subregional Experience in Conflict Resolution, Management, and Peacekeeping in Liberia* (Accra: Sedco Enterprise, 1999), pp. 229–267; Adekeye Adebajo and David Keen, "Banquet for Warlords," *The World Today* 56, no. 7 (July 2000): 8–10; Eric G. Berman and Katie E. Sams, *Peacekeeping in Africa: Capabilities and Culpabilities* (Geneva and Pretoria: UN Institute for Disarmament Research, and Institute for Security Studies, 2000), pp. 111–128; Comfort Ero, "The Future of ECOMOG in West Africa," in Jakkie Cilliers and Greg Mills (eds.), *From Peacekeeping to Complex Emergencies: Peace Support Missions in Africa* (Johannesburg and Pretoria: South African Institute of International Affairs, and Institute for Security Studies, 1999), pp. 62–65; and Robert Mortimer, "From ECOMOG to ECOMOG II: Intervention in Sierra Leone," in John W. Harbeson and Donald Rothchild (eds.), *Africa in World Politics: The African State System in Flux,* 3rd ed. (Boulder and Oxford: Westview Press, 2000), pp. 188–207.

34. Personal interview with Monie Captan, foreign minister of Liberia, Monrovia, 15 July 1999.

35. James Jonah, "Security Co-operation," p. 30.

36. Mortimer, "From ECOMOG to ECOMOG II," p. 198.

37. I thank Jimmy Kandeh for drawing my attention to this point.

38. See Julius Spencer, "Mitikishe Khobe: A Tribute," *The Guardian* (Lagos), 28 April 2000, p. 49.

39. See Richard Conroy, David Cortright, and George A. Lopez, "Sierra Leone: The Failure of Regional and International Sanctions," in David Cortright and George A. Lopez (eds.), *The Sanctions Decade: Assessing UN Strategies in the 1990s* (Boulder and London: Lynne Rienner, 2000), pp. 167–179; and Hirsch, *Sierra Leone,* pp. 65–67.

40. Quoted in Mortimer, "From ECOMOG to ECOMOG II," p. 199.

41. Cited in ibid.

42. Olusegun Obasanjo, "Nigeria, Africa, and the World in the Next Millennium" (address at the Fifty-fourth Session of the UN General Assembly, New York, 23 September 1999), p. 6.

43. Personal interview with an ECOMOG officer, Freetown, July 1999.

44. Personal interview with Lieutenant Colonel Chris Olukolade, ECOMOG chief military information officer, Freetown, 3 July 1999.

45. Personal interviews with ECOMOG officers, Freetown, July 1999.

46. Personal interview with Colonel Ibrahim Jalloh, ECOMOG deputy force commander, Conakry, 7 July 1999.

47. Personal interview with General Felix Mujakpero, ECOMOG force commander, Freetown, 6 July 1999.

48. See Ismail Rashid, "The Lomé Peace Negotiations," in Lord, *Paying the Price,* p. 27.

49. Personal interviews with ECOMOG officers, Freetown, July 1999.

50. Personal interview with General Agbevey, ECOMOG deputy force commander, Freetown, 3 July 1999.

51. Personal interviews with ECOMOG officers, Freetown, July 1999.

52. See, for example, Adekeye Adebajo, "Nigeria: Africa's New Gendarme?" *Security Dialogue* 31, no. 2 (June 2000); Bola Akinterinwa, *Nigeria and France, 1960–1995: The Dilemma of Thirty-five Years of Relationship* (Ibadan: Vantage, 1999); Bassey Ate and Bola Akinterinwa (eds.), *Nigeria and Its Immediate Neighbors* (Lagos: Nigerian Institute of International Affairs, 1992); Ibrahim Gambari, *Theory and Reality in Foreign Policy Making: Nigeria After the Second Republic* (Atlantic Highlands, N.J.: Humanities Press International, 1989); James Mayall, "Oil and Nigerian Foreign Policy," *African Affairs* 75, no. 300 (July 1976); Gabriel Olusanya and R. A. Akindele (eds.), *Nigeria's External Relations: The First Twenty-five Years* (Ibadan: University Press, 1986); Gabriel Olusanya and R. A. Akindele (eds.), *The Structure and Processes of Foreign Policy Making and Implementation in Nigeria, 1960–1990* (Lagos: Nigerian Institute of International Affairs, 1990); and John Stremlau, *The International Politics of the Nigerian Civil War, 1967–1970* (Princeton: Princeton University Press, 1977).

53. See Ade Adefuye et al., *Seven Years of IBB,* 7 vols. (Lagos: Daily Times of Nigeria, 1993); Nkem Agetua, *Operation Liberty: The Story of Major-General Joshua Nimyel Dogonyaro* (Lagos: Hona Communications, 1992); Chidi Amuta, *Prince of the Niger: The Babangida Years* (Lagos: Tanus, 1992); J. Isawa Elaigwu, *Gowon* (Ibadan: West Books, 1986); Joseph Garba, *Diplomatic Soldiering: Nigerian Foreign Policy, 1975–1979* (Ibadan: Spectrum Books, 1987); Frederick Forsyth, *Emeka* (Ibadan: Spectrum Books, 1982); Yakubu Gowon, *The Economic Community of West African States: A Study of Political and Economic Integration* (Ph.D. thesis, Warwick University, February 1984); Olusegun Obasanjo, *My Command* (London: Heinemann, 1980); and Olusegun Obasanjo, *Not My Will* (Ibadan: University Press, 1990).

54. Quoted in Berman and Sams, *Peacekeeping in Africa,* p. 117, footnote 172.

55. On Branch Mining, see Reno, *Warlord Politics and African States,* p. 134.

56. On Executive Outcomes, this point is based on my personal interview with General Julius Maada Bio.

57. Aboagye, *ECOMOG,* p. 297.

58. Personal interviews with ECOMOG officers, Freetown, July 1999.

59. Personal interview with General Theophilus Danjuma, defense minister of Nigeria, Abuja, 2 March 2001.

60. Lucy Akhigbe, "Why Peace Has Been So Elusive," *New African,* July/August 1999, pp. 32–33, 50; Comfort Ero, "British Policy and Conflict in Sierra Leone" (unpublished manuscript); and William Reno, "The Failure of Peacekeeping in Sierra Leone," *Current History,* May 2001, pp. 219–225.

61. Personal interview with Peter Penfold, British high commissioner in Sierra Leone, Freetown, 2 July 1999.

62. Personal interviews with ECOMOG officers, Freetown, July 1999.

63. Ibid.

64. Quoted in Mortimer, "From ECOMOG to ECOMOG II," p. 201.

65. See Boutros Boutros-Ghali, *Unvanquished: A U.S.-UN Saga* (London and New York: I. B. Tauris, 1999), p. 104.

66. Personal interviews with ECOMOG soldiers, Freetown, July 1999.

67. I thank Jimmy Kandeh for this point.

68. Confidential interview.

69. Personal interview with General Timothy Shelpidi, ECOMOG force commander, Abuja, July 1999.

70. Personal interviews with ECOMOG officers, Freetown, July 1999.

71. For an excellent insider's assessment of the issues surrounding the peace accord, see Rashid, "Lomé Peace Negotiations," pp. 26–35.

72. Sixth Report of the Secretary-General on the UN Observer Mission in Sierra Leone, S/1999/645, 4 June 1999, p. 2.

73. Rashid, "Lomé Peace Negotiations," p. 29.

74. The information from this paragraph is largely derived from Thomas Mark Turay, "Civil Society and Peacebuilding: The Role of the Inter-Religious Council of Sierra Leone," in Lord, *Paying the Price*, pp. 50–53.

75. Personal interview at the Ivorian foreign ministry, Abidjan, 9 July 1999.

76. Ibid.

77. Rashid, "Lomé Peace Negotiations," p. 29.

78. Personal interview with Francis Okelo, former UN Special Representative in Sierra Leone, Lomé, 8 December 1999.

79. Rashid, "Lomé Peace Negotiations," p. 29.

80. Ibid., pp. 27–28.

81. See Seventh Report of the Secretary-General on the UN Observer Mission in Sierra Leone, S/1999/836, 30 July 1999, p. 2.

82. Eighth Report of the Secretary-General on the UN Observer Mission in Sierra Leone, S/1999/1003, 23 September 1999, p. 6.

83. See First Report on the UN Mission in Sierra Leone, S/1999/1223, 6 December 1999, pp. 1–6.

84. Fourth Report on the UN Mission in Sierra Leone, S/2000/455, 19 May 2000, p. 4.

85. Third Report on the UN Mission in Sierra Leone, S/2000/186, 7 March 2000, pp. 3–4; and Fifth Report on the UN Mission in Sierra Leone, S/2000/751, 31 July 2000, p. 4.

86. Fifth Report on the UN Mission in Sierra Leone, p. 9.

87. For initial reports of the tension, see Lansana Fofana, "A Nation Self-Destructs," *NewsAfrica* 1, no. 5 (31 July 2000): 25; and Chris McGreal, "UN to Sack Its General in Sierra Leone," *Guardian Weekly*, 29 June–5 July 2000, p. 2.

88. Eleventh Report of the Secretary-General on the UN Mission in Sierra Leone, S/2001/857/Add.1, 10 September 2001, pp. 1–2.

89. On the demobilization effort, see Fourth Report on the UN Mission in Sierra Leone, p. 5.

90. Third Report on the UN Mission in Sierra Leone, p. 14.

91. Fifth Report on the UN Mission in Sierra Leone, pp. 4–5.

92. Oluyemi Adeniji (interview), "We Don't Want Another Angola," *West Africa* no. 4217 (13–19 March 2000): p. 14.

93. See Comfort Ero, *Sierra Leone's Security Complex* (working paper no. 3, Centre for Defence Studies, London, June 2000).

94. For an assessment of the UN's prospects in Sierra Leone, see John Hirsch, "War in Sierra Leone," *Survival* 43, no. 3 (Autumn 2001): 145–162.

95. See Adekeye Adebajo and Chris Landsberg, "Back to the Future: UN Peacekeeping in Africa," in Adekeye Adebajo and Chandra Lekha Sriram (eds.), *Managing Armed Conflicts in the Twenty-first Century* (London and Portland: Frank

Cass, 2001), pp. 161–188; and David M. Malone and Karin Wermester, "Boom and Bust? The Changing Nature of UN Peacekeeping," in Adebajo and Sriram, *Managing Armed Conflicts,* pp. 37–54.

5

Guinea-Bissau:
Lilliputians Without Gulliver

Always bear in mind that the people are not fighting for ideas, for the things in anyone's head. They are fighting to win material benefits, to live better and in peace, to see their lives go forward, to guarantee the future for their children.

—Amilcar Cabral, PAIGC leader, 1964–1973

This chapter provides a background to Guinea-Bissau's civil war between June 1998 and May 1999, situating the roots of the crisis in the twenty-four-year rule of the Partido Africano da Independencia da Guine e Cabo Verde (PAIGC), as well as the resource-poor and aid-dependent country's economic difficulties. The short-term explanation for the conflict lay in the deteriorating relationship between President João Bernardo Vieira and his former army chief of staff, General Ansumane Mane. The disintegration of the relationship between the men led to the division of the country's army into rival factions supporting Vieira and Mane.

Major concerns of this chapter are the peacemaking efforts by external actors, ECOWAS and the lusophone CPLP, as well as the peacebuilding efforts by the UN and Guinea-Bissau's civil society groups. We also investigate the two external military interventions in Guinea-Bissau between 1998 and 1999. The first military intervention was undertaken by troops from Senegal and Guinea in defense of Vieira. The second intervention was undertaken by an ECOMOG force consisting of Benin, Gambia, Togo, and Niger.

It has sometimes been argued that a coalition of small states can avoid the political baggage and interests that regional powers such as Nigeria carry into military interventions in places like Liberia and Sierra Leone. According to this view, a coalition of small states can help allay suspicions about the motives of external interveners and reassure belligerents about the neutrality of the peacekeeping mission.[1] However, ECOMOG's intervention into Guinea-Bissau between December 1998 and June 1999 exposed some major weaknesses in this approach. The lack of Nigeria in this intervention denied the mission of vital logistical and financial support that was at least sufficient to keep ECOMOG alive in Liberia and Sierra Leone. Lacking the regional Gulliver, the Lilliputian peacekeepers had to withdraw from Bissau by June 1999 after fierce fighting erupted amid a military coup d'état.

Within the context of these interventions, this chapter also examines the rivalry between Portugal, Guinea-Bissau's former colonial power, and France, whose influence in this tiny country increased after Vieira joined the CFA franc currency zone in 1997. France, a close ally of Senegal and Guinea, financed and transported the predominantly francophone ECO-MOG force to Bissau. Portugal remains Guinea-Bissau's principal bilateral donor; it sent warships to Bissau Guinean waters during the conflict and was perceived to be close to Mane.

The chapter explains the difficulties of peacemaking in Guinea-Bissau at three interdependent levels. At the domestic level, Guinea-Bissau's two main protagonists, Vieira and Mane, were unwilling to settle their differences through peaceful means and sought to manipulate the support of external forces. Even with ECOMOG peacekeepers on the ground, Mane resorted to military means to achieve his political objectives. At the subregional level, Senegal and Guinea were compromised as neutral peacekeepers and had to be replaced by West African troops with no prior involvement in the fighting. But the size of ECOMOG's contingent—712 men—was insufficient to protect the capital from attack and to disarm the combatants, a situation exacerbated by its logistical weaknesses. At the extra-regional level, actors like the UN, the World Bank, the EU, and several bilateral donors supported some peacebuilding efforts. But continuing instability in Guinea-Bissau has made donors reluctant to deliver on most of the pledges made at a conference in Geneva in May 1999.

BACKGROUND TO CONFLICT:
A PEASANT REVOLUTION DEVOURS ITS OWN CHILDREN

Guinea-Bissau is a tiny country of about 1.3 million people located on West Africa's Atlantic coast. One of the poorest countries in the world, its foreign exchange earnings are derived largely from cashew nuts and fishing. In the 1970s, Guinea-Bissau was widely seen as a political and economic model of a successful African peasant revolution. Under the charismatic leadership of Amilcar Cabral, and operating from bases in neighboring Guinea-Conakry during the liberation struggle from Portuguese rule, many young Bissau Guinean volunteers received military and ideological training before being sent back across the border to win support for their cause among the rural masses. A largely peasant army of about 6,000 eventually forced the withdrawal of 30,000 Portuguese troops and independence was declared in September 1974.

Amilcar Cabral tragically did not live to see the fruits of his labor: he was assassinated in Conakry in January 1973 by African agents of the Portuguese government.[2] His brother, Luis Cabral, took over the leadership of the PAIGC. The party was the symbol of the guerrilla struggle waged by peasant youths, but it inherited a country with an illiteracy rate of 95 percent and an underdeveloped economy.[3] Despite the great expectations raised by the attainment of independence, the liberation struggle soon degenerated into a feast of corruption and repressive misrule, as Guinea-Bissau's peasant revolution devoured its own children.

Once in government, the PAIGC continued the centralizing tendencies it had displayed during the liberation struggle and the party soon became indistinguishable from the state. The National Popular Assembly met only once a year to rubber-stamp decisions made by a secretive ten-member Council of State. The PAIGC thus allowed its local party organizations, painstakingly built up during the war of liberation, to disintegrate. Luis Cabral built up a repressive security service and centralized power in a close-knit cabal. A coup attempt by PAIGC politician Malam Sanha in November 1978 led to a crackdown by Cabral's *securocrat*. Strikes were banned and labor leaders jailed. Civil society activists, including youth and women's groups, were co-opted into the party.

Luis Cabral was constantly in fear of Bissau Guinean dissidents based in Senegal, though Senegalese leader Léopold Sédar Senghor later handed over some of these dissidents to the authorities in Bissau. But the strained relations between Dakar and Bissau over the harboring of each other's dissidents would remain a major source of friction and instability that carried over into Guinea-Bissau's civil war of 1998 to 1999.

The hard-won unity achieved by Amilcar Cabral during the liberation struggle soon started to disintegrate. Portuguese colonialists had used people of Cape Verdean descent as district administrators and Fulas as village administrators, thus marginalizing other groups like the Balantas and Manjocos. Many of the *civilizados,* the educated elite who were the leaders of the PAIGC, were Cape Verdeans, including the Cabral brothers. The struggle for independence in both Guinea-Bissau and Cape Verde had been waged by the PAIGC. By 1980, about 200 Cape Verdeans served in key government and administrative posts in Guinea-Bissau, creating a ground swell of resentment among the indigenous population.[4] The fact that many of the senior officers in the country's army, the Forças Armadas

Revolucionárias do Povo (FARP), were of Cape Verdean descent was a further source of tension, despite the claims of the Balanta as the largest ethnic group in the liberation army.[5]

The PAIGC repeated the practice of most postindependence African governments in using monopolistic marketing boards to force peasant farmers to sell crops to the government at lower prices in a bid to raise extra revenue. This resulted in widespread smuggling of the country's cashew nuts across the border into Senegal and Gambia in search of higher prices. Already a small, resource-poor country striving to recover from a decade-long liberation struggle, Guinea-Bissau soon became one of the world's most aid-dependent countries.

In November 1980, Guinea-Bissau's army staged a successful coup against Cabral. João Bernardo "Nino" Vieira, Cabral's prime minister since 1978 and a former military commander during the liberation struggle, became head of state. Vieira's two-decade rule continued in the security-obsessed, autocratic traditions of his predecessor. There were soon reports of torture and jailing of opponents. Vieira disbanded the National Popular Assembly and quickly established control over the army and security services, often reasserting power through periodic purges of "fifth columnists." In the first six years of his rule, Vieira announced the uncovering of three coup "plots." After the apparent discovery of the "November plot" in 1985, "Nino" had six people executed, including Paulo Correia, his first vice president. Many of those implicated in this "plot" were members of the Balanta ethnic group.[6] Mass graves believed to contain the remains of Vieira's assassinated opponents were discovered after he was ousted from power.

The election of a National Popular Assembly and adoption of a new constitution in 1984 were designed to lend a veneer of legitimacy to Vieira's autocratic rule. Barely two years later, however, Vieira launched violent reprisals against members of the Balanta ethnic group after yet another alleged coup attempt. Guinea-Bissau's first multiparty election took place in July 1994: Vieira was directly elected alongside a 100-member parliament. But discontentment with his rule continued, amid charges of cronyism and corruption within the ruling PAIGC. In what many regarded as a shift away from Portugal, the former colonial power, toward France, Vieira exchanged the peso for the CFA franc in May 1997, joining a French-dominated currency zone. The frequently postponed PAIGC party congress in May 1998 reelected Vieira to the party's presidency "by acclamation," but several party barons regarded the process as an unconstitutional usurpation of party procedures. Within four years of its first multiparty elections, the country's political and economic anomie would be glaringly exposed. Vieira himself was among the first to fall as the country collapsed into civil war. Guinea-Bissau's peasant revolution, which had promised so much to so many, would soon become mired in civil war, political instability, and financial crisis. It is to these events that we now turn our attention.

COUP, CONFLICT, AND INTERVENTION:
JUNE–NOVEMBER 1998

Mane's Mutiny

Guinea-Bissau's eleven-month civil conflict and continuing instability followed the deterioration in the personal relationship between two powerful men: President João Bernardo Vieira and General Ansumane Mane, his army chief of staff. Mane had served as Vieira's deputy commander during the liberation struggle and was regarded as a loyal and even subservient chief of staff who often avoided the limelight.[7] In January 1998, Vieira accused Mane of providing arms to Casamance secessionists of the MFDC in neighboring Senegal. The president suspended his army chief of staff from his post and ordered a parliamentary inquiry into the affair. Mane strongly denied the charges of arms trafficking leveled against him, arguing that it was Vieira himself who had supplied arms to the MFDC.[8] Before the report of the parliamentary inquiry could be published, Vieira announced the replacement of Mane by General Humberto Gomes. The report on arms trafficking, which was released in April 1999, exonerated Mane of the charges and instead implicated Vieira and some of his senior PAIGC officials in gunrunning to Casamance rebels.[9]

Vieira's attempt to arrest Mane before his departure for an OAU heads of state summit in Ouagadougou in June 1998 led to an attempted coup d'état by Mane, who, while disavowing any political ambitions, announced the establishment of a military junta. Mane had been a popular chief of army staff among both officers and rank-and-file soldiers whose interests and welfare he had tried to defend. He had called for payment of their delayed salaries and urged Vieira to improve the squalid living conditions of soldiers posted to the border region with Senegal.[10] Fighting erupted between rival factions of the army on 7 June 1998, resulting in hundreds of deaths in Bissau. Factions loyal to Mane and fighters loyal to Vieira waged a fierce battle for control of the capital. Most of the army deserted to Mane, whose soldiers seized control of the country's Bissalanca airport and soon controlled an estimated three-quarters of the country. With the bulk of his soldiers defecting to Mane's side, Vieira employed hundreds of young, often underage militias—the *aguentas*—mostly from his own Pepel ethnic group.[11] Some MFDC rebel fighters reportedly crossed the border to join Mane, himself an ethnic Mandingo.[12]

In response to these developments, Senegal, with about 2,000 troops, and Guinea, with about 400, intervened militarily in Bissau in support of Vieira. Soldiers from both countries guarded Vieira in his presidential palace. Senegalese troops deployed along the front line with Mane's troops near the airport, while Guinean troops deployed near the seaport. Senegalese troops, who were more numerous and more directly involved in the fighting, suffered more casualties than the Guineans. Senegalese forces were later accused of having laid thousands of mines on the front lines of the battle in Bissau, though the army denied this charge.[13] Like Nigeria in Liberia and Sierra Leone, Senegal overestimated its military capabilities in launching this intervention against a junta it assumed it could easily over-power. As its casualties mounted, Dakar urged Vieira to seek ECOWAS support, including the use of Alpha jets to bomb junta positions.[14]

Senegal and Guinea justified their intervention on the basis of bilateral defense pacts between Guinea-Bissau and its two neighbors. Many critics within Guinea-Bissau, however, questioned the legality of these accords, arguing that their purpose was to defend against externally instigated threats rather than to maintain internal security.[15] Like the ECOMOG inter-ventions in Liberia and Sierra Leone, the Seneguinean intervention was undertaken without the blessing of the full ECOWAS authority.

The main concern for Senegalese president Abdou Diouf was clearly the need to avoid any strengthening of Casamance separatists, by prevent-ing the emergence of a regime in Bissau that was perceived to be friendly to the MFDC. Diouf was also close to Vieira, whom he had often collected in Bissau in his presidential jet on the way to regional summits.[16] Diouf's intervention nonetheless left him open to charges of hypocrisy. Senegal had been one of the most vociferous critics of the Nigerian-led ECOMOG inter-vention in Liberia in 1990, though Senegal did later contribute troops to assist ECOMOG's efforts in Liberia between 1992 and 1993.

Guinea's leader, General Lansana Conté, intervened for two main rea-sons. First, he was acting out of solidarity with two friendly heads of state, Diouf and Vieira. Conté, who also maintained close personal relations with Sierra Leone's President Ahmed Tejan Kabbah, realized the importance of having close allies in the subregion, particularly in light of his military bat-tles with Charles Taylor's Liberia. The second consideration was the need to avoid a further destabilizing flow of refugees from Guinea-Bissau into Guinea, which was already hosting 500,000 refugees from the conflicts in Liberia and Sierra Leone.

Early Peacemaking Efforts

Following the events of June 1998, President Vieira wrote to General Abdulsalam Abubakar, ECOWAS chairman and Nigeria's head of state, requesting that an ECOMOG force be sent into Guinea-Bissau to restore order. ECOWAS foreign and defense ministers met to discuss the request on 3 July. The ministers strongly condemned Mane's coup, affirmed support for Vieira's elected government, and sanctioned the Seneguinean intervention.[17] ECOWAS's immediate support for this intervention contrasted markedly with the opposition of several of its francophone members to the Nigerian-led ECOMOG interventions in Liberia and Sierra Leone. Three factors explain this divergent response. First, Samuel Doe, Liberia's beleaguered leader, was very unpopular, even among ECOWAS leaders. Second, the camaraderie between the leaders of Senegal, Guinea, and Guinea-Bissau and their fellow ECOWAS heads of state was strong. Third, and most significantly, there was within the subregion a widespread historical fear of Nigeria, the primary contributor of the troops for the ECOMOG interventions in Liberia and Sierra Leone.

At the July 1998 ECOWAS meeting, subregional ministers recommended that ECOMOG's functions and mandate be broadened beyond Sierra Leone to include Guinea-Bissau. A Committee of Seven was established, consisting of Burkina Faso, Côte d'Ivoire, Gambia, Ghana, Guinea, Nigeria, and Senegal. This became a Committee of Nine after Cape Verde and Togo joined in October 1998. But ECOWAS was not the only mediator in Guinea-Bissau. Following consultations with the lusophone CPLP, consisting of Portugal, Angola, Brazil, Cape Verde, Mozambique, and São Tomé and Principe, Guinea-Bissau's warring factions signed a Memorandum of Understanding on a Portuguese frigate, *Corte-Real,* on 26 July 1998. The agreement called for the withdrawal of Senegalese and Guinean troops from Guinea-Bissau and their replacement by military observers from lusophone states.

Following this accord, the ECOWAS secretariat and several of its member states were uncomfortable about their subregional body being marginalized by an external mediator in a crisis involving one of their own members.[18] With continuing instability in Guinea-Bissau, ECOWAS and the CPLP together negotiated a cease-fire agreement in Praia, Cape Verde, on 26 August 1998. Two months after this accord, heavy fighting erupted in Bissau and surrounding cities in which fifty-three rebels and seven Senegalese troops were killed. Mane's forces captured Bafana, Gabu, Fulacunda, and Bambadinca.[19]

The Abuja Agreement

Another agreement was brokered by ECOWAS and the CPLP in the Nigerian capital of Abuja on 2 November 1998. For the first time, Vieira and Mane personally committed themselves to a peace agreement. The presence of both protagonists in Abuja was due to the efforts of Yaya Jammeh, Gambia's leader, who had invited them to Banjul for talks and transported them in his official aircraft to the Nigerian capital.[20] Gambia had close cultural and historical ties with neighboring Guinea-Bissau, and hosted refugees from both Guinea-Bissau and Senegal's Casamance region. It thus had a direct interest in a peaceful resolution of the conflict. General Mane also traced part of his family roots to Gambia.

The Abuja accord called for a cease-fire; the withdrawal of Senegalese and Guinean troops from Guinea-Bissau (Mane had refused their participation in any observer force) and the simultaneous deployment of ECOMOG observers from more neutral states by 28 February 1999; the establishment of a government of national unity; the deployment of observers along Guinea-Bissau's border with Senegal; the creation of a buffer zone between the warring parties until the demilitarization of the country by an ECOW-AS-led joint commission; the disarmament and demobilization of the country's estimated 28,000 fighters (an increase from a prewar level of 5,000); and the provision of security by ECOMOG to allow the delivery of humanitarian assistance and the holding of ECOWAS- and CPLP-monitored general and presidential elections no later than March 1999.[21,22]

With the signing of important peace agreements in Nigeria's capital in 1995 (for Liberia) and in 1998 (for Guinea-Bissau), Abuja was establishing itself as a capital of subregional peacemaking in fulfillment of Pax Nigeriana: the long-cherished dreams of Nigeria's leaders to play a leadership role in Africa. But unlike the ECOMOG missions in Liberia and Sierra Leone in which Nigeria had served as the pillar of both forces by providing the bulk of men and money, Nigeria declined to contribute any troops to the new mission in Guinea-Bissau. This was despite a desperate attempt by Vieira to secure Nigeria's participation in the ECOMOG force.[23]

General Abdulsalam Abubakar, who had served as Nigeria's chief of defense staff, became head of state following General Sani Abacha's sudden death in June 1998. Abubakar, having regularly attended ECOWAS chiefs of staff meetings, had been closely involved in the protracted ECOMOG missions in Liberia and Sierra Leone. He felt that Nigeria's troops and resources were already overstretched and had witnessed firsthand the difficulty of convincing other subregional states to contribute troops to the ECOMOG mission in Sierra Leone.[24] At the time that the conflict erupted in Guinea-Bissau, General Abubakar was about to undertake a difficult transition to civilian rule and was wary of embroiling Nigeria in another financially costly and domestically unpopular subregional intervention. Though Abubakar played a key role, as ECOWAS chairman, in the decision to send ECOMOG observers to Guinea-Bissau, Nigerian troops would play no part in this contingent.[25]

Nigeria did, however, play a role in military preparations for the deployment of ECOMOG observers to Guinea-Bissau. General Timothy Shelpidi, Nigeria's ECOMOG force commander in Freetown, carried out a needs assessment for the proposed force in November 1998, shuttling between Banjul and Bissau. In his final report, Shelpidi recommended a 5,000-strong ECOMOG force to oversee Guinea-Bissau's peace process, with an initial 2,000 troops replacing the departing Senegalese and Guineans. The report called for disarmament and elections, based on the recent experience in Liberia, and outlined plans for reopening the airport and for making the country's seaport functional.[26] The number of ECO-MOG observers for the transition period was later reduced by ECOWAS leaders to 1,450, and that of the initial force to 600 troops. This was largely due to financial and logistical problems.

Shortly after the signing of the Abuja agreement, foreign ministers of the ECOWAS Committee of Nine went to New York to brief the UN Security Council on the ECOMOG mission. They won the council's approval for the new peacekeeping mission. Interest was maintained in Guinea-Bissau at the UN by the fact that a few interested friends of Guinea-Bissau sat on the Security Council during this period: France is one of the five permanent members, while Portugal and Gambia had two-year stints as nonpermanent members.

FAILED PEACEKEEPING: DECEMBER 1998–JUNE 1999

The Government of National Disunity

In fulfillment of the Abuja accord, Francisco Fadul, a technocrat of Syrian-Lebanese descent, was appointed prime minister of Guinea-Bissau on 3 December 1998. Fadul inherited an economy with an external debt of U.S.$964 million and a real GDP that had shrunk by 28 percent during the previous, turbulent year.[27] On 8 January 1999, ministries were shared out between representatives of Vieira and Mane after an agreement brokered by new ECOWAS chairman Gnassingbé Eyadéma in Lomé on 15 December 1998. Senegalese and Guinean troops started to leave Bissau in January 1999. But a full withdrawal was delayed by Seneguinean fears of leaving a security vacuum that General Mane's forces could exploit pending gradual

deployment of the proposed ECOMOG force. Further complicating matters, Mane, supported by Fadul, continued to demand the participation of
CPLP states in any peacekeeping mission, expressing suspicion that France
and Senegal would manipulate the proposed francophone-dominated ECO-
MOG force. Vieira, meanwhile, continued to accuse Portugal of supporting
Mane.[28] Adding to the confusion, Prime Minister Fadul refused to take
office until the departure of Senegalese and Guinean troops.[29]

Fighting broke out again along the front line in the north of Bissau on
31 January 1999. Many of the 200,000 civilians who had recently returned
to Bissau were forced to flee the city or to seek shelter in churches and
embassies, as junta troops shelled government positions in the city center.
Eighty people were reported killed and 200 wounded in four days of fighting, while an estimated 130,000 people were internally displaced.[30] The
battle raged even as 300 ECOMOG troops from Benin and Niger aboard
the French warship *Sirrocco* were approaching the port of Bissau to begin
their peacekeeping mission. In a cruel twist, Settimo Arturo Ferrazeta, the
bishop of Bissau, one of Guinea-Bissau's most effective peacemakers and a
leading civil society activist who had often risked his life to mediate
between Vieira and Mane, died of a heart attack four days before the latest
bout of bloodshed.

Eyadéma dispatched his foreign minister, Joseph Kokou Koffigoh, to
Bissau to present a draft cease-fire, which Vieira and Mane signed on 3
February 1999. The government of national unity was formally inaugurated
on 20 February, with five cabinet ministers nominated by Vieira and four
by Mane. None of the opposition parties were included in the new government and the country's largest ethnic group, the Fulas, had no representa-
tion in the new cabinet.[31] The government's smooth running was hampered
by lack of offices, staff, and resources, as many buildings had been
destroyed in the fighting and many civil servants had fled abroad.

The Politics of Peacekeeping

In fulfillment of the military aspects of Abuja, Togo deployed 110 troops to
Guinea-Bissau between 26 December 1998 and 2 January 1999. This
deployment was undertaken without the knowledge of General Shelpidi,
ECOMOG's commander in Freetown, who had prepared the plans for the
deployment. Shelpidi had heard about the deployment on the BBC's Africa
service. Having submitted his assessment report to ECOWAS executive
secretary Lansana Kouyaté, Shelpidi had heard nothing further until news
of the Togolese deployment.[32] Eyadéma had apparently secured French
support for this deployment during a visit to Paris, having previously gar-
nered the support of the leaders of Benin, Mali, and Niger for a subregional

force in Guinea-Bissau.[33] As with his role in negotiating the Lomé accord in Sierra Leone in 1999, many felt that the Togolese leader was presenting himself as a subregional peacebroker partly in an attempt to deflect attention from his domestic failings following international criticism of flawed national elections and repressive policies toward Togo's opposition leaders.

By 12 February 1999, a 600-strong battalion from Benin, Gambia, Niger, and Togo, the core of ECOMOG III, had arrived in Guinea-Bissau. The number of ECOMOG military observers eventually rose to 712. Benin, whose troops had been trained under the U.S. African Crisis Response Initiative (ACRI), and Togo provided about 150 troops each. A promised 125-strong contingent from Mali never arrived. By the end of March 1999, Senegal and Guinea had finally withdrawn their troops from Guinea-Bissau. Vieira, backed by Dakar, had opposed the departure of Senegalese and Guinean troops, arguing that the ECOMOG contingent could not guarantee his security against Mane's army.[34] Mane, for his part, expressed fears of collusion between ECOMOG, Vieira, and Senegal, arguing that the late deployment of the peacekeepers was a ploy to allow government forces time to regroup. Vieira called for 4,000 ECOMOG peacekeepers, while Mane insisted that 750 troops were sufficient to do the job.[35] Subregional peacekeepers entered Guinea-Bissau under a cloud of total mistrust between the two parties.

On arrival, the peacekeepers secured the seaport and reopened the international airport. ECOMOG representatives chaired a special disarmament commission, which included representatives of both parties and reported some success in recovering heavy weapons. The subregional force also collected some light weapons and small arms, though the country remained awash with such weapons.[36] The disarmament of 5,000 troops stationed in and around Bissau started in March 1999 following a meeting between Vieira and Mane at the EU mission in Bissau on 15 February, the first such encounter on Guinean soil since the start of the conflict. The EU's commissioner for humanitarian affairs, Emma Bonino, was instrumental in brokering these talks, demonstrating again the influence of donors on an excessively aid-dependent country like Guinea-Bissau. In late April 1999, the peacekeepers had to defuse tensions between the junta and government forces after the government-appointed mayor of Bissau, Paulo Medina, refused to cede his position to his successor, Francisca Vaz.

Although the ECOMOG observers in Guinea-Bissau were led by task force commander Colonel Gnakoudé Berema of Togo, it was at first assumed that the force would be under the overall command of General Shelpidi, ECOMOG's force commander in Freetown. This could have been a way of retaining Nigerian support for the force. However, establishing a unified ECOMOG command was difficult in practice due to the lack of effective communication between Bissau and Freetown, the uncoordinated deployment of ECOMOG troops in Guinea-Bissau, and the lack of Nigerian observers in Bissau. General Shelpidi never received any directive from the ECOWAS chairman or secretariat instructing him to take over command of the ECOMOG force in Bissau.[37] The Nigerian general visited Togolese troops in Bissau in December 1998 and was bluntly told by their commander, Colonel Berema, that the force was under Togolese and not Nigerian command. Shelpidi then told Berema that the force had to call itself something other than ECOMOG since there was already an ECO- MOG force operating under his control in Freetown. As Shelpidi put it: "You cannot have two captains on one ship."[38] These tensions revealed the interstate rivalries and highly improvised and uncoordinated nature of yet another ECOMOG deployment.

The delay in deploying the ECOMOG force to Guinea-Bissau was due to the same logistical and financial difficulties evident in ECOMOG's missions in Liberia and Sierra Leone. This situation had prevented many subregional states from contributing peacekeepers to these missions. The ECOMOG force in Guinea-Bissau could in the end not have been deployed without French logistical and financial support. The troops arrived in Bissau aboard a French naval vessel, while Paris supplied military trucks and some communication equipment and paid the U.S.$16 daily stipends of the troops.

France and Portugal: Shades of Fashoda

France's contribution of logistical and financial support for the ECOMOG force, while generous, must still be seen in the light of its overall Africa policy and its desire to maintain influence and retain the confidence of its former colonies. Senegal and Guinea, which intervened militarily in Bissau, remain key countries in France's West Africa policy, while Benin, Togo, and Mali, which all pledged peacekeepers to the ECOMOG mission in Bissau, have traditionally been part of the Francophonie. France strongly supported the Seneguinean intervention in Bissau and adopted a hostile attitude toward Mane's junta, suspending aid to the transition government in Bissau.[39] The ECOMOG mission to Bissau was undertaken under the French initiative to strengthen African peacekeeping capacity, Renforcement des Capacités Africaines de Maintien de la Paix (RECAMP).[40] Gambia was the only nonfrancophone member of the ECOMOG force, while Guinea-Bissau had joined the francophone UEMOA in 1997 and was thus a member of the CFA franc currency zone.

Guinea-Bissau effectively became a stage on which anachronistic European "gunboat diplomacy" was played out as France and Portugal bat-

tled for geopolitical preeminence in this tiny African country. As fighting
raged in Bissau on 2 February 1999, Francisco Fadul accused the French
warship *Sirrocco,* transporting Nigerien and Beninois troops to Guinea-
Bissau, of bombarding junta positions.[41] Others, including some missionar-
ies, reported seeing 300 white, French-speaking soldiers, possibly mercenaries, supporting Vieira's forces during the battle for Bissau.[42]

Portugal responded by sending several warships to the Guinean coast,
without any authorization from the Vieira government, to conduct military
exercises and humanitarian operations. This was a clear effort to ward off
any possible French intervention. Jacques Chirac, France's president,
denied any French military involvement in Bissau during a visit to Portugal
in early February 1999.[43] Vieira responded to the Portuguese action by suspending a long-standing military cooperation agreement with Lisbon.
Prime Minister Fadul soon restored these ties during a visit to Lisbon,
where he also called for a defense pact between Portugal and other lusophone states to ward off any future Senegalese military intervention into
Guinea-Bissau.[44]

ECOMOG "Observes" a Putsch

Once deployed, the ECOMOG force in Guinea-Bissau had very few vehicles, and these frequently broke down.[45] The troops could not patrol much
beyond Bissau and had to return to the capital to sleep every night due to
the lack of radios and vehicles and the fear of being isolated from their
headquarters.[46] The small size of the force also prevented its observers
from deploying along Guinea-Bissau's border with Senegal, as envisaged
under the Abuja agreement. ECOMOG's difficulties in deploying troops on
the border with Senegal were exacerbated by political differences between
the parties: Vieira insisted on additional troops to undertake the deployment; Mane and Fadul argued that sufficient progress had been made in the
peace process to negate the need for more observers.[47]

While neither of Guinea-Bissau's warring factions fully complied with
the cease-fire, Vieira proved to be the more frequent violator of the Abuja
agreement. Whereas ECOMOG disarmed 600 of Mane's fighters, Vieira
refused to allow the peacekeepers to disarm an equal number of his own
troops. Mane decided to take matters into his own hands. Taking advantage
of the weak ECOMOG force in Guinea-Bissau, the former army chief
moved to oust Vieira on 7 May 1999, routing his depleted forces in Bissau.
ECOMOG troops did not intervene in the fighting. Vieira's presidential
term had been due to expire on 29 September 1999. However, even without
Mane's coup, it is unlikely that he would have survived beyond his term.
Vieira was increasingly unpopular even within his own party. On 16 April

1999, the country's parliament had voted to put Vieira and about forty of his senior aides on trial for arms trafficking to Casamance separatists.

Vieira sought shelter at the French Cultural Center in Bissau before fleeing to the Portuguese embassy after the French Cultural Center was destroyed by an angry crowd. The beleaguered president's plight was symbolic of his political fortunes: having moved closer to France through establishing closer monetary and political ties, he was forced to fall back on the "Mother Country" that he had abandoned and accused of supporting his enemy. Many of Guinea-Bissau's political and military leaders insisted that Vieira stand trial for treason and crimes against humanity. They were particularly incensed by his use of Senegalese and Guinean troops to prop up his regime.[48]

Prime Minister Fadul, ECOWAS, and key external donors eventually prevailed on Vieira's opponents to let him leave the country for Lisbon, where he arrived on 11 June 1999. As a condition of his safe departure, Vieira had been forced to sign a declaration renouncing his claim to the presidency. France, ECOWAS, the UN, the OAU, and the EU all condemned Mane's coup as domestically unconstitutional and a breach of the Abuja accord. Some of them threatened economic sanctions if Vieira suffered any harm. However, the coup was hugely popular within Guinea-Bissau itself.

Shortly after Mane's putsch, ECOWAS foreign ministers met in Lomé on 24 and 25 May, condemned the coup, and decided to withdraw the ECO-MOG contingent from Guinea-Bissau by early June, citing the deteriorating security situation and the force's financial and logistical weaknesses.[49] In Lomé, the pleas of Bissau Guinean foreign minister Hilla Barber for the force to stay in the country until forthcoming elections were held, fell on deaf ears. Colonel Berema, the ECOMOG commander, offered a somewhat disingenuous appraisal of the peacekeeping mission: "We fulfilled our mission because we intervened at the right moment. Now that they are not two sides, we can leave."[50] But a coup d'état in which one side routed the other militarily under the noses of subregional peacekeepers could hardly have been the means through which ECOMOG had hoped to fulfill its mission.

PEACEBUILDING ON A SHOESTRING: 1999–2001

United Nations, Divided Country

On 3 March 1999, the UN Security Council approved the creation of a small UN Peacebuilding Support Office in Guinea-Bissau (UNOGBIS), with an international staff of only eighteen in July 2001, and a fourfold mandate: first, to create an environment that would allow the consolidation of peace and enable the holding of democratic elections; second, to work with the government of Guinea-Bissau, ECOWAS, and other parties to implement the Abuja accord; third, to seek the parties' compliance in collecting and destroying the large quantity of arms circulating in the country; and finally, to harmonize the UN's political, humanitarian, and economic activities in Guinea-Bissau.[51] Gambia was appointed to chair the "Group of Friends of Guinea-Bissau" at the UN under Baboucarr Jagne, its respected former Permanent Representative to the UN and current foreign minister. The group, consisting of fourteen countries, meets periodically to mobilize resources for the reconstruction of Guinea-Bissau, define priority areas for such assistance, and keep the attention of the international community on developments in the country.[52] A UN Trust Fund for Guinea-Bissau was also established, and on 30 April 1999, Cameroonian diplomat Samuel Nana-Sinkam was appointed as the Special Representative of the UN Secretary-General in Guinea-Bissau.

In April 1999, Bissau Guinean premier Francisco Fadul traveled to Europe with a begging bowl. He secured U.S.$4 million of assistance in Lisbon, U.S.$2.3 million in Stockholm, and mended political fences in Paris. Following the establishment of a transitional government in Guinea-Bissau, international donors attended a meeting in Geneva on 4 and 5 May convened by the UN Development Programme (UNDP). At the meeting, donors pledged U.S.$200 million to support peacebuilding activities including organizing elections, demobilizing and disarming combatants and reintegrating them into civilian life, reunifying the army, rehabilitating the country's infrastructure, investing in its public administration and private sector, and destroying 20,000 land mines. Two days after the donor conference, Mane's military coup removed Vieira from power. The funds pledged in Geneva have since largely remained on hold, though the World Bank and EU have since provided U.S.$3 million each, and the IMF U.S.$2 million, for postconflict emergency assistance. Portugal and France also resumed assistance after elections in early 2000, while the World Bank approved a U.S.$25 million economic rehabilitation and recovery credit in May 2000.

Bissau Guinean civil society actors have played an important role in promoting peace and human rights by organizing seminars and sensitization programs on these issues. In recognition of these efforts, UN Secretary-General Kofi Annan requested the UN Security Council to broaden UNOGBIS's mandate to support national efforts, including those of civil society, in order to promote reconciliation and the pacific settlement of disputes. Guinea-Bissau's respected League of Human Rights (LDH) organized a three-day National Reconciliation Conference for 300 civil society participants in Bissau in August 1999 that called for accountability for crimes committed during the country's civil war and urged the military to stop interfering with the political process. The LDH has also been involved in efforts to protect child soldiers from public hostility and has called for the release of political prisoners.

This call has been backed by UN Special Representative Nana-Sinkam, who publicly called on the government either to release or to speed up the trials of political prisoners jailed on charges of treason, corruption, and collaborating with foreign troops from Senegal and Guinea. Nana-Sinkam also issued strong warnings to the military junta to stay out of politics. But the UN's mission in Guinea-Bissau has been dogged by reports of tensions between Nana-Sinkam and the UNDP Resident Coordinator, Philoméne Makolo, leading to a failure to coordinate the UN's efforts effectively.[53] UNOGBIS hosted conferences for parliamentarians in June and September 2000, and helped to train Bissau Guinean magistrates in a bid to revive the judiciary and to speed up the trial of the 600 prisoners arrested after the May 1999 coup. In March 2001, the Netherlands funded a UNOGBIS seminar that brought together 120 representatives of political parties, the media, civil society, and trade unions.

The UN's mandate in Guinea-Bissau also called for UNOGBIS to help build good relations between Guinea-Bissau and its neighbors.[54] In furtherance of this goal, Nana-Sinkam traveled to Dakar and Conakry in November 1999 amid continuing concerns about instability on the common border between the three countries. This situation led to Kofi Annan proposing to the UN Security Council the deployment, between October and December 1999, of military observers and joint monitoring measures along these borders.[55] The council, wary of being drawn into what some of its members regarded as another protracted African conflict, did not approve such a force.

By the end of 1999, the subregional dimensions of Guinea-Bissau's instability were evident. Bissau Guinean refugees still remained in Senegal, Guinea, Gambia, and Cape Verde, while Guinea-Bissau hosted over 6,300 refugees, including about 5,500 from Senegal's troubled Casamance region and 800 from Liberia and Sierra Leone.[56] Within Guinea-Bissau itself, about 60,000 people remained internally displaced outside the capital.[57] In late December 1999, Guinea-Bissau attempted to mediate in peace negotiations held in Banjul between MFDC separatists and the Senegalese government. Gambia, which was also playing a more high-profile role in the disputes in Guinea-Bissau and Casamance, had itself often been accused of hosting Casamance rebels.[58]

From Bullets to Ballots

Following Mane's coup in May 1999, Prime Minister Fadul confirmed that elections would still go ahead as scheduled on 28 November 1999. Malam Bacai Sanha, the speaker of the National Assembly and the leader of an anti-Vieira faction within the PAIGC, was sworn in on 14 May as interim president. Sanha quickly sought to improve relations with neighboring states. He visited Abdou Diouf in Dakar in late June, where both leaders pledged to work together to resolve the Casamance problem. Fadul had earlier visited Dakar and apologized for the involvement of Bissau Guinean officials in arms trafficking to Casamance rebels.

On 8 July 1999, an increasingly assertive parliament voted by a two-thirds majority for a new constitution that would limit elected presidents to two five-year terms and prevent anyone whose parents were not born in Guinea-Bissau from holding the highest offices in the land. Given that prominent figures including Francisco Fadul and General Mane had family roots outside Guinea-Bissau, that Cape Verde had produced Guinea-Bissau's first head of state, and that many Cape Verdeans had adopted Bissau Guinean citizenship, this last clause contained the seeds of future social upheavals. In late July, the transition government arrested over a dozen of Vieira's closest associates for "incitement to war."

Guinea-Bissau's powerful military continued to cast an ominous shadow over the dawn of a democratic era. In October 1999, General Mane stated that the junta would not be disbanded after the elections and warned that the army could return if the "interests of the people" were threatened. In early November, the military produced its own Magna Carta in which it stated its plans to continue to play a role alongside an elected government. Two days before elections, the army was still trying to sell a power-sharing arrangement to a future government, including a proposal for an upper council including the country's executive and senior military officials.[59] Most of the country's politicians rejected these proposals.

Before elections in Guinea-Bissau in November 1999, some newspapers were revived and private radio stations started to broadcast again. Twelve candidates competed for the presidential election itself. The most competitive candidates included: interim president Sanha of the ruling PAIGC, Kumba Yala of the Partido para a Renovção Social (PRS), Joaquim Balde of the Partido Social Democratico (PSD), and Abubacan Balde of the União Nacional para a Democracia e o Progresso. Thirteen parties in all contested for 102 legislative seats.

Guinea-Bissau's poorly-resourced national electoral commission was aided in its tasks by the UNDP, which provided assistance in registering 502,678 electors, 91.2 percent of eligible voters. UNDP also assisted in

civic education, computerization of the voter list, training election workers, and procuring and delivering ballot boxes. The EU, the Netherlands,
and Japan contributed about U.S.$4.5 million to support the election.
Portugal and Sweden also contributed generously. The CPLP, the OAU,
and the Francophonie sent electoral observers to monitor the poll, in
which over 400,000 people, about 80 percent of registered voters, participated.[60]

Voting took place peacefully in Guinea-Bissau following an election
campaign between 5 and 26 November 1999. No party won an outright
majority in the legislative election, though the ruling PAIGC lost its twen-
ty-five-year monopoly on power. The PRS won 38 out of 102 seats, compared to 29 for the Resistência da Guiné-Bissau–Movimento Ba-Fata
(RGB-MB) and 24 for the PAIGC (down from 62 in 1994). In the first
round of the presidential election, Kumba Yala won the majority of votes
with 38.81 percent, followed by interim president Sanha with 23.37 percent.[61] A presidential runoff between the two leading candidates on 16
January 2000 resulted in a comfortable 72 percent victory for Yala, who
had narrowly lost to Vieira in the 1994 presidential election. Yala's power
base was built around his Balanta ethnic group, which constitutes about a
third of Guinea-Bissau's population. Sanha had been the favorite candidate
of the military junta.[62]

The Elusive "Democracy Dividend"

In a portent of future problems for the new civilian regime, a group of disaffected soldiers demonstrated for their pay on the eve of elections. A week
before the presidential runoff, doctors, nurses, and teachers staged a series
of strikes to press for payment of nine months of salary arrears. Guinea-
Bissau's new government was inaugurated in February 2000 with a parliamentary coalition government of the PRS and the RGB. It soon released
most of the political prisoners held following the May 1999 coup. Though
most Bissau Guinean refugees returned to their country after the elections,
armed banditry continued to be a major source of insecurity. A lack of
trained personnel and logistical support for the police forced the recently
mutinous army to take on policing tasks.[63]

As previously feared, problems soon developed for Yala's government
in handling elements of Mane's military junta. Mane turned down the offer
of a position as military adviser to the presidency, while his deputy,
Colonel Verissimo Correia Seabre, refused to take up his appointment as
minister of defense. The junta also fought against the restructuring of the
army in a dispute mediated by civil society groups, including most promi-
nently Bishop Jose Camnate of Bissau, as well as former Gambian foreign

minister Sedate Jobe. In May 2000, Mohammed Lamine Sanha, the commander of the navy, defied President Yala's order, relieving him of his post for releasing a Korean trawler that was fishing illegally in Guinean waters. The situation in Guinea-Bissau was worrying enough for ECOWAS leaders, meeting in Abuja on 28 and 29 May, to express concern over continuing tensions between the president and members of the former military junta. Subregional leaders sternly reminded the soldiers that the president had been democratically elected.[64]

In a further disturbing sign for Guinea-Bissau's fledgling democracy, two journalists at the state-run television service and an opposition politician, Fernando Gomes, were arrested in May 2000 after Gomes, during a public broadcast, denied charges of corruption by the prime minister, Caetano N'tchama, and leveled the same charges against N'tchama. All three were later released by a judge. This followed protests by civil society representatives and political groups. In March 2001, the UN reported that three people were shot by police during a student demonstration.[65] Further complicating peacebuilding efforts, religious and ethnic tensions erupted between Fula and Felupe communities in the north and between Fula and Mandingo communities in the east.

External Friends and Foes

The situation along Guinea-Bissau's border with Senegal also continues to worsen amid continuing reports of cross-border banditry. This has resulted in the frequent closing of the common border and the detention of nationals from the opposite side of the border. In April 2000, Senegalese troops pursued MFDC rebels across the border into Guinea-Bissau; Senegalese planes bombed the northern border areas of Cutima and Iumbembem; and fighting in the Bissau village of Djagur displaced 1,000 villagers.[66] Amid this deteriorating situation, newly elected Senegalese president Abdoulaye Wade visited Bissau on 29 April 2000. As an opposition leader, Wade had been a vociferous critic of Senegal's peacekeeping role in Liberia. He had described its 1998 intervention in Guinea-Bissau as a mistake, and during his visit to Bissau asked for forgiveness for Diouf's actions. But relations soon soured between Bissau and Dakar after Wade asked for UN observers to monitor what he described as rebel infiltration into Casamance from Guinea-Bissau. Yala responded by saying there was no need for UN observers, though he finally supported the idea in September 2000.

Following Wade's visit to Bissau, the chiefs of staff of both countries met, and in August 2000 their interior ministers, the prefect of the Senegalese province of Kolda, and the governor of the Bissau Guinean province of Bafata all met with communities on both sides of the divide, leading to the reopening of their common border.[67] Yala went on a state visit to Dakar in August 2000 and both countries signed agreements on border issues, though Guinea-Bissau's army rejected the idea of joint patrols by both national armies. The situation soon deteriorated again, and by March 2001 increased fighting between rival factions of Casamance's MFDC spilled over into northwestern Guinea-Bissau, resulting in president Yala ordering a military offensive against the MFDC in which both sides suffered heavy casualties. Fighting was also reported between Senegalese troops and MFDC factions. The continuing presence of over 3,000 refugees from Casamance in Guinea-Bissau's northwest, some with alleged links to MFDC rebels, remains a major source of concern.[68]

President Yala visited two other important subregional states during this period. He went to Conakry from 30 April to 2 May 2001, where he signed a protocol of friendship with Lansana Conté, who had sent troops into Guinea-Bissau with Senegal three years earlier. During a visit to Abuja from 13 to 15 June 2001, Nigerian president Olusegun Obasanjo presented Yala with U.S.$1 million as a contribution toward the restructuring of Guinea-Bissau's armed forces.[69] This was a clear sign that despite its own domestic problems, Nigeria still intended to continue to play a leadership role within West Africa.

From Ballots to Bullets?

Despite the most democratic election in the country's history, Guinea-Bissau's domestic political problems continue. Opposition leaders were arrested following an alleged coup attempt in November 2000 involving General Mane. They were later released and confined to Bissau. One hundred fifty military officers were also detained, as well as 108 MFDC rebels accused of supporting Mane. Another government crisis was triggered in January 2001 when all the legislators of the coalition RGB party withdrew their support from Yala's government, depriving him of a governing majority. Yala has often been accused of making decisions without consulting with relevant ministers, but much of the political class has demonstrated similar traits of a lack of experience and political judgment. In February 2001, the government announced that it had foiled yet another assassination "plot" against Yala and senior Balanta officials. Bissau Guinean security officials accused the MFDC of involvement in the failed plot, and there was an exchange of gunfire in Bissau involving suspected MFDC rebels and Yala's security officials.[70]

Guinea-Bissau's political instability has been accompanied by a profound economic crisis. With a budget of only around 86 billion CFA francs in 2000, its main bank is close to collapse, its fishery industry continues to be ravaged by illegal fishing and insufficient vessels, and its cashew crop revenues, the principal government earnings, were expected to be 50 percent lower in 2001 than in the previous year.[71] Even amid these difficulties, sections of Guinea-Bissau's political class continued to demonstrate signs of the corruption that had helped keep the country near the bottom of global development–league tables. In June 2001, a parliamentary commission of inquiry started investigating the disappearance of U.S.$17 million of World Bank funds from the national treasury. At the end of the same month, President Yala visited New York and addressed a meeting of the "Friends of Guinea-Bissau" at the UN. Yala urged donors to deliver on their pledges, assured them that his government was respecting the rule of law, and noted that a new generation of Bissau Guineans wanted peace.[72] But for many donors, these words rang hollow amid the continuing political, financial, and security situation in Guinea-Bissau.

As the domestic governance and security situation in Guinea-Bissau has worsened, most of the external assistance pledged to Guinea-Bissau at the donor conference in Geneva in 1999 has not been delivered. France and the Netherlands have contributed to the demobilization of some ex-combatants; Australia, Britain, Germany, and the United States have contributed to clearing land mines; and the World Bank has provided some assistance for the demobilization of combatants and their reintegration into a new national army, and provided funds for the payment of civil service salaries. But these funds are scarcely enough to meet the country's postconflict peacebuilding needs. As Baboucarr Jagne, Gambia's foreign minister, noted: "The ball is really in the court of the international community to help the people of Guinea-Bissau consolidate what they have achieved."[73] But it is highly unlikely that a wary donor community will play ball until it sees genuine signs of financial probity and political stability.

The continuing instability in Guinea-Bissau remains a serious obstacle to the consolidation of its fledgling democracy. The country has now had three governments in less than two years. In disturbing moves that could yet trigger a backlash, there are growing complaints of "Balantaization," as the president, prime minister, defense minister, and thirty-five out of thirty-seven sector administrators all belong to the Balanta ethnic group. This pattern was perpetuated on 16 November with the promotion, disproportionately favoring Balantas, of thirty army officers. General Mane immediately rejected the promotions. Instead, he promoted himself to commander in chief, reversed these decisions, and prepared for yet another military insurrection against a civilian government. But Mane, the military cat with umpteen lives, had finally run out of lives. After fighting erupted in Bissau on 23 November 2000, forces loyal to President Yala managed to defeat General Mane's forces, killing Mane in the process and purging the army of his loyalists.

In January 2001, the political squabbling among Guinea-Bissau's fractious parties continued. President Yala was forced to appoint a new government and depend on the PAIGC for support on critical parliamentary bills after the RGB left the ruling coalition. Three months later, Yala finally replaced his unpopular premier, Caetano N'tchama, with Foreign Minister Faustino Imbali. The RGB had demanded N'tchama's sacking as a condition for continuing to support the government. But Imbali's appointment was also strongly opposed by opposition parliamentarians as well as by some members of Yala's own party, leading to near governmental paralysis in April and May. After encouragement by civil society actors, particularly Bishop Camnate, Imbali's government and budget were finally approved by the end of May. In December 2001, Yala replaced Imbali with Interior Minister Alamara Whasse, amid allegations of corruption. Yala was also accused of unconstitutional acts in dismissing four supreme court justices and expelling the leaders of a Muslim group from the country for allegedly fueling instability.[74]

Eighty percent of Guinea-Bissau's budget continues to be provided by external donors, and the EU is believed to have helped pay salaries for civil servants and soldiers in March and April 2000 and for striking teachers in February 2001.[75] This financial dependence leaves the country vulnerable to shifts in the mood of wary donors. But there are some glimmers of hope: Guinea-Bissau has been ruled eligible for some debt relief under the IMF's heavily indebted poor countries (HIPC) initiative, while the government has managed to convince a Canadian firm, Champion Resources, to invest U.S.$80 million in efforts to exploit its rich phosphate reserves.[76]

Guinea-Bissau's notoriously cantankerous political class must still find a way to establish political stability in order to sustain such investor interest and to attract more donor support. For its part, the international donor community will have to dig deeper into its pockets and find creative ways of channeling support to priority areas like disarmament, employment schemes, education, and infrastructure rehabilitation to take advantage of this window of opportunity to consolidate peace in Guinea-Bissau. As the May 2001 report of the Inter-Agency Mission to West Africa, led by Ibrahima Fall, a UN Assistant Secretary-General, warned: "Without national political will to overcome internal divisions and without concerted international support, this situation may lead to the collapse of the State, with tremendous security and humanitarian implications for neighboring countries."[77] The future looks bleak, indeed, for the heirs of Guinea-Bissau's peasant revolutionaries.

CONCLUSION

This chapter has examined the actions of domestic actors and their external allies in fueling conflict, and the role of external actors in efforts to end the civil war in Guinea-Bissau between 1998 and 1999. We have focused on three interdependent levels of analysis. At the domestic level, we have assessed the role of Guinea-Bissau's internal parties in triggering the civil war and the efforts of Bissau Guinean civil society actors in ending the conflict. In postelectoral Guinea-Bissau, we have analyzed the country's sources of instability and the difficult relations between the civilian government and military junta, as well as the instability of the fractious ruling coalition. At the subregional level, we have examined the Seneguinean military intervention into Guinea-Bissau in 1998, as well as the reasons for the failure of the ECOMOG mission, which led to its premature withdrawal in 1999. At the extra-regional level, we have analyzed the political rivalry between Portugal and France and assessed the role of the UN and external donors in peacebuilding efforts.

The chapter has noted that there remain major reasons for concern in postconflict Guinea-Bissau and for the future of its fledgling democracy. The military junta that had sought to continue to exert influence over and challenge the authority of the elected government appeared to have been struck a devastating blow following the assassination of General Mane by government troops in November 2000. But the disproportionate role of Balanta indigenes in the country's military and political leadership does not augur well for the country's future political stability. Equally disturbing is the destabilizing effect on the subregion of the continuing fighting in Guinea-Bissau's border area with Senegal involving Casamance rebels. The UN established a peacebuilding office in Guinea-Bissau in 1999 and has sought to play a role in supporting the consolidation of democracy and mobilizing resources for reconstruction. But the UN's role, while useful, continues to be difficult in light of ineffective coordination, political instability, and a lack of substantial donor funds for postconflict peacebuilding.

NOTES

1. See Adekeye Adebajo and Chris Landsberg, "Pax Africana in the Age of Extremes," *South African Journal of International Affairs* 7, no. 1 (Summer 2000): 21–22; and Chris Landsberg, "Willing but Unable: Small States and Peacekeeping in Africa," in Jakkie Cilliers and Greg Mills (eds.), *From Peacekeeping to Complex Emergencies: Peace Support Missions in Africa* (Johannesburg and Pretoria: South African Institute of International Affairs, and Institute for Security Studies, 1999), pp. 45–54.

2. See Basil Davidson, *The People's Cause: A History of Guerrillas in Africa* (Essex: Longman, 1981), pp. 135–138.

3. Rosemary E. Galli and Jocelyn Jones, *Guinea-Bissau: Politics, Economics, and Society* (Boulder and London: Lynne Rienner and Frances Pinter, 1987), p. 78.

4. Ibid., p. 93.

5. Ibid., p. 97.

6. Ibid., p. 108.

7. I thank Anthony Ohemeng-Boamah, UNDP program specialist, for drawing my attention to this point during an interview in New York on 20 August 2001.

8. Comfort Ero, "The Future of ECOMOG in West Africa," in Cilliers and Mills, *From Peacekeeping to Complex Emergencies*, p. 67.

9. *Economist Intelligence Unit*, Country Report, "Guinea-Bissau," 3rd Quarter 1999, p. 30.

10. Personal interview with General Timothy Shelpidi, former ECOMOG force commander, Abuja, 10 July 2001.

11. *Economist Intelligence Unit*, Country Report, "Guinea-Bissau," 4th Quarter 1999, p. 30.

12. Ibid., 1st Quarter 2000, p. 30.

13. Ibid., January 2001, p. 34.

14. Personal interview with General Timothy Shelpidi.

15. I thank Galina Kuznetsova, desk officer for Guinea-Bissau, UN Department of Political Affairs, for drawing my attention to this point during an interview in New York on 16 August 2001.

16. I thank Anthony Ohemeng-Boamah for drawing my attention to this point.

17. Eric G. Berman and Katie E. Sams, *Peacekeeping in Africa: Capabilities and Culpabilities* (Geneva and Pretoria: UN Institute for Disarmament Research and Institute for Security Studies, 2000), p. 129.

18. Personal interview with General Timothy Shelpidi.

19. Ero, "Future of ECOMOG in West Africa," p. 67.

20. Personal interview with Baboucarr Jagne, foreign minister of Gambia, New York, 30 July 2001.

21. *Economist Intelligence Unit*, Country Report, "Guinea-Bissau," January 2001, p. 30.

22. See Report of the Secretary-General Pursuant to Security Council Resolution 1216 (1998) Relative to the Situation in Guinea-Bissau, S/1999/294, 17 March 1999, pp. 1–2.

23. Maxwell Khobe, "The Evolution and Conduct of ECOMOG Operations in West Africa," in Mark Malan (ed.), *Boundaries of Peace Support Operations: The African Dimension,* ISS monograph no. 44 (February 2000), p. 111.

24. Personal interview with General Timothy Shelpidi.

25. Eboe Hutchful, "Peacekeeping Under Conditions of Resource Stringency: Ghana's Army in Liberia," in Cilliers and Mills, *From Peacekeeping to Complex Emergencies,* p. 111.

26. Personal interview with General Timothy Shelpidi.

27. *Economist Intelligence Unit*, Country Report, "Guinea-Bissau," 1st Quarter 2000, p. 30.

28. Ibid., 2nd Quarter 2000, p. 31.

29. Report of the Secretary-General Relative to the Situation in Guinea-Bissau, S/1999/294, 17 March 1999, p. 2.

30. On the killed and wounded, see *Economist Intelligence Unit,* Country Report, "Guinea-Bissau," 2nd Quarter 2000, p. 32.

31. Ibid., p. 33.

32. Personal interview with General Timothy Shelpidi.

33. Confidential interview.

34. *Economist Intelligence Unit,* Country Report, "Guinea-Bissau," 2nd Quarter 2000, p. 30.

35. Ibid., p. 31.

36. Report of the Secretary-General Relative to the Situation in Guinea-Bissau, S/1999/294, 17 March 1999, p. 4.

37. Personal interview with General Timothy Shelpidi.

38. Ibid.

39. *Economist Intelligence Unit,* Country Report, "Guinea-Bissau," 4th Quarter 1999, p. 34.

40. See Eboe Hutchful, "Peacekeeping Under Conditions of Resource Stringency," p. 115; and Rocklyn Williams, "Beyond Old Borders: Challenges to Franco-South African Security Relations in the New Millennium," *African Security Review* 8, no. 4 (1999): pp. 3–19.

41. *Economist Intelligence Unit,* Country Report, "Guinea-Bissau," 2nd Quarter 2000, p. 32.

42. Ibid., p. 33.

43. Ibid.

44. Ibid., 3rd Quarter 1999, p. 33.

45. I thank Galina Kuznetsova for drawing my attention to this point.

46. Berman and Sams, *Peacekeeping in Africa,* p. 134.

47. Report of the Secretary-General Relative to the Situation in Guinea-Bissau, S/1999/294, 17 March 1999, p. 3.

48. *Economist Intelligence Unit,* Country Report, "Guinea-Bissau," 3rd Quarter 1999, p. 32.

49. See Meeting of the ECOWAS Ministers of Foreign Affairs, Final Communiqué, Lomé, 24–25 May 1999, p. 4.

50. Quoted in *Economist Intelligence Unit,* Country Report, "Guinea-Bissau," 3rd Quarter 1999, p. 32.

51. Report of the Secretary-General Relative to the Situation in Guinea-Bissau, S/1999/741, 1 July 1999, p. 4.

52. The "Group of Friends" consists of Brazil, Canada, France, Gambia, Germany, Guinea, Italy, the Netherlands, Nigeria, Portugal, Senegal, Sweden, Togo, and the United States.

53. Report of the Joint Review Mission on the UN postconflict peacebuilding offices, UN Department of Political Affairs/UNDP, 20 July 2001, p. 14.

54. Report of the Secretary-General Relative to the Situation in Guinea-Bissau, S/1999/741, 1 July 1999, p. 4.

55. Report of the Secretary-General on Developments in Guinea-Bissau and on the Activities of the UN Peacebuilding Support Office in that Country, S/1999/1276, 23 December 1999, p. 5.

56. Ibid., p. 6.

57. Report of the Secretary-General Relative to the Situation in Guinea-Bissau, S/1999/741, 1 July 1999, p. 4.

58. *Economist Intelligence Unit,* Country Report, "Guinea-Bissau," 2nd Quarter 2000, p. 31.

59. Ibid., 1st Quarter 2000, p. 26.

60. Report of the Secretary-General on Developments in Guinea-Bissau, pp. 2–3.

61. Ibid., p. 4.

62. *Economist Intelligence Unit,* Country Report, "Guinea-Bissau," 1st Quarter 2000, p. 24.

63. Report of the Secretary-General on Developments in Guinea-Bissau, S/2000/250, 24 March 2000, p. 2.

64. Ibid., S/2000/632, 28 June 2000, p. 2.

65. Ibid., S/2001/237, 16 March 2001, p. 3.

66. *Economist Intelligence Unit,* Country Report, "Guinea-Bissau," July 2000, p. 29.

67. Report of the Secretary-General on Developments in Guinea-Bissau, S/2000/920, 29 September 2000, p. 2.

68. Ibid., S/2001/622, 22 June 2001, p. 3.

69. Ibid., p. 2.

70. Ibid., S/2001/237, 16 March 2001, p. 2.

71. Ibid., p. 3.

72. Personal interview with Baboucarr Jagne.

73. Ibid.

74. Report of the Secretary-General on Guinea-Bissau, S/2001/915, 27 September 2001, p. 1.

75. On external donor budget support, see Report of the Secretary-General on Developments in Guinea-Bissau, S/2001/622, 22 June 2001, p. 3.

76. *Economist Intelligence Unit,* Country Report, "Guinea-Bissau," 4th Quarter 1999, p. 36.

77. Report of the Inter-Agency Mission to West Africa, "Towards a Comprehensive Approach to Durable and Sustainable Solutions to Priority Needs and Challenges in West Africa," UN Security Council document, S/2001/434, 2 May 2001, p. 4.

The ECOWAS Security Mechanism: Toward a Pax West Africana

> Africa has the ability to solve its problems, where there is clarity of vision and firmness of will.
> —Amara Essy, secretary-general of the OAU

We will conclude this study by offering some lessons for developing a new security mechanism in West Africa based on our three case studies of Liberia, Sierra Leone, and Guinea-Bissau. Before discussing the ECOWAS security mechanism and offering proposals on how to make it more effective, we will first focus on nine important issues that emerge from our three case studies: first, the role of autocracy in fueling conflicts in West Africa; second, the disturbing trend of government support for armed factions and rebels from other states; third, the improvised nature of the ECOMOG interventions; fourth, the need for subregional actors to apply lessons from prior peacemaking efforts in undertaking new missions; fifth, the need for Nigeria to learn important lessons from these three cases in pursuing its leadership ambitions in West Africa; sixth, the role of external actors in fueling and/or managing conflicts in West Africa; seventh, the role of local civil society actors in managing conflicts; eighth, the potential cooperation between ECOWAS and the UN; and ninth, the importance of developing strategies and sanctions to deal with "spoilers" who are bent on destroying peace processes.

LEARNING LESSONS:
LIBERIA, SIERRA LEONE, AND GUINEA-BISSAU

West Africa's Tragic Triplets

In all three cases of Liberia, Sierra Leone, and Guinea-Bissau, personalized autocracies played a part in triggering the civil conflicts resulting in the tragic tale of West Africa's hapless triplets. Samuel Doe in Liberia (and Charles Taylor in postwar Liberia), Siaka Stevens and Joseph Momoh in Sierra Leone, and João Bernardo Vieira in Guinea-Bissau all displayed antidemocratic tendencies and often ethnic favoritism, which lost them the support of their people in the process. Placing ethnic kinsmen in senior political positions in states like Liberia, Guinea-Bissau, and even Côte d'Ivoire will only fuel violent confrontations by disaffected groups. This points to the importance of the ECOWAS security mechanism of 1999 (discussed below) applying democratic principles consistently and sanctioning military and civilian autocrats. Only through such actions will ECOWAS's security mechanism avoid becoming a defense pact for autocrats to protect their allies.

An alarming trend that is evident in all three cases is the support of dissident factions by subregional leaders to destabilize neighboring regimes. Burkina Faso and Côte d'Ivoire assisted the NPFL in Liberia; Liberia and Burkina Faso assisted the RUF in Sierra Leone. Nigeria, Sierra Leone, and Guinea also backed anti-NPFL factions in Liberia. The ECOWAS security mechanism cannot be successful if member states continue to support warring factions. A key lesson for the ECOWAS security mechanism is to learn the lessons from the fact that all three ECOMOG interventions were highly improvised. There was no clear mandate on exactly what the troops would be doing. Peacekeepers were sent into fragile environments without adequate logistical support and funding, and without a political settlement. Unsurprisingly, when things turned difficult, ECOMOG struggled to respond decisively in all three cases and was criticized for using too little or too much force and for compromising its stated neutrality.

ECOMOG as Guinea Pig

Like experimental guinea pigs, ECOWAS states seem to have repeated some of the same mistakes of previous interventions in undertaking new missions. The Sierra Leone intervention in February 1998 clearly revealed that Nigeria did not learn four important lessons from the Liberia experience. First, Nigeria failed to secure a clear mandate for its intervention from both ECOWAS and the UN before the intervention. Second, it failed to act in concert with other important subregional states to garner key francophone support for the intervention. Third, its disastrous intelligence failures before the invasion of Monrovia in 1992 were repeated in Freetown in 1999. Fourth, Nigeria's leaders failed to secure military and logistical equipment and the necessary financial support before undertaking the intervention.

But the Sierra Leone intervention also showed that a few lessons had been learned from the ECOMOG experience in Liberia. In Sierra Leone, francophone countries were actively involved in ECOWAS's peacemaking efforts from the start, resulting in less hostility and criticism of Nigeria's intervention in Sierra Leone. With Côte d'Ivoire having negotiated the Abidjan peace agreement in 1996, the most important francophone state in West Africa had a stake in the success of the mission in Sierra Leone. Likewise in Lomé in 1999, francophone Togo took the lead, along with the UN, in peacemaking, while Burkina Faso was actively involved in efforts to reach agreement with the RUF.

The ECOMOG intervention in Guinea-Bissau, however, repeated some of the mistakes of the Liberia and Sierra Leone interventions. The peacekeepers were logistically ill equipped for their mission; the number of troops was grossly insufficient to maintain security in the country; and the funding for the mission depended entirely on France, an external power that had its own interest in the outcome of the conflict in Guinea-Bissau. This intervention raised serious questions about the soundness of widespread claims by many analysts that Nigeria's own interventions in Liberia and Sierra Leone were undertaken in a bid to dominate its subregion. Here was Senegal, a middle-size West African power leading an intervention with Guinea in defense of what it saw as its national security interests without an ECOWAS mandate. The contrasting subregional and external reactions to the Senegalese and Nigerian interventions underlined the continuing fears and suspicions about Nigeria's domineering ambitions in West Africa.

Nigeria: Bull in a Community China Shop

The three ECOMOG interventions in Liberia, Sierra Leone, and Guinea-Bissau demonstrated the importance of Nigeria to any peacekeeping mission in West Africa.[1] Despite continuing fears expressed by several ECOWAS states and numerous commentators of a bullying Nigeria clumsily rampaging through West Africa like a bull in a china shop, Nigeria appears to be an indispensable presence to the success of any future subregional peacekeeping initiatives. General Cheick Diarra, ECOWAS's Malian deputy executive secretary, expressed the dilemma eloquently: "Nigeria is the problem and the solution to the problem."[2] The absence of the Nigerian Gulliver from the ECOMOG force in Guinea-Bissau was critical to the premature end of the peacekeeping mission in Guinea-Bissau in 1999. In Liberia and Sierra Leone, Nigerian-led ECOMOG forces had been able to overcome their logistical shortcomings to protect Monrovia and Freetown from being overrun by rebels in 1992 and 1999, respectively. The Nigerians had also been able to repel the NPFL from Monrovia in 1990 and restore the Kabbah government to power in Freetown in 1998. This suggests the indispensability of Nigeria's military and financial muscle to largely subregional peacekeeping efforts.

The conditions in post–Cold War West Africa, with two Nigerian-led interventions, a declining French military role, and increasing Franco-Nigerian diplomatic cooperation, would seem particularly propitious for Nigeria to pursue its historic hegemonic ambitions in the subregion. But Nigeria faces both opportunities and obstacles. The country's enormous political and socioeconomic problems and the aversion of Nigerian public opinion to such costly interventions in the future will prove to be major constraints for the elected government of Olusegun Obasanjo. The Nigerian military is also in a state of decay after sixteen years of corrupt neglect and politicization, which has eroded its professionalism. Plans announced in 1999 by Nigerian defense minister General Theophilus Danjuma to reduce the military from about 94,500 to 50,000 had to be shelved due to concerns about the socioeconomic impact of demobilizing 44,500 soldiers. The Nigerian army is also not short of trouble spots to police: nearly one-third of the army is being used for international missions in Sierra Leone and on the border with Cameroon as well as in the Niger Delta and various parts of the country where religious and ethnic-based conflicts have erupted.[3] Nigerian soldiers have also been involved in massacres of civilians in Odi and Gbeji under Obasanjo's rule, during military reprisals for the killing of soldiers by local youths.

Another key prerequisite to Nigeria fulfilling its leadership ambitions in West Africa is for its leaders to learn to treat its neighbors with respect and to consult more closely with them. An arrogant unilateralism was evident in Nigerian diplomacy particularly during the time of Tom Ikimi, Foreign Minister from 1995 to 1998. Ikimi's brusque style was subsequently dubbed "area boy diplomacy" by his Nigerian critics.[4] As Yéro Boly, Burkina Faso's interior minister, put it: "Nigeria cannot do what it wants and then go to ECOWAS for approval."[5] Despite these criticisms, most ECOWAS countries no longer question the need for Nigerian leadership, but rather its penchant for a unilateral diplomatic style that offends the sensibilities of smaller, poorer, and weaker states. Nigeria must learn to speak softly even when it carries a big stick. Sule Lamido, Nigeria's foreign minister, recognized these fears in noting: "It is important that while you are playing the role of Big Brother, you have to recognize that the countries you are dealing with are sovereign nations. You have to know this and recognize that psychological feeling of independence."[6]

There still remains much unease in West Africa about Nigeria's domination of the ECOMOG military High Commands in Liberia and Sierra Leone.[7] As Liberian defense minister Daniel Chea noted: "We all want to learn to respect Nigeria. The problem with Nigeria is that they are roasting too many nuts in the fire. They have a hand in every conspiracy from Liberia to Sierra Leone."[8] Most subregional diplomats and military officers I interviewed during research trips to West Africa between 1999 and 2001 consistently made the point that, regardless of whether one country is disproportionately represented in an ECOMOG peacekeeping force, there has to be equality in the distribution of command posts in order for the force to be politically acceptable to others. As Mamadou Sermé, director-general in Burkina Faso's foreign ministry, noted: "You cannot have a security mechanism without equal distribution. Everyone has to be represented."[9]

While it is indisputable that Nigeria has an interest in stabilizing its subregion in order to promote its economic and political goals in West Africa, its domestic political and economic problems will continue to take up much of its attention.[10] Nigeria's decisions not to contribute troops to the ECOMOG mission in Guinea-Bissau in 1998 and to reduce significantly Nigerian troops in Sierra Leone in 1999 are clear signs of a growing wariness of the costs and frustrations with subregional peacekeeping, even among the Nigerian leadership. Nigerian casualties in Liberia and Sierra Leone were estimated at nearly 1,000 and its treasury released billions of dollars to these two missions. It is unlikely that the civilian government in Nigeria will be able to sustain these casualties and costs without some loss of political support. It is therefore vital that the new ECOWAS security mechanism find a way of using Nigeria's military and financial muscle, while institutionalizing a mechanism that does not depend entirely on Nigeria to survive.

External Friends and Foes

The role of external actors was important in all three cases. France's military interventions in support of African despots between 1960 to the early 1990s had already made many West Africans suspicious of the intentions of external actors. In Liberia, U.S. support for Doe during the Cold War fueled these suspicions further and also helped fuel the civil conflict in the 1990s. In Guinea-Bissau, France and Portugal resorted to "gunboat diplomacy" in backing different factions during the civil war.

But external actors have also sometimes played a positive role in peacemaking efforts in West Africa. The U.S. provision of logistical assistance to ECOMOG in Liberia before disarmament and its contributions to elections helped end the war temporarily in 1997. The EU and UN agencies also provided vital financial, logistical, and humanitarian support that assisted peacemaking efforts in Liberia. In Sierra Leone, Britain led international efforts to mobilize donor support and used its permanent seat on the UN Security Council to increase the size of the UN peacekeeping force and to impose sanctions against Charles Taylor. In Guinea-Bissau, France provided financial and logistical support to ECOMOG's peacekeepers, and both France and Portugal contributed to peacebuilding activities following the cessation of hostilities.

But the support of the West for peacebuilding activities in Africa has been derisory compared to similar efforts in the Balkans and East Timor. Even in countries like Liberia and Guinea-Bissau, where donors understandably have doubts about political stability and democratic rule, they must still find creative ways of channeling resources to affected communities through the UN and international and local nongovernmental organizations (NGOs) to disarm fighters, rebuild state institutions, restore judiciaries and police forces, and consolidate democracy. Such a conflict prevention strategy is crucial to ensuring that wars do not erupt again in these countries and that long-suffering populations are not punished for the excesses of their unaccountable leaders.

Civil Societies as Peacebuilders

Civil society actors in Liberia, Sierra Leone, and Guinea-Bissau contributed to the management of civil conflicts. In Liberia, the Inter-Faith Mediation Committee (IFMC) crafted the ECOWAS peace plan of 1990, while ECOMOG supported an interim government in Monrovia between 1990 and 1994 with active civil society participation. In Sierra Leone, a cross section of women's organizations pressured the military government to hold democratic elections in February 1996, while the Inter-Religious Council of Sierra Leone played a crucial role during the negotiation of the Lomé peace agreement of 1999. In Guinea-Bissau, the bishop of Bissau played an important role in mediating between both sides during the war, while civil society groups have played an important role in postelectoral peacebuilding activities.

But despite the often courageous role of civil society, this role had its limits during civil wars in which armed factions controlled large parts of the country. In the end, ECOWAS, frustrated by military stalemate and the financial burden of protracted peacekeeping, pursued a policy of appeasing warlords and rebels in all three cases, often in the face of vociferous opposition from civil society groups. In Liberia, the warlords were brought into an interim government in 1995 and their allies were given government posts; in Sierra Leone, Foday Sankoh was given the vice presidency in 1999 and the RUF was handed cabinet posts; in Guinea-Bissau, a deal was brokered in 1998 that established an interim government between representatives of Mane and Vieira. These deals proved to be unstable: Mane launched a coup against Vieira; Sankoh attacked UN peacekeepers; and Taylor used his war chest to win elections before continuing his destabilization policies in the subregion. This suggests that neither an exaggerated faith in the ability of civil society to manage uncivil conflicts nor the blatant appeasement of warlords can bring stability to West Africa. However, ECOWAS leaders will have to work closely with civil society actors in developing their security mechanism, since these actors are often closest to conflicts and can contribute to preventive efforts.

ECOWAS and the UN:
From Burden Shedding to Burden Sharing

In discussing the lessons of ECOWAS/UN cooperation in the three cases of Liberia, Sierra Leone, and Guinea-Bissau, it is important to emphasize that the UN Security Council has primary responsibility for international peace and security and has simply shifted its responsibilities to ECOWAS due to the reluctance of the council to sanction UN missions in Africa.[11] The three ECOMOG interventions underlined the importance of an active UN role in subregional peacekeeping efforts. As in Liberia and Sierra Leone, the UN eventually became involved in Guinea-Bissau, though it played different roles in all three cases. In Liberia, the UN played a very limited monitoring role to ECOMOG. It helped organize and monitor Liberia's 1997 election and established a small peacebuilding office in Monrovia following this election. In Sierra Leone, the UN played a similar military monitoring role in support of ECOMOG, as it had done in Liberia, until it took over ECOMOG's peacekeeping duties and subsumed some of its troops under UN command in 2000. In Guinea-Bissau, the UN played no military role, but was involved in development work through UN agencies like the UNDP as well as in helping to organize and monitor elections in Guinea-Bissau in 1999 and 2000. The UN currently has a small peacebuilding office in Bissau.

The creation of UN peacebuilding offices in Liberia and Guinea-Bissau represents a potentially significant innovation in the UN's conflict management strategy. The UN peacebuilding office in Liberia, established in 1997, was the first-ever such office established by the UN. If the current progress continues in Sierra Leone, the UN will almost certainly have to consider the establishment of a peacebuilding office in that country. These offices have been mandated to perform such tasks as providing electoral assistance, promoting human rights and the rule of law by working through both governments and civil society actors, mobilizing donor support for disarmament, demobilizing and reintegrating ex-combatants into local communities, supporting the rebuilding of administrative capacity, and rehabilitating local infrastructure.

Many of these goals have often not been met in fragile situations in which parties fail to honor their commitments and donors fail to deliver on their pledges. The UN office in Liberia was regarded as too close to Charles Taylor's government. It narrowly interpreted its mandate as mobilizing donor support for peacebuilding and declined working closely with civil society groups and reporting on human rights abuses. But the UN peacebuilding office in Guinea-Bissau (UNOGBIS) interpreted its mandate more flexibly and was able to monitor human rights violations, support the training of judges and legislators, and work with civil society groups to pressure the government to observe the rule of law.[12] It is vital that the UN collaborate with ECOWAS in its future peacebuilding tasks.

Following the recommendations of the UN's Inter-Agency Task Force on West Africa of May 2001, the decisions to establish a UN office in West Africa and to appoint a Special Representative of the UN Secretary-General to head this office in Dakar both represent positive steps for ECOWAS/UN cooperation. The UN has been asked to help strengthen ECOWAS's peacekeeping and electoral capacities and to work with civil society groups in West Africa. The UN office in West Africa is to perform the following specific tasks: assist the UN and its subregional offices to coordinate strategies in West Africa; monitor and report on political, humanitarian, and human rights developments; harmonize UN activities with those of ECOWAS; monitor ECOWAS's decisions and activities; and support national and subregional peacebuilding efforts.[13] While these are all noble objectives, the curious decision to locate this office in Dakar rather than Abuja, site of the ECOWAS secretariat, will lessen its effectiveness in fulfilling its mandate, particularly in light of the complications of communication and travel within West Africa.

Spoilers and Sanctions

Finally, the three cases of Liberia, Sierra Leone, and Guinea-Bissau underline the importance of developing effective strategies and sanctions to deal with subregional "spoilers" like Taylor, Sankoh, Mane, and Vieira.[14] In Guinea-Bissau, General Mane resorted to military means to achieve his political objectives in 1999, resulting in the withdrawal of ECOMOG peacekeepers. In Liberia and Sierra Leone, warring factions killed and kidnapped ECOMOG and UN peacekeepers and stole their weapons and vehicles. At Abuja in 1999, Mane refused to allow Senegal or Guinea to contribute troops to any ECOMOG force. His demands echoed those made by the RUF in Sierra Leone, which insisted that Nigerian, Ghanaian, and Guinean troops depart as a condition for signing the Abidjan accord of 1996. In Liberia, Charles Taylor consistently demanded the departure of Nigerian troops as a condition for implementing various peace agreements.

In all three cases, ECOMOG sent peacekeepers into countries in which there was no peace to keep and in which certain parties were determined to use violence to force the withdrawal of its peacekeepers. It is difficult to remain neutral under such circumstances, and the economic, political, and legal sanctions of the sort that were applied to the RUF in Sierra Leone and Charles Taylor in Liberia would seem appropriate in such cases. European, North American, and Asian commercial firms also played a negative role in supporting Liberian and Sierra Leonean warlords through the illicit export of natural resources and minerals in both countries. In devising sanctions against factions or subregional states, the actions of these firms will also need to be carefully scrutinized and, if necessary, punished.

BUILDING A NEW SECURITY
ARCHITECTURE IN WEST AFRICA

The Creation of an ECOWAS Security Mechanism

Fresh from the successful Liberian election five months earlier, ECOWAS leaders met in Lomé on 17 December 1997 and approved a Nigerian suggestion to establish a Mechanism for Conflict Prevention, Management, Resolution, Peacekeeping, and Security. Francophone Côte d'Ivoire and Senegal, the host and head of the all-francophone security body ANAD, respectively, were said to have only reluctantly supported the Nigerian proposal.[15] The revised ECOWAS treaty of 1993 had envisaged such a security mechanism.[16]

ECOWAS foreign ministers met in Abidjan in January 1998 to endorse the plan to create a security mechanism based on ECOMOG's experiences in Liberia and Sierra Leone. At the meeting, Senegal, Togo, and Burkina Faso, all francophone states, insisted on a more restricted ECOMOG force with specially trained units remaining with their national contingents, rather than joining a permanent, centralized force.[17]

ECOWAS ministers of foreign affairs, defense, internal affairs, and security held their first meeting in Yamoussoukro on 11 and 12 March 1998. The meeting set out guidelines for experts from member states and the executive secretariat to prepare a draft report on ECOWAS's security mechanism. But Yamoussoukro revealed the continuing tensions within ECOWAS, and continued francophone apprehensions about Nigeria's domineering diplomatic style. This meeting was marked by a clash between Nigerian foreign minister Tom Ikimi and his Senegalese counterpart, Moustapha Niasse. In a barely veiled criticism of France, which a fortnight before had sponsored an all-francophone military training exercise in Senegal, Ikimi criticized "foreign countries working to weaken our inter-African organizations by dividing us along anglophone-francophone lines."[18] Niasse's riposte was swift and equally undiplomatic: "No one can prevent Senegal or any other state from organizing such military maneuvers as it wishes . . . nor can anyone prevent states from training their police, gendarmerie and army or freely choosing their partners."[19] Côte d'Ivoire expressed support for the Senegalese position. These exchanges suggest that the true test of the success of the ECOWAS security mechanism will not be the signing of diplomatic protocols, but the management and overcoming of lingering subregional suspicions.

In May 1998 ECOWAS military chiefs of staff weighed in with their ideas on the creation of a security mechanism. A meeting of experts was held in Banjul from 13 to 22 July 1998 to prepare a draft report for the consideration of ECOWAS ministers. ECOWAS ministers of defense, internal affairs, and security met in Banjul on 23 and 24 July 1998 to review the proposed mechanism for conflict resolution. The ministers started their meeting by acknowledging three main problems in deploying ECOMOG in both Liberia and Sierra Leone: the mode of deployment, the composition of the force, and the command and control of the operations, especially the lack of involvement of ECOWAS members and the secretariat in managing both missions.[20]

One of the main issues of discussion in Banjul was whether prior UN Security Council authorization was needed before launching future ECOMOG interventions. ECOWAS leaders determined in the end that based on the extreme reluctance of Western members of the Security Council to sanction a UN peacekeeping mission in Liberia and Sierra Leone, it would be better to retain autonomy over the decision to intervene and not to let the UN Security Council, itself unwilling to intervene, prevent ECOWAS from taking urgent action to maintain subregional stability.[21] After much discussion and refinement of these ideas, ECOWAS heads of state met in Lomé in December 1999 and signed the protocol to establish a Mechanism for Conflict Prevention, Management, Resolution, Peacekeeping, and Security.[22] It is worth assessing this important document in some detail, since it has attempted to draw lessons from ECOMOG's experience in Liberia and Sierra Leone and, to a lesser extent, Guinea-Bissau.

The ECOWAS Mechanism: Institutions and Actors

There are five major flaws of the three ECOMOG interventions that are particularly relevant to the establishment of a security mechanism. First, ECOMOG peacekeepers were deployed to Liberia, Sierra Leone, and Guinea-Bissau before detailed logistical and financial arrangements were made. The peacekeepers were ill equipped and ill prepared, and not all members were informed before full-scale deployment occurred. Second, the ECOMOG forces in Liberia and Sierra Leone were dominated by Nigeria, resulting in a lack of subregional unity and depriving the force of important legitimacy in fulfilling its tasks. Third, the ECOMOG force in Guinea-Bissau was deployed without Nigeria, denying the peacekeepers the logistical and financial muscle of the subregion's dominant force. Fourth, the ECOMOG missions in Liberia and Sierra Leone were under the operational control of ECOMOG commanders in the field, rather than the ECOWAS secretariat. Since these were, with the brief exception of Ghana's General Arnold Quainoo in 1990, all Nigerian, as were the bulk of the troops, Nigeria's military leaders were kept closely informed of operations on the ground. This information, however, did not always filter speedily, if at all, to other ECOWAS members and the secretariat. Finally, the ECO-MOG mission in Guinea-Bissau, under a Togolese commander, reported directly to Togolese leader Gnassingbé Eyadéma, the ECOWAS chairman.

The ECOWAS security protocol of 1999 set out to correct these flaws. The protocol called for the establishment of the following organs: a Mediation and Security Council, a Defense and Security Commission, and a Council of Elders. The Mediation and Security Council has since met to discuss the crises in Sierra Leone, the border area between Liberia and Guinea, and Côte d' Ivoire. The ECOWAS protocol of 1999 also called for improved cooperation in early warning, conflict prevention, peacekeeping operations, and cross-border crime and proliferation in the trafficking of small arms and narcotics.[23] Many of these suggestions were based on the Liberia, Sierra Leone, and Guinea-Bissau experiences, with the concern about cross-border crimes and arms trafficking being a direct result of the deleterious effect of civil wars on neighboring states like Côte d' Ivoire, Guinea, Sierra Leone, Liberia, and Senegal.

The Mediation and Security Council aims to accelerate decisionmaking in crisis situations by making decisions on deploying military and political missions and by informing the UN and the OAU of such decisions on behalf of the ECOWAS Authority of Heads of State. Clearly inspired by the ECOWAS Committee of Nine on the Liberian crisis, the body was to have nine members elected to a two-year term. ECOWAS leaders have since increased the membership of the committee to ten. A Committee of

Ambassadors of the ten countries meets in Abuja once a month, their foreign, defense, and internal affairs ministers meet quarterly, and their heads of state are mandated to meet at least twice a year. Decisions are to be made by a two-thirds majority of six members.[24]

These decisions represent a clear effort to improve on decisionmaking and to build wider subregional support for ECOMOG peacekeepers following the experiences of the five-member Standing Mediation Committee that sent ECOMOG into Liberia, of the Committee of Seven on Sierra Leone, and of the Committee of Nine on Guinea-Bissau. ECOWAS leaders hope that with a more representative and diverse group of members in decision-making, such subregional divisions as occurred in Liberia and Sierra Leone, and to a lesser extent in Guinea-Bissau, can be avoided for future peacekeeping missions. But the ECOWAS mechanism does not state what would occur if the council failed to secure two-thirds support for future peacekeeping missions, a serious omission that will need to be corrected if future subregional divisions that hampered the Liberia and Sierra Leone interventions are to be avoided.

The Defense and Security Commission is to advise the Mediation and Security Council on mandates, terms of reference, and the appointment of force commanders for future military missions. The commission, made up of army chiefs of staff, police chiefs, experts from foreign ministries, and heads of immigration, customs, narcotics, and border guards, is also to advise the Mediation and Security Council on administration and logistics support for military operations.[25]

The Council of Elders consists of eminent personalities from Africa and outside the continent, including women and traditional, religious, and political leaders appointed to mediate conflicts. Seventeen of its thirty-two members met for the first time in Niamey, Niger, from 2 to 4 July 2001. At the meeting, former Nigerian head of state General Yakubu Gowon was elected as the council's chairman, with Niger's Ide Oumarou and Burkina Faso's Alimata Salambere elected as vice chairmen. ECOWAS chairman Lansana Kouyaté and his deputy, General Cheick Diarra, briefed the Council of Elders on their mandate and on the progress of the ECOWAS security mechanism. Council members urged the ECOWAS secretariat to expand the council's membership to ensure that all members of the subregional body were represented, and appealed to members to implement the protocol related to the community levy for financing the work of the mechanism (see below).[26]

As earlier noted, though traditional leaders and civic groups can and do contribute immensely to the resolution of conflicts at the local level, the three ECOMOG interventions examined in this study offer cautionary tales as to the efficacy of such efforts on a nationwide basis during a civil war in which warlords control most of the country. Despite various efforts to involve traditional rulers and civic groups in mediation efforts in all three countries, it was clear that the key to the resolution of the war often lay with warlords and rebel groups, who were usually unwilling to lay down their arms. Thus, while the involvement of civil society actors in mediation efforts may serve a useful purpose, its efficacy as a method of resolving national conflicts should not be overestimated.

ECOWAS's security mechanism further proposes that the powers of the ECOWAS executive secretary be broadened, giving him (there has yet to be a female executive secretary!) the authority to initiate prevention and management of conflicts including fact-finding, mediation, facilitation, negotiation, and reconciliation of parties. The ECOWAS executive secretary also appoints members of the Council of Elders and recommends the appointment of special representatives and force commanders, for approval by the Mediation and Security Council. A deputy executive secretary for political affairs, defense, and security, General Cheick Diarra of Mali, has been appointed to manage field operations in support of cease-fires and/or peace agreements.[27] This position will be important in coordinating activities between the ECOWAS secretariat and field missions and, it is hoped, will help avoid the experiences of ECOMOG's three interventions, in which force commanders often reported directly to their own leaders rather than to the ECOWAS secretariat. The deputy executive secretary will also oversee the Departments of Political Affairs, Humanitarian Affairs, and Defense and Security, as well as the Observation and Monitoring Center.

The three ECOMOG experiences, however, suggest that it might in the future be worth considering making the deputy executive secretary a full executive secretary with his/her own separate organization, which can be physically close to but bureaucratically separate from ECOWAS. This would allow ECOWAS to concentrate on its raison d'être of regional integration while recognizing the crucial link between security and economic integration. Under the ECOWAS protocol, the executive secretary could end up being overburdened with security tasks that prevent total concentration on economic integration issues. The Liberia experience in particular, but also those in Sierra Leone and Guinea-Bissau, demonstrated how much ECOWAS's attention can be diverted from its economic goals to focus on security issues.

One error of the three ECOMOG interventions that the 1999 protocol attempts to rectify is the appointment of a special representative of the ECOWAS executive secretary to peacekeeping operations. This is an attempt to ensure a high-level diplomatic presence on the ground and better coordination and information sharing between the ECOWAS secretariat and peacekeeping missions in the field. The special representative would lead peacemaking efforts and coordinate humanitarian and peacebuilding operations of ECOWAS, international organizations, and NGOs.[28] This idea seems particularly sensible since in Liberia, Sierra Leone, and Guinea-Bissau, delicate diplomatic tasks were often left in the hands of military commanders who were ill equipped and untrained to handle such matters. These problems also took away from the commanders' time to focus on purely military and security issues.

ECOWAS's Evolving Early Warning System

As envisaged in the ECOWAS security protocol of 1999, an Observation and Monitoring Center is currently being established within the ECOWAS secretariat. The EU is funding this project and the director of the center, program manager, and the heads of ECOWAS's four zonal bureaus have now been recruited. But the EU insisted that recruitment be done according to its own bureaucratic rules, and not those of ECOWAS, again revealing how donors can sometimes act in a heavy-handed manner even as they claim to support "ownership" of subregional mechanisms by local actors.

ECOWAS's three departments—Political Affairs, Humanitarian Affairs, and Defense and Security—are mandated to formulate and implement all military, peacekeeping, and humanitarian operations, as well as organize, manage, and provide support for political activities related to conflict prevention and formulate and implement policies on cross-border crime, the circulation of light arms, and drug control.

ECOWAS's protocol also calls for a peace and security observation mechanism as well as an early warning system, with observation centers in four reporting zones based in Banjul (to cover Cape Verde, Gambia, Guinea-Bissau, and Senegal), Cotonou (to cover Benin, Nigeria, and Togo), Monrovia (to cover Ghana, Guinea, Liberia, and Sierra Leone), and Ouagadougou (to cover Burkina Faso, Côte d'Ivoire, Mali, and Niger). From these four zonal headquarters, officials are expected to assess political (human rights, democracy), economic (food shortages), social (unemployment), security (arms flows, civil-military relations), and environmental (drought, flooding) indicators on a daily basis.[29] By July 2001, agreements had been signed with the governments of Benin, Burkina Faso, and Gambia to host these bureaus, but not yet with the government of Liberia.

One encouraging development of ECOWAS's early warning system is the involvement of civil society actors in its establishment. The African Strategic and Peace Research Group (AFSTRAG), a small Nigerian-based research institute, is leading a project on developing ECOWAS's early warning system with a forum of twenty-six mostly West African NGOs under a West African Network for Peacebuilding (WANEP), which has already met in Abuja on 24 to 27 March 2001 to discuss the potential contributions of civil society groups to ECOWAS's early warning system by sending reports to the ECOWAS secretariat. AFSTRAG is planning to coordinate activities and civil society groups participating in the four observation zones of ECOWAS's early warning system. It plans to use satellite networks for this work, after establishing two zonal coordinating offices in Freetown and Dakar.[30]

While the observation system and plans surrounding it are all laudable goals, these tasks will need to be reduced and made more focused to reflect better the political realities in West Africa. Monitoring human rights, press freedom, and civil-military relations would have been politically impossible for the ECOWAS secretariat, for example, under a repressive regime like that of Nigeria's General Sani Abacha between 1993 and 1998. In a subregion in which seven of the current fifteen leaders initially came to power through a military coup, such political tasks seem simply beyond the reach of international civil servants serving at the behest of governments. It would appear more sensible for the observation mechanisms to focus on less politically sensitive issues like economic, social, and environmental indicators, while perhaps leaving some of the more sensitive political analysis to civil society groups to send to the ECOWAS secretariat.

Entente Cordiale? ECOWAS and ANAD

One issue on which a decision has been made but that is yet to be implemented is the role of ANAD, the all-francophone West African security organization, within the ECOWAS security mechanism. In 1996, ANAD leaders revived a plan to establish a *force de paix* to serve as a rapid intervention force (see Chapter 2). The force, which was never established, was to have been based on standby troops trained in individual countries and funded by ANAD members as well as external subventions. The proposal was discussed at a meeting in Nouakchott, Mauritania, on 18 and 19 April 1996. ANAD chiefs of staff held an additional meeting in Niamey, Niger, a week later to discuss the idea of the force, which was to be used for conflict prevention and management, humanitarian aid operations, and for combating illicit arms trafficking and crime. The force could be deployed under the aegis of the OAU and the UN, but significantly not ECOWAS.[31]

Since the ANAD proposal clearly reflected the same ideas behind the ECOWAS security mechanism, there is a feeling among many nonfrancophone West Africans that ANAD remains another potential tool for France to maintain a "sphere of influence" in West Africa and prevent unity within a Nigerian-led ECOWAS. Senior ANAD staff, however, denied this, asserting that France had not contributed a single franc to ANAD and that the organization was barely known within French military and political circles.[32]

In 1999, ANAD had a forty-five-person secretariat and a budget of about 350 million CFA francs. But its members were meeting irregularly, its staff was irregularly paid, and member states did not keep their accounts current. Several ANAD states conducted two military exercises under French funding: *Exercise le Nangbeto* in Togo in March 1997 and *Exercise Guidimakha* in Senegal in February 1998. But the *force de paix* remained an unachieved dream. There were also some cracks within ANAD, as Togo was said to have been disappointed not to have secured more support from ANAD in its historical tensions with neighboring Ghana, and Lomé was said to have become lukewarm toward the organization as a result.[33] Togo was one of the strongest supporters of the decision to integrate ANAD into the ECOWAS security mechanism.

At the suggestion of former Senegalese president Abdou Diouf, it was decided that ANAD be integrated into the ECOWAS security mechanism. The option of ANAD becoming a specialized ECOWAS agency to control cross-border crime was rejected. In April 2000, General Ishola Williams, the acting director of AFSTRAG, met with staff of the ANAD secretariat to discuss plans of how to integrate the organization into the ECOWAS security mechanism.[34] While ANAD staff were apparently keen to be integrated into ECOWAS, there was some resistance to this within ECOWAS itself amid alleged concerns that the arrival of senior ANAD staff (the executive secretary, the director of studies, and the legal adviser) could lead to the demotion of some ECOWAS staff.[35] As General Amadou Touré, Mali's former head of state, noted: "ANAD . . . seems to be searching for a role for itself. Its survival would seem to depend on either expanding or adapting to present times."[36]

The Institutionalization of ECOMOG

Based largely on the experience of ECOMOG in Liberia, Sierra Leone, and Guinea-Bissau, the ECOWAS protocol of 1999 called for the establishment of a standby force of brigade size consisting of specially trained and equipped units of national armies ready to be deployed at short notice. All fifteen ECOWAS states have pledged one battalion each to the proposed new force. It now remains to be seen whether this pledge can be translated into reality.

The force is to be called ECOMOG, and its main tasks will involve observation and monitoring, peacekeeping, humanitarian intervention, enforcement of sanctions and embargoes, preventive deployment, peacebuilding operations, disarmament and demobilization, and policing activities, including anti-smuggling and anti-criminal activities.[37] These were among the tasks that ECOMOG attempted to perform in Liberia, Sierra Leone, and Guinea-Bissau. The new subregional force is to embark on periodic training exercises to enhance the cohesion of its troops and compatibility of equipment. ECOMOG's soldiers will also undertake training exchange programs in West African military training institutions, as well as external training involving the UN and the OAU. Four thousand troops from Benin, Burkina Faso, Chad, Côte d'Ivoire, Niger, Togo, and Ghana have already taken part in war games in the Burkinabè town of Kompienga and in northern Togo in May 1998, with Nigeria involved in the military planning.[38] Some analysts have proposed that ECOWAS establish a subregional peacekeeping training center to enhance cooperation.[39]

It is important to examine three important issues related to the new ECOMOG force: first, the criteria for mandating military interventions; second, the importance of distinguishing between keeping and enforcing peace; and third, the danger of the force becoming a defense pact for the protection of local autocrats. The proposed ECOMOG force is to be used in four cases: first, aggression or conflict within a member state; second, a conflict between two or more member states; third, internal conflicts that threaten to trigger a humanitarian disaster, pose a serious threat to subregional peace and security, result in serious and massive violation of human rights, and/or follow the overthrow or attempted overthrow of a democratically elected government; and fourth, any other situation that the council deems appropriate.[40]

While the first two scenarios for justifying military interventions were included in the ECOWAS Protocol on Mutual Assistance and Defense of 1981 (see Chapter 2), the third scenario is a conscious attempt to provide legal cover for future interventions, based on ECOMOG's three interventions. In Liberia and Guinea-Bissau, ECOMOG had intervened by arguing that the situation had threatened a humanitarian disaster and posed a threat to subregional peace and security. In Sierra Leone, ECOMOG had restored a democratically elected government to power after its overthrow by soldiers. The interventions in Liberia and Sierra Leone were controversial and questioned on legal grounds, even by some ECOWAS members.

It must also be recognized that decisions to intervene in countries will be political in subregional conflicts where member states often have parochial national interests. Unlike the collective security system of the UN, whose universal membership often allows it to send peacekeepers from countries that have no direct interest in the conflicts to be settled, ECOWAS does not have this luxury. ECOWAS will have to find a way of excluding countries whose presence is strongly opposed by the parties to the dispute and might sometimes have to borrow troops from outside its own subregion, as it did in Liberia with OAU and UN peacekeepers, and as it has done with Sierra Leone where ECOMOG was subsumed under a UN peacekeeping mission while retaining a subregional core of peacekeepers. Such innovative divisions of labor will have to be devised for future interventions. ECOMOG must learn from the Liberia and Sierra Leone experiences the importance of diversifying troop-contributing contingents to include both ECOWAS and non-ECOWAS members to avoid charges of Nigerian or anglophone domination.

Political discretion will still have to be exercised in decisions to intervene in conflicts, even when ECOWAS's criteria for intervention are met. It is clear that if a military regime took power in Nigeria, for example, with popular support from a democratically elected but politically discredited civilian regime (as occurred in 1983), an ECOMOG intervention force would be practically impossible to deploy. Likewise, if a military coup were to succeed in a francophone state with popular domestic support or tacit French and francophone support, a Nigerian-led ECOMOG intervention would be fraught with political and military risks that could lead to the force being regarded as foreign invaders.

Interventions will always have to be determined on a case-by-case basis. The requirement of a two-thirds majority is an important check that allows for a blocking minority. The experts meeting in Banjul in 1998 to discuss the ECOWAS mechanism did not suggest alternatives to break this possible deadlock for fear of creating negative loopholes that could be exploited by member states.[41] But this still leaves ECOWAS with a dilemma: if the needs of an intervention are so pressing on humanitarian grounds of saving lives and rescuing citizens trapped in fighting, but at least five subregional states on the Mediation and Security Council veto the action because they have an interest in the victory of a domestic party they are supporting, ECOMOG can be blocked by parochial, partisan interests from undertaking action that could benefit the interests of the wider community.

The ECOMOG intervention in Liberia parallels such a scenario with Burkina Faso and Côte d'Ivoire opposing ECOMOG due largely to their own interest in seeing an NPFL victory. Under the ECOWAS protocol of 1999, ECOMOG would probably not have found the six votes necessary to intervene in Liberia. With eight out of fifteen members in ECOWAS, the Francophonie possesses the most united, though not monolithic, political bloc in a relationship cemented through cooperation in the institutions of the franc zone often under French leadership. It does not seem difficult to imagine five francophone states on the Mediation and Security Council saying *"non"* to a Nigerian-led intervention that they perceive to be against their own interests.

It is also important to establish conceptual clarity in determining the mandate of the proposed ECOMOG force. The ECOWAS protocol talks of peacemaking, peacekeeping, and peacebuilding but does not explicitly address the issue of peace enforcement, which occurred in both Liberia and Sierra Leone, suggesting a certain conceptual confusion. It seems that peace enforcement has simply been subsumed into peacekeeping without differentiating clearly traditional peacekeeping, which involves defensive lightly armed troops monitoring an agreed peace and defending themselves only when attacked, from peace enforcement, which involves offensive heavily armed troops imposing peace against recalcitrant parties.[42] This distinction will need to be more clearly defined for future ECOMOG missions, since such decisions will be crucial in determining the needs and mandate of forces to be dispatched into conflict zones.

Finally, the fourth criterion for intervention, which leaves the situation under which military interventions can occur to the discretion of the Mediation and Security Council, introduces the possibility, expressed particularly by many African civil society actors, of the abuse of the mechanism.[43] The fear is that autocratic subregional leaders who have lost the support of their citizens could convince their fellow leaders to sanction interventions to protect their regimes. Such an allegation was made against ECOMOG, and particularly Nigeria, in relation to Liberian leader Samuel Doe when its peacekeepers entered Liberia in 1990. ECOWAS members are still allowed, under the 1999 protocol, to enter into bilateral arrangements that could lead to allies sending troops to help each other.

Sékou Touré had sent Guinean troops into Siaka Stevens's Sierra Leone in 1973 and into William Tolbert's Liberia in 1979 to help restore internal stability following civil disturbances. More recently, Senegal and Guinea sent troops to assist Vieira's regime in Guinea-Bissau in 1998, while Nigerian, Guinean, and Ghanaian troops were sent to Freetown to assist successive regimes in Sierra Leone between 1991 and 2000. Most of these interventions were justified on the basis of prior bilateral defense accords. Despite genuine fears about the abuse of an ECOWAS security mechanism to support illegitimate regimes, the fact that six out of ten ECOWAS states have to approve any military interventions could help curb abuses, provided that these regimes are democratically elected and enjoy domestic and international legitimacy.

Of Men, Money, and Military Matériel

Many of the institutions proposed by the 1999 protocol represent an important step to improving ECOWAS's ability to manage conflicts, but they will also be expensive to staff. Based on the experience of member states in failing to pay their dues to maintain existing ECOWAS institutions, there are genuine grounds for skepticism as to whether these institutions will receive consistent funding. More detailed financial arrangements need to be made to ensure continued funding both from within and outside the subregion.

All three ECOMOG interventions clearly exposed the logistical weaknesses of West Africa's armies. It is no secret, however, as to what is required to improve the effectiveness of such forces: serviceable weapons, good communications equipment, tactical mobility and logistical support, knowledge of basic doctrine, individual skills training, and realistic exercises involving whole units. Convoy escort operations through hostile territory during military interventions are best undertaken with the support of scout and attack helicopters. West African peacekeepers do not have such assets in significant quantities. Attacks against resisting forces in urban areas are difficult without access to gunships, precise-fire weaponry such as attack helicopters, and night-vision equipment.

For operations to establish order in even relatively small countries, over 10,000 troops are likely to be needed. ECOMOG had roughly this number at the height of its peacekeeping missions in Liberia and Sierra Leone, while it had only 712 peacekeepers in Guinea-Bissau. Ten thousand soldiers would usually be enough to maintain security for several hundred thousand people located over tens or hundreds of square kilometers, and for policing and monitoring borders. In 1996, ECOMOG's military planners calculated that they would need at least 18,000 troops to fulfill their peacekeeping and disarmament tasks satisfactorily in Liberia. In the end, they had to settle for 10,500. External support in the form of weaponry, transportation, and communication equipment will still need to be provided by external actors for ECOMOG's peacekeepers for the foreseeable future, and there is a continuing need for logistical support in the form of trucks, transport helicopters, water purification equipment, tents, uniforms, and boots. Associated costs for such equipment could reach U.S.$1 billion for a total force of 30,000 to 50,000, but this would be the only way of ensuring that the force could operate autonomously once it was deployed.[44]

Several subregional military analysts have suggested that ECOWAS establish strategic reserves of equipment that could be used for peacekeeping missions, much like the UN's central depot in Italy.[45] But this issue was discussed in Banjul in 1998 by the experts who drafted the ECOWAS security mechanism and they decided that it would be too risky to establish military reserves that could be stolen and used if conflict broke out in the country where they were stored.[46] General Maxwell Khobe, the late Nigerian ECOMOG task force commander in Sierra Leone, offered some sensible ideas for overcoming ECOWAS's logistical deficiencies. Khobe suggested among other things: the standardization of equipment, arms, ammunition, training standards, and doctrine of ECOMOG's standby forces; the establishment of an ECOMOG standing command staff to harmonize military policies; and the creation of an ECOMOG support command with ships and airlift capability.[47] As noted above, the implementation of these ideas will require both finance and political will.

The issue of financing is particularly important to the building of ECOMOG's proposed force. The ECOWAS protocol of 1999 foresees troop-contributing countries bearing financial costs for the first three months of military operations before the ECOWAS secretariat takes over the costs of the mission. The initial agreement for the ECOMOG mission in Liberia was for each contingent to fund its own troops for the first month of the mission, after which time all ECOWAS members would assume responsibility for ECOMOG. But Nigeria ended up footing about 90 percent of the costs and francophone countries opposed to ECOMOG were unwilling to contribute to a mission they did not support. Similarly in Sierra Leone, Nigeria shouldered much of the financial burden for the mission. In Guinea-Bissau, France underwrote the financial costs of the mission, providing stipends, transportation, and some communication equipment to the subregional peacekeepers. Under the ECOWAS protocol, funds for the mechanism are to be raised from the annual budget until a community levy comes into existence. Funding is also expected to be provided by the UN, international agencies, the OAU, and voluntary contributions and grants from bilateral and multilateral sources.[48]

This is an unsatisfactory system that does not correct a critical flaw in ECOMOG's peacekeeping experiences. All three ECOMOG missions clearly demonstrated the importance of securing financial support *before* embarking on a military intervention. The ECOMOG missions in Liberia and Sierra Leone cost the Nigerian treasury billions of dollars (though large portions of these funds were embezzled by corrupt military leaders in Nigeria). Such costs can prove a disincentive to future interventions in a subregion saddled with a crippling external debt. Tanzania and Uganda withdrew from ECOMOG in large part because their financial and logistical needs were not being met. Other ECOWAS states declined to contribute troops to ECOMOG due to the costs of maintaining peacekeepers in Liberia, Sierra Leone, and Guinea-Bissau.

The Nigerian-led OAU intervention in Chad between 1979 and 1981 was forced to withdraw largely because it lacked the funding and logistical support to sustain itself.[49] In 1997, only Nigeria, Benin, and Côte d'Ivoire had paid their ECOWAS dues in full, and since 1975 only these three countries and Togo have contributed regularly to the ECOWAS budget. By July 1992, the arrears to the ECOWAS budget was equivalent to three years of its operating budget, while unpaid arrears stood at U.S.$38.1 million in

December 1999.[50] The move of the ECOWAS secretariat from Lagos to Abuja in 1998 was delayed by seven years due to lack of funds, and its staff is irregularly paid, with the Nigerian government having had to loan ECOWAS money to pay its personnel in September 1998.[51] This hardly appears to be a promising basis for securing financial support for a future ECOMOG force. A sounder financial base must be built through the acceleration of the community levy in order for ECOWAS's security mechanism to be successful.

In concluding this section, we briefly assess efforts by three external actors, France, Britain, and the United States, to contribute to building ECOWAS's security capacity. France has invited nonfrancophone states to participate in RECAMP and established a peacekeeping training center in Abidjan. The changing French role coincides with increasing but limited U.S. and British security roles in West Africa.[52] Britain currently has a small military contingent in Sierra Leone that is training a new national army and has supported the larger but poorly equipped UN force. The British government has established an African Peacekeeping Training Support Program involving officer training projects in Ghana, South Africa, and Zimbabwe. The United States has provided military assistance to Benin, Ghana, Mali, and Senegal as part of its 1996 African Crisis Response Initiative to strengthen the military capabilities of African states for regional peacekeeping. But with a total annual contribution of only about U.S.$25 million to selected African states, the ACRI is unlikely to contribute substantially to ECOWAS's logistical deficiencies. The United States has also trained three Nigerian, one Ghanaian, and one Senegalese battalion for participation in the UN mission in Sierra Leone.

Critical voices in Africa have argued that external security initiatives have not been coordinated, that Africans have not been adequately consulted on these initiatives, and that emphasis on training is misplaced, since logistical and financial support are more essential for African peacekeepers. ECOWAS also must not be overdependent on external funding for its operations, since this could not only compromise its independence of action but could also lead to funding shortfalls as a result of the changing political interests of unpredictable external donors. As former ECOWAS executive secretary Lansana Kouyaté recognized: "If we depend 100 percent on donors, all the good ideas mentioned may never be realized."[53]

The ECOWAS security mechanism has so far received funding from the OAU and several donor governments. The OAU gave ECOWAS U.S.$300,000 for its deployment in Sierra Leone and Liberia. The European Union (2 million euros), the U.S. Agency for International Development (USAID) (U.S.$250,000), and the governments of the United Kingdom, Japan (U.S.$100,000), and Germany have made contributions in support of the ECOWAS mechanism. The governments of the Netherlands and Canada have also expressed an interest in funding the mechanism, and Canada has contributed U.S.$300,000 for the establishment of an ECOWAS Child Protection Unit.

Armed Humanitarianism

The ECOWAS security mechanism foresees humanitarian and logistical support being provided by ECOWAS.[54] Based on the three ECOMOG experiences, however, it is obvious that such resources are in short supply within the subregion. ECOMOG did play a role in revitalizing ports, electricity stations, and communication facilities in Liberia and Sierra Leone, and its engineers rebuilt some roads and bridges.[55] This experience should be built on for future missions. But in the humanitarian field, ECOWAS simply lacks the resources and experience provided by UN agencies and the NGO community, while in the area of logistics, such basic equipment as radios, tents, medical equipment, boots, and uniforms, as well as trucks and helicopters, had to be provided by the United States, France, and the European Union.

It would seem sensible for future ECOMOG missions to emulate the division of labor established in Liberia, where ECOMOG concentrated on disarmament and providing security for humanitarian convoys, while leaving the bulk of humanitarian tasks in the hands of the UN and NGOs. Although the ECOWAS protocol of 1999 foresees a role in peacebuilding for ECOMOG, a division of labor between ECOWAS and international actors would appear to be more realistic. ECOWAS could take the lead in elections, supported by the UN and other groups, while ECOMOG, or UN peacekeepers, could provide security after completing its disarmament tasks. But the reintegration of fighters and food-for-work projects are better left to the UN, the World Bank, and the EU, which have both the experience and the resources, though sometimes not the political will, to undertake these tasks.

TOWARD A PAX WEST AFRICANA

West Africa remains today among the world's poorest and most conflict-prone subregions. Four ECOWAS states, Guinea, Guinea-Bissau, Liberia, and Sierra Leone, all of them significantly involved in recent conflicts, are among the ten poorest countries in the world. But despite these difficulties, there are some rays of hope in West Africa's bleak security prospects. ECOWAS has survived for twenty-six years despite its members' political

and cultural divisions and economic disparities. Following three unprecedented military interventions in the 1990s, the organization has managed to
overcome these obstacles to establish one of the world's first subregional
security mechanisms. Mali and Niger have imaginatively used civil society
groups and government mediation to manage their long-running Tuareg
problems. ECOWAS's citizens travel visa-free and work throughout its fifteen countries. Highways have been built linking Lagos to Nouakchott and
Dakar to Ndjamena. A West African gas pipeline is being built to transport
gas throughout the subregion. A semblance of democratic rule appears to be
emerging in Benin, Cape Verde, Ghana, Nigeria, and Senegal after years of
autocratic rule. There are plans afoot to create a common currency, an
ECOWAS Court of Justice, and a 120-member subregional parliament.

ECOWAS has also won praise for taking steps to control the proliferation of light weapons and small arms within its subregion. An estimated 7
million such weapons are currently circulating in West Africa. On 31
October 1998, ECOWAS heads of state signed a three-year moratorium on
the importation, exportation, and manufacture of light weapons from
November 1998 until November 2001. The moratorium has since been
extended to 2004. Technical assistance to support implementation of the
moratorium is being provided through the UNDP and the UN regional disarmament center in Lomé.[56] Much work remains to be done to ensure the
effectiveness of efforts to halt the spread of these lethal weapons across
West Africa's porous borders.

There is a glimmer of hope in the birth of a new security mechanism in
West Africa. ECOWAS has finally started to fulfill the ambition of establishing what Kenyan political scientist Ali Mazrui described as a Pax
Africana in its own subregion by creating an indigenous system for managing its own conflicts.[57] Usually, theory and conceptualization precedes
practice in the establishment of security structures. In ECOWAS's case,
however, practice of three subregional interventions has preceded theory.
This gives ECOWAS a golden opportunity to draw from its experiences in
Liberia, Sierra Leone, and Guinea-Bissau in building its security mechanism. The lessons of these three cases must be properly applied if West
Africa, arguably the world's most troubled subregion, is to build peace and
achieve prosperity in a new millennium.

NOTES

1. This section draws heavily from Adekeye Adebajo, "Nigeria: Africa's New
Gendarme?" *Security Dialogue* 31, no. 2 (June 2000): 185–199.
2. Personal interview with General Cheick Diarra, ECOWAS deputy executive secretary, Abuja, 10 July 2001.

3. Personal interview with General Theophilus Danjuma, defense minister of Nigeria, Abuja, 2 March 2001.

4. This phrase was coined by Gabriel Olusanya, Nigeria's former ambassador to France. "Area boys" are thuggish local youths. See also Tunde Asaju and Dotun Oladipo, "Ikimi's Jungle Diplomacy," *Newswatch* (28 September 1998): 8–16.

5. Personal interview with Yéro Boly, interior minister of Burkina Faso, Ouagadougou, 22 July 1999.

6. Sule Lamido (interview), "I Will Surprise My Critics," *ThisDay,* 8 August 1999, p. 10.

7. Personal interviews with diplomatic and military officials on a research trip to Burkina Faso, Côte d'Ivoire, Guinea, Liberia, Nigeria, and Sierra Leone in July and August 1999.

8. Personal interview with Daniel Chea, defense minister of Liberia, Monrovia, 13 July 1999.

9. Personal interview with Mamadou Sermé, director-general, foreign ministry of Burkina Faso, Ouagadougou, 22 July 1999.

10. See Stephen Wright and Julius Emeka Okolo, "Nigeria: Aspirations of Regional Power," in Stephen Wright (ed.), *African Foreign Policies* (Boulder and Oxford: Westview Press, 1999), pp. 125–130.

11. For interesting African perspectives on this issue, see IPA/Center on International Cooperation, *Refashioning the Dialogue: Regional Perspectives on the Brahimi Report on UN Peace Operations,* Regional Meetings February–March 2001, pp. 6–11.

12. This view was confirmed by an internal UN assessment of these missions. See Report of the Joint Review Mission on the UN postconflict peacebuilding offices, UN Department of Political Affairs/UNDP, 20 July 2001, p. 12.

13. Report of the Inter-Agency Mission to West Africa, "Towards a Comprehensive Approach to Durable and Sustainable Solutions to Priority Needs and Challenges in West Africa," UN Security Council document, S/2001/434, 2 May 2001, p. 15.

14. See, for example, David Cortright and George A. Lopez (eds.), *The Sanctions Decade: Assessing UN Strategies in the 1990s* (Boulder and London: Lynne Rienner, 2000); and Stephen Stedman, "Spoiler Problems in Peace Processes," *International Security* 22, no. 2 (Fall 1997): 5–53.

15. Personal interview with General Ishola Williams, acting director of AFSTRAG, Lagos, 6 August 1999.

16. See Article 58 of the Revised ECOWAS Treaty of 1993.

17. Desmond Davies, "Peacekeeping African Style," *West Africa* no. 4190 (4–17 May 1998).

18. Quoted in Robert Mortimer, "From ECOMOG to ECOMOG II: Intervention in Sierra Leone," in John W. Harbeson and Donald Rothchild (eds.), *Africa in World Politics: The African State System in Flux,* 3rd ed. (Boulder and Oxford: Westview Press, 2000), p. 200.

19. Quoted in ibid.

20. ECOWAS Draft Mechanism for Conflict Prevention, Management, Resolution, Peacekeeping, and Security; Meeting of the Ministers of Defense, Internal Affaires, and Security, Banjul, 23–24 July 1998, pp. 2–3.

21. Personal discussions with Margaret Vogt, director of IPA's Africa Program at the time, who headed the team of experts in Banjul. New York, 8 August 2001.

22. See Protocol Relating to the Mechanism for Conflict Prevention, Management, Resolution, Peacekeeping, and Security; Lomé, 10 December 1999.

23. Ibid., p. 7.

24. Ibid., p. 10.

25. Ibid., pp. 14–15.

26. Inaugural Meeting of the ECOWAS Council of Elders, Final Communiqué, Niamey, 2–4 July 2001, pp. 2–4.

27. Protocol Relating to the Mechanism for Conflict Prevention, Management, Resolution, Peacekeeping, and Security, p. 13.

28. Ibid., p. 23.

29. Ibid., pp. 17–19.

30. Personal interview with General Ishola Williams.

31. Synpotic Report on the Proceedings of the Workshops of the Expert Committee at the Level of Chiefs of Staff of the Armed Forces of ANAD, Niamey, 24–26 April 1997, pp. 3–9.

32. Personal interviews with Admiral Alexandre Diam, ANAD secretary-general, and Colonel Ahmadou Touré, ANAD director of studies, Abidjan, 19 July 1999.

33. I thank Colonel Daprou Kambou, secretary-general, defense ministry of Burkina Faso, for the Togo-Ghana observation during an interview in Ouagadougou on 22 July 1999.

34. See AFSTRAG Roundtable, "Harmonization of Conflict Management Mechanisms in West Africa: The Facilitating Role of AFSTRAG," serial no. 1, vol. 2, 1998.

35. Confidential interview.

36. Amadou Toumani Touré, "Mastering African Conflicts," in Adebayo Adedeji (ed.), *Comprehending and Mastering African Conflicts: The Search for Sustainable Peace and Good Governance* (London and New York: Zed Books, 1999), p. 25.

37. Protocol Relating to the Mechanism for Conflict Prevention, Management, Resolution, Peacekeeping, and Security, pp. 16–17

38. See Ebow Godwin, "'Cohesion Kompienga' 98," *West Africa* no. 4191 (18–31 May 1998): 474–475.

39. See, for example, Joses Gani Yoroms, "Mechanisms for Conflict Management in ECOWAS" (Accord occasional paper no. 8, 1999), p. 6.

40. Protocol Relating to the Mechanism for Conflict Prevention, Management, Resolution, Peacekeeping, and Security, pp. 19–20.

41. I thank Lateef Aminu, one of the experts in Banjul in 1998, for this point, which I learned during an interview with him in Lagos on 6 August 1999.

42. See Boutros Boutros-Ghali, *An Agenda for Peace* (New York: United Nations, 1992); and Alan James, *Peacekeeping in International Politics* (London: Chatto and Windus, 1990).

43. This point was made particularly forcefully at an IPA/Council for the Development of Social Science Research in Africa (CODESRIA) seminar of African civil society actors in Senegal. See IPA/CODESRIA, *War, Peace, and Reconciliation in Africa,* November–December 1999.

44. I thank my coauthor, Michael O'Hanlon, for the observations in this and the paragraph above, cited in Adekeye Adebajo and Michael O'Hanlon, "Africa: Toward a Rapid-Reaction Force," *SAIS Review* 17, no. 2. (Summer/Fall 1997): 157–159.

45. Colonel Festus Aboagye, *ECOMOG: A Subregional Experience in Conflict Resolution, Management, and Peacekeeping in Liberia* (Accra: Sedco Enterprise, 1999), p. 300; and personal interview with General Emmanuel Erskine, New York, 21 June 1999.

46. I thank Lateef Aminu for this point.

47. Maxwell Khobe, "The Evolution and Conduct of ECOMOG Operations in West Africa," in Mark Malan (ed.), *Boundaries of Peace Support Operations: The African Dimension,* ISS monograph no. 44 (February 2000), pp. 118–119.

48. Protocol Relating to the Mechanism for Conflict Prevention, Management, Resolution, Peacekeeping, and Security, p. 25.

49. See, for example, Margaret Vogt and Lateef Aminu (eds.*), Peacekeeping as a Security Strategy in Africa: Chad and Liberia as Case Studies,* 2 vols. (Enugu: Fourth Dimension, 1996).

50. Regarding the 1992 arrears, see Daniel Bach, "Institutional Crisis and the Search for New Models," in Réal Lavergne (ed.), *Regional Integration and Cooperation in West Africa* (Trenton, N.J., and Asmara, Eritrea: Africa World Press, 1997), p. 85.

51. Eric G. Berman and Katie E. Sams, *Peacekeeping in Africa: Capabilities and Culpabilities* (Geneva and Pretoria: UN Institute for Disarmament Research and Institute for Security Studies, 2000), p. 146.

52. See Adebajo and O'Hanlon, "Africa," pp. 153–164; Jendayi Frazer, "The Africa Crisis Response Initiative: Self-Interested Humanitarianism," *The Brown Journal of World Affairs* 4, no. 2 (Summer/Fall 1997): 103–118; Oliver Furley and Roy May (eds.), *Peacekeeping in Africa* (Aldershot and Brookfield, Vt.: Ashgate, 1998); Eboe Hutchful, "Peacekeeping Under Conditions of Resource Stringency," in Jakkie Cilliers and Greg Mills (eds.), *From Peacekeeping to Complex Emergencies: Peace Support Missions in Africa* (Johannesburg and Pretoria: South African Institute of International Affairs, and Institute for Security Studies, 1999), pp. 113–117; Paul Omach, "The African Crisis Response Initiative: Domestic Politics and Convergence of National Interests," *African Affairs* 99, no. 394 (January 2000): 73–95; and Rocklyn Williams, "Beyond Old Borders: Challenges to Franco-South African Security Relations in the New Millennium," *African Security Review* 8, no. 4 (1999): 3–19.

53. Quoted in Berman and Sams, *Peacekeeping in Africa,* p. 146.

54. Protocol Relating to the Mechanism for Conflict Prevention, Management, Resolution, Peacekeeping, and Security, pp. 25–27.

55. I thank General Ishola Williams, one of the experts in Banjul in 1998, for this insight.

56. See ECOWAS/UNDP, *Programme for Coordination and Assistance on Security and Development.*

57. Ali Mazrui, *Towards a Pax Africana* (Chicago: University of Chicago Press, 1967).

Acronyms

AAFC	Allied Armed Forces of the Community
ACDL	Association for Constitutional Democracy in Liberia
ACP	African, Caribbean, and Pacific
ACRI	African Crisis Response Initiative
AFL	Armed Forces of Liberia
AFRC	Armed Forces Ruling Council
AFSTRAG	African Strategic and Peace Research Group
ANAD	Accord de Non-Aggression et d'Assistance en Matière de Défense
APC	All People's Congress
BBC	British Broadcasting Corporation
CDF	Civil Defense Force
CEAO	Communauté Économique de l'Afrique de l'Ouest
CEDE	Center for Democratic Empowerment
CFA	Communauté Financière Africaine
CNN	Cable News Network
CODESRIA	Council for the Development of Social Science Research in Africa
CPLP	Community of Portuguese-Speaking Countries
CRC	Central Revolutionary Council (of NPFL)
ECOMOG	Economic Community of West African States Cease-fire Monitoring Group
ECOWAS	Economic Community of West African States
EEC	European Economic Community
EU	European Union
FARP	Forças Armadas Revolucionárias do Povo
GDP	gross domestic product
GNP	gross national product

HIPC	heavily indebted poor countries
IFMC	Inter-Faith Mediation Committee
IGNU	Interim Government of National Unity
IMF	International Monetary Fund
INPFL	Independent National Patriotic Front of Liberia
IPA	International Peace Academy
IRCSL	Inter-Religious Council of Sierra Leone
LDF	Lofa Defense Force
LDH	League of Human Rights
LEON	Liberian Elections Observer Network
LNC	Liberian National Conference
LNTG	Liberian National Transitional Government
LPC	Liberia Peace Council
LURD	Liberians United for Reconciliation and Democracy
MAD	(Protocol Relating to) Mutual Assistance on Defense
MFDC	Mouvement des Forces Démocratiques de Casamance
NGO	nongovernmental organization
NMG	Neutral Monitoring Group
NNPC	Nigerian National Petroleum Corporation
NPFL	National Patriotic Front of Liberia
NPP	National Patriotic Party
NPRAG	National Patriotic Reconstruction Assembly Government
NPRC	National Provisional Ruling Council
NRP	National Reconstruction Program
OAU	Organization of African Unity
OPEC	Organization of Petroleum Exporting Countries
PA&E	Pacific Architects and Engineers
PAIGC	Partido Africano da Independencia da Guine e Cabo Verde
PRS	Partido para a Renovação Social
PSD	Partido Social Democratico
RECAMP	Renforcement des Capacités Africaines de Maintien de la Paix
RGB-MB	Resistência da Guiné-Bissau–Movimento Ba-Fata
RUF	Revolutionary United Front
SLA	Sierra Leone Army
SLPP	Sierra Leone People's Party
SLWMP	Sierra Leone Women's Movement for Peace
SMC	Standing Mediation Committee
UEMOA	West African Economic and Monetary Union
ULIMO	United Liberation Movement of Liberia for Democracy
UN	United Nations
UNAMSIL	UN Mission in Sierra Leone

UNDP	UN Development Programme
UNOGBIS	UN Peacebuilding Support Office in Guinea-Bissau
UNOL	UN Office in Liberia
UNOMIL	UN Observer Mission in Liberia
UNOMSIL	UN Observer Mission in Sierra Leone
USAID	U.S. Agency for International Development
WANEP	West African Network for Peacebuilding

Selected Bibliography

AUTHOR INTERVIEWS

Agbevey, H. W. K. ECOMOG deputy force commander. Freetown, 3 July 1999.

Aminu, Lateef. Expert in Banjul (1998). Lagos, 6 August 1999.

Boly, Yéro. Interior minister of Burkina Faso. Ouagadougou, 22 July 1999.

Captan, Monie. Foreign minister of Liberia. Monrovia, 15 July 1999.

Chea, Daniel. Defense minister of Liberia. Monrovia, 13 July 1999.

Cohen, Herman. Former U.S. assistant secretary of state for African affairs. Washington, D.C., July 1997.

Danjuma, Theophilus. Defense minister of Nigeria. Abuja, 2 March 2001.

Diam, Alexandre. ANAD secretary-general. Abidjan, 19 July 1999.

Diarra, Cheick. ECOWAS deputy executive secretary. Abuja, 10 July 2001.

Erskine, Emmanuel. New York, 21 June 1999.

Gordon-Somers, Trevor. UNDP. New York, May 1997.

Jagne, Baboucarr. Foreign minister of Gambia. New York, 30 July 2001.

Jalloh, Ibrahim. ECOMOG deputy force commander. Conakry, 7 July 1999.

Jeter, Howard. U.S. presidential envoy to Liberia. Washington, D.C., 3 April 1997.

Jonah, James. Former finance minister of Sierra Leone. New York, 2 July 2001.

Kambou, Daprou. Secretary-general, defense ministry of Burkina Faso. Ouagadougou, 22 July 1999.

Kouamé, Maes. Chief of the Division of African Conflicts in the Ivorian foreign ministry. Côte d'Ivoire, 9 July 1999.

Kuznetsova, Galina. Desk officer for Guinea-Bissau, UN Department of Political Affairs. New York, 16 August 2001.

Lamido, Sule. Foreign minister of Nigeria. Lomé, 8 December 1999.

Maada Bio, Julius. Former head of state of Sierra Leone. Washington, D.C., 19 January 2001.

Mujakpero, Felix. ECOMOG force commander. Freetown, 6 July 1999.

Ohemeng-Boamah, Anthony. UNDP program specialist. New York, 20 August 2001.

Okelo, Francis. Former UN Special Representative in Sierra Leone. Lomé, 8 December 1999.

169

Olukolade, Chris. ECOMOG chief military information officer. Freetown, 3 July 1999.
Olurin, Adetunji. ECOMOG force commander 1992–1993. Lagos, 9 August 1999.
Penfold, Peter. British high commissioner in Sierra Leone. Freetown, 2 July 1999.
Sawyer, Amos. President of Liberia 1990–1994. Monrovia, 14 July 1999.
Seck, Mamadou. Former chief of staff of the Senegalese army. Washington, D.C., 21 July 1997.
Sermé, Mamadou. Director-general, foreign ministry of Burkina Faso. Ouagadougou, 22 July 1999.
Sey, Omar. Foreign minister of Gambia 1987–1994. Baghdad, 14 December 1997.
Shelpidi, Timothy. Former ECOMOG force commander. Abuja, 10 July 2001.
Touré, Ahmadou. ANAD director of studies. Abidjan, 19 July 1999.
Vokouma, Prosper. Foreign minister of Burkina Faso 1989–1991. Ouagadougou, 22 July 1999.
Williams, Ishola. Expert in Banjul (1998). Lagos, 6 August 1999.

BOOKS AND ARTICLES

Abdullah, Ibrahim, and Patrick Muana. "The Revolutionary United Front of Sierra Leone: A Revolt of the Lumpenproletariat." In Christopher Clapham (ed.), *African Guerrillas*. Oxford, Kampala, and Bloomington: James Currey, Fountain, and Indiana University Press, 1998.
Aboagye, Festus. *ECOMOG: A Subregional Experience in Conflict Resolution, Management, and Peacekeeping in Liberia*. Accra: Sedco Enterprise, 1999.
Adebajo, Adekeye. "Nigeria: Africa's New Gendarme?" *Security Dialogue* 31, no. 2 (June 2000).
————. *Liberia's Civil War: Nigeria, ECOMOG, and Regional Security in West Africa*. Boulder and London: Lynne Rienner, forthcoming 2002.
Adebajo, Adekeye, and David Keen. "Banquet for Warlords." *The World Today* 56, no. 7 (July 2000).
Adebajo, Adekeye, and Chris Landsberg. "Pax Africana in the Age of Extremes." *South African Journal of International Affairs* 7, no. 1 (Summer 2000).
————. "Back to the Future: UN Peacekeeping in Africa." *International Peacekeeping* 7, no. 4 (Winter 2000).
————. "The Heirs of Nkrumah: Africa's New Interventionists." *Pugwash Occasional Paper* 2, no. 1 (January 2001).
Adebajo, Adekeye, and Michael O'Hanlon. "Africa: Toward a Rapid-Reaction Force." *SAIS Review* 17, no. 2. (Summer/Fall 1997).
Adefuye, Ade, et al. *Seven Years of IBB*. 7 vols. Lagos: Daily Times of Nigeria, 1993.
Adeniji, Olu (interview). "We Don't Want Another Angola." *West Africa* no. 4217 (13–19 March 2000).
Adibe, Clement. "The Liberian Conflict and the ECOWAS-UN Partnership." *Third World Quarterly* 18, no. 3 (1997).
AFSTRAG Roundtable. "Harmonization of Conflict Management Mechanisms in West Africa: The Facilitating Role of AFSTRAG." Serial no. 1, vol. 2, 1998.
Agetua, Nkem. *Operation Liberty: The Story of Major-General Joshua Nimyel Dogonyaro*. Lagos: Hona Communications, 1992.

Akhigbe, Lucy. "Why Peace Has Been So Elusive." *New African,* July/August 1999.

Akinterinwa, Bola. *Nigeria and France, 1960–1995: The Dilemma of Thirty-five Years of Relationship.* Ibadan: Vantage, 1999.

Alao, Abiodun, John Mackinlay, and Funmi Olonisakin. *Peacekeepers, Politicians, and Warlords: The Liberian Peace Process.* Tokyo, New York, and Paris: UN University Press, 1999.

Amuta, Chidi. *Prince of the Niger: The Babangida Years.* Lagos: Tanus, 1992.

ANAD. Synoptic Report on the Proceedings of the Workshops of the Expert Committee at the Level of Chiefs of Staff of the Armed Forces of ANAD. Niamey, 24–26 April 1997.

Anderson, Jon Lee. "The Devil They Know." *New Yorker,* 27 July 1998.

Aning, Emmanuel Kwezi. "Managing Regional Security in West Africa: ECOWAS, ECOMOG, and Liberia." Working paper no. 94.2, Centre for Development Research, Copenhagen, February 1994.

Ankomah, Baffour. "Knives Out for Taylor." *New African,* September 1998.

Asaju, Tunde, and Dotun Oladipo. "Ikimi's Jungle Diplomacy." *Newswatch* (28 September 1998).

Ate, Bassey, and Bola Akinterinwa (eds.). *Nigeria and Its Immediate Neighbors.* Lagos: Nigerian Institute of International Affairs, 1992.

Atkinson, Philippa. *The War Economy in Liberia: A Political Analysis.* London: Overseas Development Institute, 1997.

Bach, Daniel. "Institutional Crisis and the Search for New Models." In Réal Laverge (ed.), *Regional Integration and Cooperation in West Africa* (Trenton, N.J., and Asmara, Eritrea: Africa World Press, 1997).

Bangura, Yusuf. "Understanding the Political and Cultural Dynamics of the Sierra Leone War: A Critique of Paul Richards's *Fighting for the Rainforest.*" *African Development* 22, nos. 2–3 (1997) (special issue on "Youth Culture and Political Violence: The Sierra Leone Civil War").

Barrett, Lindsay. "Why Senegal Withdrew." *West Africa* no. 3931 (25–31 January 1993).

Bartholet, Jeffrey. "Liberia's Charles Taylor: Inside the Mind of a Tyrant." *Newsweek,* 14 May 2001.

Berman, Eric G., and Katie E. Sams. *Peacekeeping in Africa: Capabilities and Culpabilities.* Geneva and Pretoria: UN Institute for Disarmament Research and Institute for Security Studies, 2000.

Bienen, Henry. *Armed Forces, Conflict, and Change in Africa.* Boulder, San Francisco, and London: Westview Press, 1989.

Boley, G. E. Saigbe. *Liberia: The Rise and Fall of the First Republic.* New York: St. Martin's Press, 1983.

Boutros-Ghali, Boutros. *Unvanquished: A U.S.-UN Saga.* London and New York: I. B. Tauris, 1999.

Bundu, Abass. "The Case Against Intervention." *West Africa* no. 4156 (30 June–6 July 1997).

Cohen, Herman. *Intervening in Africa: Superpower Peacemaking in a Troubled Continent.* Hampshire, London, and New York: Macmillan and St. Martin's Press, 2000.

Conroy, Richard. "Sierra Leone: The Failure of Regional and International Sanctions." In David Cortright and George A. Lopez (eds.), *The Sanctions Decade: Assessing UN Strategies in the 1990s.* Boulder and London: Lynne Rienner, 2000.

Davidson, Basil. *The People's Cause: A History of Guerrillas in Africa*. Essex: Longman, 1981.

Davies, Desmond. "Peacekeeping African Style." *West Africa* no. 4190 (4–17 May 1998).

Decalo, Samuel. *Coups and Army Rule in Africa*. 2nd ed. New Haven and London: Yale University Press, 1990.

Economist Intelligence Unit. "Liberia." 4th Quarter 1997.

——. "Liberia." 3rd Quarter 1998.

——. "Liberia." 1st Quarter 1999.

——. "Liberia." 2nd Quarter 1999.

——. Country Report. "Guinea-Bissau." 3rd Quarter 1999.

——. Country Report. "Guinea-Bissau." 4th Quarter 1999.

——. "Liberia." 4th Quarter 1999.

——. Country Report. "Guinea-Bissau." 1st Quarter 2000.

——. Country Report. "Guinea-Bissau." 2nd Quarter 2000.

——. Country Report. "Guinea-Bissau." July 2000.

——. Country Report. "Guinea-Bissau." January 2001.

——. "Liberia." March 2001.

ECOWAS charter of 1975 and security protocols of 1979 and 1981.

——. First Session of the ECOWAS Standing Mediation Committee. Final Communiqué. Banjul, 6–7 August 1990.

——. First Extraordinary Session of the Authority of Heads of State and Government. Final Communiqué. Bamako, 27–28 November 1990.

——. Second Meeting of the ECOWAS Committee of Five. Final Communiqué. Yamoussoukro, 16–17 September 1991.

——. Third Meeting of the ECOWAS Committee of Five. Final Communiqué. Yamoussoukro, 29–30 October 1991.

——. Informal Consultative Group Meeting of the ECOWAS Committee of Five on Liberia. Final Communiqué. Geneva, 6–7 April 1992.

——. Economic Community of West African States Consultative Meeting on the Liberia Peace Process. Final Report. ECW/MINFA/CTTE9/VI/2. Abuja, 16–19 August 1995.

——. Seventh Meeting of ECOWAS Committee of Nine Foreign Ministers. Final Report (Restricted). ECW/MINFA/CTTE9/VII/2/Rev.1. Accra, 7 May 1996.

——. Fourth Meeting of ECOWAS Heads of State and Government of the Committee of Nine. Final Communiqué. Abuja, 17 August 1996.

——. ECOWAS Draft Mechanism for Conflict Prevention, Management, Resolution, Peacekeeping, and Security. Meeting of the Ministers of Defence, Internal Affaires, and Security. Banjul, 23–24 July 1998.

Elaigwu, J. Isawa. *Gowon*. Ibadan: West Books, 1986.

Ellis, Stephen. "Liberia 1989–1994: A Study of Ethnic and Spiritual Violence." *African Affairs* 94, no. 375 (April 1995).

——. *The Mask of Anarchy*. London: Hurst, 1999.

Ero, Comfort. "The Future of ECOMOG in West Africa." In Jakkie Cilliers and Greg Mills (eds.), *From Peacekeeping to Complex Emergencies: Peace Support Missions in Africa* (Johannesburg and Pretoria: South African Institute of International Affairs, and Institute for Security Studies, 1999).

——. "British Policy and Conflict in Sierra Leone." Unpublished manuscript.

Fofana, Lansana. "A Nation Self-Destructs." *NewsAfrica* 1, no. 5 (31 July 2000).

Foltz, William, and Henry Bienen (eds.). *Arms and the African: Military Influences on Africa's International Relations.* New Haven and London: Yale University Press, 1985.

Forsyth, Frederick. *Emeka.* Ibadan: Spectrum Books, 1982.

Frazer, Jendayi. "The Africa Crisis Response Initiative: Self-Interested Humanitarianism." *The Brown Journal of World Affairs* 4, no. 2 (Summer/Fall 1997).

Furley, Oliver, and Roy May (eds.). *Peacekeeping in Africa.* Aldershot and Brookfield, Vt.: Ashgate, 1998.

Galli, Rosemary E., and Jocelyn Jones. *Guinea-Bissau: Politics, Economics, and Society.* Boulder and London: Lynne Rienner and Frances Pinter, 1987.

Gambari, Ibrahim. *Theory and Reality in Foreign Policy Making: Nigeria After the Second Republic.* Atlantic Highlands, N.J.: Humanities Press International, 1989.

————. *Political and Comparative Dimensions of Regional Integration: The Case of ECOWAS.* Atlantic Highlands, N.J., and London: Humanities Press International, 1991.

Garba, Joseph. *Diplomatic Soldiering: Nigerian Foreign Policy, 1975–1979.* Ibadan: Spectrum Books, 1987.

Godwin, Ebow. "A Cohesion Kompienga 98." *West Africa,* 18–31 May 1998.

Gowon, Yakubu. *The Economic Community of West African States: A Study of Political and Economic Integration.* Ph.D. thesis, Warwick University, February 1984.

Harris, Katherine. *African and American Values: Liberia and West Africa.* Lanham, New York, and London: University Press of America, 1985.

Hayward, Fred. "Sierra Leone: State Consolidation, Fragmentation, and Decay." In Donal B. Cruise O'Brien, John Dunn, and Richard Rathbone (eds.), *Contemporary West African States.* Cambridge: Cambridge University Press, 1989.

Hirsch, John. *Sierra Leone: Diamonds and the Struggle for Democracy.* Boulder and London: Lynne Rienner, 2001.

Howe, Herbert. "Lessons of Liberia: ECOMOG and Regional Peacekeeping." *International Security* 21, no. 3 (Winter 1996/1997).

Huband, Mark. *The Liberian Civil War.* London and Portland: Frank Cass, 1998.

Human Rights Watch/Africa. "Waging War to Keep the Peace: The ECOMOG Intervention and Human Rights." Vol. 5, no. 6 (June 1993).

————. "Liberia: Emerging from Destruction." Vol. 9, no. 7 (November 1997).

Hutchful, Eboe. "Peacekeeping Under Conditions of Resource Stringency: Ghana's Army in Liberia." In Jakkie Cilliers and Greg Mills (eds.), *From Peacekeeping to Complex Emergencies: Peace Support Missions in Africa.* Johannesburg and Pretoria: South African Institute of International Affairs, and Institute for Security Studies, 1999.

Independent Elections Commission. *Special Elections Law for the 1997 Elections.* Monrovia: Sabanoh Press, 1997.

IPA/CODESRIA. *War, Peace, and Reconciliation in Africa.* Seminar of African civil society actors in Senegal, November–December 1999.

Iweze, Cyril. "Nigeria in Liberia: The Military Operations of ECOMOG." In M. A. Vogt and A. E. Ekoko (eds.), *Nigeria in International Peacekeeping, 1960–1992.* Lagos and Oxford: Malthouse Press, 1993.

Jusu-Sheriff, Yasmin. "Sierra Leonean Women and the Peace Process." In David Lord (ed.), *Paying the Price: The Sierra Leone Peace Process, Accord* no. 9 (2000).

Keen, David. "War and Peace: What's the Difference?" *International sPeacekeeping* 7, no. 4 (Winter 2000).

Khobe, Maxwell. "The Evolution and Conduct of ECOMOG Operations in West Africa." In Mark Malan (ed.), *Boundaries of Peace Support Operations: The African Dimension,* ISS monograph no. 44 (February 2000).

Kramer, Reed. "Liberia: A Casualty of the Cold War's End?" *CSIS Africa Notes* no. 174 (July 1995).

Lamido, Sule (interview). "I Will Surprise My Critics." *ThisDay,* 8 August 1999.

Landsberg, Chris. "Willing but Unable: Small States and Peacekeeping in Africa." In Jakkie Cilliers and Greg Mills (eds.), *From Peacekeeping to Complex Emergencies: Peace Support Missions in Africa.* Johannesburg and Pretoria: South African Institute of International Affairs, and Institute for Security Studies, 1999.

Langley, Norwood. "The National Reconstruction Program in Liberia." In *State Rebuilding After State Collapse: Security, Democracy, and Development in Post-War Liberia.* Report of the Strategic Planning Workshop on Liberia, 19 June 1998. London: Center for Democracy and Development, 1998.

Lardner, Tunji. "An African Tragedy." *Africa Report* 35, no. 5 (November/December 1990).

Liebenow, Gus. *The Evolution of Privilege.* Ithaca: Cornell University Press, 1969.

———. *Liberia: The Quest for Democracy.* Bloomington and Indianapolis: Indiana University Press, 1987.

Lyons, Terrence. *Voting for Peace: Post Conflict Elections in Liberia.* Washington, D.C.: Brookings Institution, 1998.

Magyar, Karl, and Earl Conteh-Morgan (eds.). *Peacekeeping in Africa: ECOMOG in Liberia.* Hampshire, London, and New York: Macmillan and St. Martin's Press, 1998.

Mayall, James. "Oil and Nigerian Foreign Policy." *African Affairs* 75, no. 300 (July 1976).

McGreal, Chris. "UN to Sack Its General in Sierra Leone." *Guardian Weekly,* 29 June–5 July 2000.

Mortimer, Robert. "Senegal's Role in ECOMOG: The Francophone Dimension." *Journal of Modern African Studies* 34, no. 2 (1996).

———. "From ECOMOG to ECOMOG II: Intervention in Sierra Leone." In John W. Harbeson and Donald Rothchild (eds.), *Africa in World Politics: The African State System in Flux,* 3rd ed. Boulder and Oxford: Westview Press, 2000.

Nowrojee, Binaifir. "Joining Forces: UN and Regional Peacekeeping, Lessons from Liberia." *Harvard Human Rights Journal* 18 (Spring 1995).

Obasanjo, Olusegun. *My Command.* London: Heinemann, 1980.

———. *Not My Will.* Ibadan: University Press, 1990.

———. "Nigeria, Africa, and the World in the Next Millennium." Address at the Fifty-fourth Session of the UN General Assembly, New York, 23 September 1999.

Olonisakin, Funmi. "UN Co-operation with Regional Organizations in Peacekeeping: The experience of ECOMOG and UNOMIL in Liberia." *International Peacekeeping* 3, no. 3 (Autumn 1996).

Olusanya, Gabriel, and R. A. Akindele (eds.). *Nigeria's External Relations: The First Twenty-five Years.* Ibadan: University Press, 1986.

———. *The Structure and Processes of Foreign Policy Making and Implementation in Nigeria, 1960–1990.* Lagos: Nigerian Institute of International Affairs, 1990.

Omach, Paul. "The African Crisis Response Initiative: Domestic Politics and Convergence of National Interests." *African Affairs* 99, no. 394 (January 2000).

Osaghae, Eghosa. *Ethnicity, Class, and the Struggle for State Power in Liberia.* Dakar: CODESRIA, 1996.

Rashid, Ismail. "The Lomé Peace Negotiations." In David Lord (ed.), *Paying the Price: The Sierra Leone Peace Process, Accord* no. 9 (2000).

Reno, William. "The Business of War in Liberia." *Current History,* May 1996.

————. *Warlord Politics and African States.* Boulder and London: Lynne Rienner, 1998.

Richards, Paul. "Rebellion in Liberia and Sierra Leone: A Crisis of Youth?" In Oliver Furley (ed.), *Conflict in Africa.* New York and London: Tauris Academic Studies, 1995.

————. *Fighting for the Rainforest: War, Youth, and Resources in Sierra Leone.* Oxford and New Hampshire: James Currey and Heinemann, 1996.

Sawyer, Amos. *The Emergence of Autocracy in Liberia: Tragedy and Challenge.* San Francisco: ICS Press, 1992.

————. "Foundations for Reconstruction in Liberia: Challenges and Responses." In *State Rebuilding After State Collapse: Security, Democracy, and Development in Post-War Liberia.* Report of the Strategic Planning Workshop on Liberia, 19 June 1998. London: Center for Democracy and Development, 1998.

Schraeder, Peter. "Senegal's Foreign Policy: Challenges of Democratization and Marginalization." *African Affairs* 96 (1997).

Stremlau, John. *The International Politics of the Nigerian Civil War, 1967–1970.* Princeton: Princeton University Press, 1977.

Tanner, Victor. "Liberia: Railroading Peace." *Review of African Political Economy* 25 (March 1998).

Thorin, Valérie. "Lune de Miel." *Jeune Afrique-L'Intelligent* no. 2040 (15–21 February 2000).

Turay, Thomas Mark. "Civil Society and Peacebuilding: The Role of the Inter-Religious Council of Sierra Leone." In David Lord (ed.), *Paying the Price: The Sierra Leone Peace Process, Accord* no. 9 (2000).

United Nations. Seventeenth Progress Report of the Secretary-General on the UN Observer Mission in Liberia. S/1996/362. 21 May 1996.

————. Report of the Secretary-General on Sierra Leone. 26 January 1997.

————. Twenty-second Progress Report of the Secretary-General on the UN Observer Mission in Liberia. S/1997/237. 19 March 1997.

————. Final Report of the Secretary-General on the UN Observer Mission in Liberia. S/1997/712. 12 September 1997.

————. Report of the Secretary-General Pursuant to Security Council Resolution 1216 (1998) Relative to the Situation in Guinea-Bissau. S/1999/294. 17 March 1999.

————. Sixth Report of the Secretary-General on the UN Observer Mission in Sierra Leone. S/1999/645. 4 June 1999.

————. Report of the Secretary-General Pursuant to Security Council Resolution 1216 (1998) Relative to the Situation in Guinea-Bissau. S/1999/741. 1 July 1999.

————. Seventh Report of the Secretary-General on the UN Observer Mission in Sierra Leone. S/1999/836. 30 July 1999.

———. Eighth Report of the Secretary-General on the UN Observer Mission in Sierra Leone. S/1999/1003. 23 September 1999.

———. First Report on the UN Mission in Sierra Leone. S/1999/1223. 6 December 1999.

———. Report of the Secretary-General on Developments in Guinea-Bissau and on the Activities of the UN Peacebuilding Support Office in That Country. S/1999/1276. 23 December 1999.

———. Third Report on the UN Mission in Sierra Leone. S/2000/186. 7 March 2000.

———. Report of the Secretary-General on Developments in Guinea-Bissau. S/2000/250. 24 March 2000.

———. Fourth Report on the UN Mission in Sierra Leone. S/2000/455. 19 May 2000.

———. Report of the Secretary-General on Developments in Guinea-Bissau. S/2000/632. 28 June 2000.

———. Fifth Report on the UN Mission in Sierra Leone. S/2000/751. 31 July 2000.

———. Sixth Report of the Secretary-General on the UN Mission in Sierra Leone. S/2000/832. 24 August 2000.

———. Report of the Secretary-General on Developments in Guinea-Bissau. S/2000/920. 29 September 2000.

———. Report of the Security Council Mission to Sierra Leone. S/2000/992. 16 October 2000.

———. Report of the Panel of Experts Appointed Pursuant to Security Council Resolution 1306 (2000), para. 19, in Relation to Sierra Leone. S/2000/1195. 20 December 2000.

———. Ninth Report of the Secretary-General on the UN Mission in Sierra Leone. S/2001/228. 14 March 2001.

———. Report of the Secretary-General on Developments in Guinea-Bissau. S/2001/237. 16 March 2001.

———. First Report of the Secretary-General Pursuant to Security Council Resolution 1343 (2001) Regarding Liberia. S/2001/424. 30 April 2001.

———. Report of the Inter-Agency Mission to West Africa. "Towards a Comprehensive Approach to Durable and Sustainable Solutions to Priority Needs and Challenges in West Africa." UN Security Council document. S/2001/434. 2 May 2001.

———. Report of the Secretary-General on Developments in Guinea-Bissau. S/2001/622. 22 June 2001.

———. Report of the Joint Review Mission on the UN postconflict peacebuilding offices. UN Department of Political Affairs/UNDP. 20 July 2001.

Van Walraven, Klaas. *The Netherlands and Liberia: Dutch Policies and Interventions with Respect to the Liberian Civil War.* The Hague: Netherlands Institute of International Relations, 1999.

———. *The Pretence of Peace-keeping: ECOMOG, West Africa, and Liberia (1990–1998).* The Hague: Netherlands Institute of International Relations, 1999.

Vogt, Margaret (ed.). *The Liberian Crisis and ECOMOG: A Bold Attempt at Regional Peacekeeping.* Lagos: Gabumo Press, 1993.

Vogt, Margaret, and Lateef Aminu (eds.). *Peacekeeping as a Security Strategy in Africa: Chad and Liberia as Case Studies.* 2 vols. Enugu: Fourth Dimension, 1996.

West Africa. No. 3892 (20–26 April 1992).
————. No. 4067 (18–24 September 1995).
————. No. 4073 (6–12 November 1995).
————. No. 4109 (22–28 July 1996).
————. No. 4251 (6–12 November 2000). Charles Taylor (interview). "The West Wants to Suffocate Liberia."
Williams, Rocklyn. "Beyond Old Borders: Challenges to Franco-South African Security Relations in the New Millennium." *African Security Review* 8, no. 4 (1999).
Wippmann, David. "Enforcing the Peace: ECOWAS and the Liberian Civil War." In Lori Fisler Damrosch (ed.), *Enforcing Restraint: Collective Intervention in Internal Conflicts.* New York: Council on Foreign Relations, 1993.
Wright, Stephen, and Julius Emeka Okolo. "Nigeria: Aspirations of Regional Power." In Stephen Wright (ed.), *African Foreign Policies.* Boulder and Oxford: Westview Press, 1999.
Yoroms, Joses Gani. "Mechanisms for Conflict Management in ECOWAS." Accord occasional paper no. 8, 1999.
Zack-Williams, A. B., and Steve Riley. "Sierra Leone: The Coup and Its Consequences." *Review of African Political Economy* no. 56 (1993).

Index

About This Publication

Among all of Africa's troubled regions, West Africa has gone the furthest toward establishing a security mechanism to manage its own conflicts. The ECOMOG intervention in Liberia in 1990–1997 was the first by a subregional African organization relying principally on its own personnel, money, and military matériel; and ECOMOG's 1998 intervention in Sierra Leone to restore a democratic government to power was equally unprecedented. Adekeye Adebajo explores these two cases, as well as the brief and unsuccessful intervention in Guinea-Bissau in 1999, in this study of regional peacebuilding efforts.

After discussing the political, economic, and security contexts of West Africa since independence, Adebajo assesses the domestic and external dynamics of the three conflicts and examines the roles and motivations of the full range of actors. Dissecting the successes and failures of external intervention in each case, he draws crucial policy lessons for building peace through the ECOWAS Mechanism for Conflict Prevention, Management, Resolution, Pecekeeping, and Security.

Adekeye Adebajo is director of the Africa Program at the International Peace Academy and adjunct professor at Columbia University's School of International and Public Affairs. Dr. Adebajo has served on UN missions in South Africa, Western Sahara, and Iraq. He is coeditor (with Chandra Sriram) of *Managing Armed Conflicts in the Twenty-first Century.*

The International Peace Academy

The International Peace Academy (IPA) is an independent, international institution dedicated to promoting the prevention and settlement of armed conflicts between and within states through policy research and development.

Founded in 1970, the IPA has built an extensive portfolio of activities in fulfillment of its mission:

- Symposiums, workshops, and other forums that facilitate strategic thinking, policy development, and organizational innovation within international organizations.
- Policy research on multilateral efforts to prevent, mitigate, or rebuild after armed conflict.
- Research, consultations, and technical assistance to support capacities for peacemaking, peacekeeping, and peacebuilding in Africa.
- Professional-development seminars for political, development, military, humanitarian, and nongovernmental personnel involved in peacekeeping and conflict resolution.
- Facilitation in conflict situations where its experience, credibility, and independence can complement official peace efforts.
- Outreach to build public awareness on issues related to peace and security, multilateralism, and the United Nations.

The IPA works closely with the United Nations, regional and other international organizations, governments, and nongovernmental organizations, as well as with parties to conflicts in selected cases. Its efforts are enhanced by its ability to draw on a worldwide network of government and business leaders, scholars, diplomats, military officers, and leaders of civil society.

The IPA is a nonprofit organization governed by an international Board of Directors. The organization is funded by generous donations from governments, major philanthropic foundations, and corporate donors, as well as contributions from individuals and its Board members.

International Peace Academy Publications

Available from Lynne Rienner Publishers, 1800 30th Street, Boulder, Colorado 80301 (303-444-6684), www.rienner.com.

Ending Civil Wars: The Implementation of Peace Agreements, Stephen John Stedman, Donald Rothchild, and Elizabeth M. Cousens (2002)

Sanctions and the Search for Security: Challenges to UN Action, David Cortright and George A. Lopez, with Linda Gerber (2002)

Ecuador vs. Peru: Peacemaking Amid Rivalry, Monica Herz and João Pontes Nogueira (2002)

Liberia's Civil War: Nigeria, ECOMOG, and Regional Security in West Africa, Adekeye Adebajo (2002)

Building Peace in West Africa: Liberia, Sierra Leone, and Guinea-Bissau, Adekeye Adebajo (2002)

Kosovo: An Unfinished Peace, William G. O'Neill (2002)

From Reaction to Conflict Prevention: Opportunities for the UN System, edited by Fen Osler Hampson and David M. Malone (2002)

Peacemaking in Rwanda: The Dynamics of Failure, Bruce D. Jones (2001)

Self-Determination in East Timor: The United Nations, the Ballot, and International Intervention, Ian Martin (2001)

Civilians in War, edited by Simon Chesterman (2001)

Toward Peace in Bosnia: Implementing the Dayton Accords, Elizabeth M. Cousens and Charles K. Cater (2001)

Sierra Leone: Diamonds and the Struggle for Democracy, John L. Hirsch (2001)

Peacebuilding as Politics: Cultivating Peace in Fragile Societies, edited by Elizabeth M. Cousens and Chetan Kumar (2001)

The Sanctions Decade: Assessing UN Strategies in the 1990s, David Cortright and George A. Lopez (2000)

Greed and Grievance: Economic Agendas in Civil War, edited by Mats
   Berdal and David M. Malone (2000)
Building Peace in Haiti, Chetan Kumar (1998)
Rights and Reconciliation: UN Strategies in El Salvador, Ian Johnstone
   (1995)